The Apostles' Creed

The Apostles' Creed

Truth with Passion

Jonathan F. Bayes

WIPF & STOCK · Eugene, Oregon

THE APOSTLES' CREED
Truth with Passion

Copyright © 2010 Jonathan F. Bayes. All rights reserved. Except for brief quotations in critical publications or reviews, no part of this book may be reproduced in any manner without prior written permission from the publisher. Write: Permissions, Wipf and Stock Publishers, 199 W. 8th Ave., Suite 3, Eugene, OR 97401.

Wipf & Stock
An Imprint of Wipf and Stock Publishers
199 W. 8th Ave., Suite 3
Eugene, OR 97401
www.wipfandstock.com

ISBN 13: 978-1-60899-539-4

Manufactured in the U.S.A.

Unless otherwise stated, all Scripture citations are from the New King James Version of the Bible © 1982 by Thomas Nelson, Inc., Nashville, Tennessee.

Contents

Abbreviations vii

1. Introduction 1
2. I believe 4
3. In God 12
4. The Father 25
5. Almighty 34
6. Creator of heaven and earth 40
7. And in Jesus Christ, his only Son, our Lord 48
8. He was conceived by the Holy Spirit, and born of the virgin Mary 63
9. He suffered under Pontius Pilate, was crucified, died and was buried 75
10. He descended to hell 87
11. On the third day he rose from the dead 108
12. He ascended to the heavens 119
13. And sat down at the right hand of God the Father almighty 133
14. From there he will come to judge the living and the dead 151
15. I believe in the Holy Spirit 160
16. The holy catholic church 170
17. The communion of saints 185
18. The remission of sins 204
19. The resurrection of the flesh 219
20. Eternal life 232
21. Amen 241

Bibliography 253
Scripture Index 265

Abbreviations

ANF   *Ante Nicene Fathers*. 10 vols. Edited by Alexander Roberts and John Donaldson, 1867–86. Digital Edition on CD-Rom, Albany, OR: Books for the Ages, 1997.

CB   *The Century Bible*. 17 vols. Edited by Walter F. Adeney. London: Caxton, no date.

CEPC   *The Creeds of the Evangelical Protestant Churches*. With Translations. By Philip Schaff. London: Hodder and Stoughton, 1877.

CTS   *Calvin's Commentaries*. Originally printed for the Calvin Translation Society, Edinburgh. Reprint, Grand Rapids, Baker, 1979, 22 vols.

CWC   *Conversations with the Confessions*. Edited by Joseph D. Small. Louisville: Geneva Press, 2005

DCT   *A Dictionary of Christian Theology*. Edited by Alan Richardson. London: SCM, 1969.

EBC   *Expositor's Bible Commentary*. Edited by Frank E. Gaebelein, 1976–92. Digital Edition on CD-Rom, Grand Rapids: Zondervan NIV Study Bible Library, 2001.

IBD   *The Illustrated Bible Dictionary*. 3 parts. Edited by James D. Douglas and Norman Hillyer. Leicester: UCCF, 1980.

JCBRF   *The Journal of the Christian Brethren Research Fellowship*.

JND   *The Collected Writings of John Nelson Darby*. Edited by William Kelly. Kingston-on-Thames: Stow Hill, 1962.

LCL   *The Apostolic Fathers*. Translated by Kirsopp Lake. 2 vols. London: Heinemann, 1912, 13. Loeb Classical Library. Edited by George Patrick Goold, Nos. 24 and 25.

NBC   *The New Bible Commentary: Revised.* Edited by Donald Guthrie and J. Alec Motyer, Leicester: IVP, 1970.

NCB   *New Century Bible.* General Editors: Ronald E. Clements and Matthew Black.

NICNT   *The New International Commentary on the New Testament.* General Editor: Frederick Fyvie Bruce.

NICOT   *The New International Commentary on the Old Testament.* General Editor: R. K. Harrison.

NIDNTT   *The New International Dictionary of New Testament Theology.* 3 vols. Edited by Colin Brown. Grand Rapids: Zondervan, 1975, 76, 78.

NIDOTTE   *The New International Dictionary of Old Testament Theology and Exegesis.* 5 vols. Edited by Willem A. van Gemeren. Grand Rapids: Zondervan, 1997.

NPNF   *Nicene and Post-Nicene Fathers.* 28 vols. Edited by Philip Schaff, 1886–98. Digital Edition on CD-Rom, Albany, OR: Books for the Ages, 1997.

SJT   *Scottish Journal of Theology.*

TNTC   *Tyndale New Testament Commentary.* General Editors: First Series: R. V. G. Tasker. Second Series: Leon Morris.

TOTC   *Tyndale Old Testament Commentary.* General Editor: Donald J. Wiseman.

WBC   *Word Biblical Commentary.* 52 vols. Edited by David A. Hubbard and Glenn W. Barker. Digital Edition on CD-Rom: Nashville, TN: Thomas Nelson, 2002.

1

Introduction

ONE SUNDAY AFTER THE evening service I was chatting to a member of my congregation whose background is Anglican. He suggested that the Anglican practice of regularly reciting the Apostles' Creed is one that we would do well to imitate in our Independent Evangelical Churches. His reason was that anyone who can say the Apostles' Creed and genuinely mean it is a real Christian.

I suspect he is right. If you can repeat the words given to us in this creed from the heart with joyful and unreserved seriousness, it is hard to doubt that God has done a true work of grace within you.

Although this creed has become known as the *Apostles' Creed*, it was not written by the apostles. It is true that a legend grew up in the early centuries, claiming that each of the apostles (including Matthias) contributed his own clause, and that all twelve clauses were put together to form the creed. However, the legend began to be questioned in the fifteenth century, and was largely discredited by the seventeenth. Most probably the Apostles' Creed grew out of a statement of faith in use in the church at Rome in the second century.[1] It had attained its present form by the end of the sixth century.[2] Because the Apostles' Creed is not authentically apostolic, William Cunningham argues that it "is not entitled to much respect, and is not fitted to be of much use as a summary of the leading doctrines of Christianity."[3]

However, this assessment seems unduly negative. It is not unfair to recognize in the Apostles' Creed a concise summary of genuinely apostolic doctrine, a distillation of the essence of the apostolic writings of the New Testament. Moreover, as Christopher Stead points out, the

1. See Kelly, *Creeds*, 172–81, 404–20.
2. Quasten, *Patrology*, Vol. 1, 23, 27; McGiffert, *Creed*, 3.
3. Cunningham, *Historical Theology*, 90.

usefulness of the creed is the link which it provides between our own age and "the historic faith of Christendom."[4] That is something from which we, as Reformed Evangelicals, can benefit. We have a tendency to look no further back than the eighteenth century heyday of the evangelical movement, or than the Reformation period at best. To be reminded that we, like our Reformed and Evangelical forefathers, stand in an ongoing heritage of faith stretching back across twenty centuries of godly reflection on the inspired documents of Scripture, must give us a fuller and fresher perspective on the faith which we profess.

Certainly, our Reformed predecessors were far more aware than we have become of their fellowship with the saints of earlier ages. For that reason they gave their sanction to the Apostles' Creed, in which they found a "consistent guide" for "their identification of fundamental teachings of the faith."[5]

Calvin, for example, writes:

> The Apostles' Creed . . . states the leading articles of redemption in a few words, and may thus serve as a tablet in which the points of Christian doctrine most deserving of attention are brought separately and distinctly before us. . . . It gives, in clear and succinct order, a full statement of our faith, and in everything which it contains is sanctioned by the sure testimony of Scripture.[6]

The Heidelberg Catechism dissects the Apostles' Creed clause-by-clause and expounds its meaning in detail, labeling it "our universally acknowledged confession of faith."[7] The Westminster Assembly included the Apostles' Creed in an appendix to its work, describing it as "a brief sum of the Christian faith, agreeable to the Word of God, and anciently received in the churches of Christ."[8]

Our concern is the *teaching* of the creed. Kelly rightly sees the creeds as "theological manifestos, shot through with doctrinal significance," and the Apostles' Creed as "a compendium of popular theology."[9] What did each clause mean to those who first used it? What did it come to mean as the Church had to cope with the challenges thrown at it with the

4. Stead, "Apostles' Creed," 10.
5. Muller, *After Calvin*, 51.
6. Calvin, *Institutes*, 2.16.18.
7. *Heidelberg Catechism*, Q. 22.
8. *Westminster Confession*, 704.
9. Kelly, *Creeds*, 131.

passage of time? How did the Reformers understand the creed in their writings, and especially in their Confessions of Faith? And what does the Apostles' Creed still mean for us today? The answers to these questions are not necessarily identical, because there is truth in Alexander Stewart's remark that "a form of words may remain the same and yet the meaning attached to it vary from time to time."[10]

But we do not wish to be merely theoretical. Friedrich Schleiermacher was right when he said, "The dogmatic procedure has reference entirely to preaching, and only exists in the interests of preaching."[11] These studies of the creed will, without apology, be sermonic.

The most important question of all is this: given that the Apostles' Creed summarizes our Christian faith, how should we then live in the twenty-first century world? God has placed us here now in this heritage of faith to know him and to live for him in our time and place. What do the insights of our spiritual ancestors imply for our discipleship today? How does the form of words which they have handed down to us inspire us in our knowledge of God in Christ by the Spirit?

Stewart is correct to say that "the Apostles' Creed . . . comes down to us from long past ages. It has sustained and cheered thousands of Christian hearts."[12] May our study of this creed prove to be sustenance to our souls too and a source of cheering encouragement in our Christian walk.

---

10. Stewart, *Creeds*, 52.
11. Schleiermacher, *Christian Faith*, 88.
12. Stewart, *Creeds*, 63.

2

I believe

In his expositions of the Apostles' Creed and its precursor, the Old Roman Creed, Kelly omits any reference to these opening words. And yet they are important. They characterize the Apostle's Creed as a statement of personal faith. This creed differs from the Nicene Creed, for example, in that it begins, "I believe," whereas the latter starts, "We believe." The Nicene Creed is a statement of universal Christian faith. So is the Apostles' Creed. But in reciting this creed each of us is saying, this faith, which the Church as a whole professes and has always professed, is my personal faith too: I am one with all my fellow Christians from every place and every generation.

The Apostles' Creed is not a statement which can be made in theoretical detachment. In declaring, "I believe," I am making a commitment. I am voicing my passion. I am gladly claiming as my own that story in which all believers have always rejoiced. Moreover, as Wolfhart Pannenberg has observed, "the declaration 'I believe' . . . means that the person who makes this profession of faith is committing himself to this God—to the Father, the Son and the Spirit. By so doing he is binding himself in solemn form."[1]

The nature of Christian commitment combines these two emotions—joy in the God who has become real to me as grace, and seriousness in the recognition that he is none other than the true and only God who is gloriously, even frighteningly, holy.

In his Commentary on the creed, written in the early years of the fifth century, Rufinus quotes Hebrews 11:6, "he who comes to God must believe that he is, and that he is a rewarder of those who diligently seek him."[2]

1. Pannenberg, *Creed*, 2.
2. Rufinus, *Commentary*, para. 3, 1099.

This text emphasizes the fact that believing in the reality of God is more than just a notional thing. "Mere belief in the existence of God is not enough: it could be belief in a god remote and unconcerned."[3] To believe, in any true sense, that God is, is already to believe something about him, namely that he willingly condescends to make himself accessible and available to those who seek him with earnestness and seriousness. To believe in God is not merely to assume that he is out there somewhere. It is to make him the goal of all our searching. It is to devote oneself to a quest for God, motivated by the assurance that he will not hide himself, but will give himself to the earnest seeker as his "exceedingly great reward" (Gen. 15:1).

For the reward of faith is nothing less than the possession of the living God himself—not to possess so as to manipulate or control or conquer, but to possess as the one overarching reality without which all other possessions are meaningless, to possess as the single inheritance which makes life as a whole significant. "The reward desired by those who seek him is the joy of finding him; he himself proves to be their 'exceeding joy' (Ps. 43:3)."[4] The final words of Hebrews 11:6 could be translated, "he **becomes** a rewarder to those who seek him." God, amazingly, places himself in the position of responding to our search. When from the heart we long for God, we shall not be disappointed.

But this quest must be wholehearted. It is the diligent seeker, the one who seeks God out with determination, who enters into the reward. As the Lord says through the prophet, "you will seek me and find me, when you search for me with all your heart" (Jer. 29:13). Our heart's desire should be nothing less than that we truly find God. Miss out on this ultimate discovery, and we are relegated to a life of frustration.

Andrew Murray put it so well: "Desire is the root of faith; without a hunger for God his existence is a matter of indifference; the knowledge of his being does not affect the soul. Faith seeks for God; it believes that he is; it keeps the heart open towards him; it bows in humility and hope for him to make himself known."[5]

Immediately after quoting the Hebrews text Rufinus goes on to cite "the prophet": "except you believe, you shall not understand." Exactly the same statement with the same attribution to "the prophet" occurs in

---

3. Wilson, *Hebrews*, 204.
4. F. F. Bruce, *Hebrews*, 290.
5. A. Murray, *Holiest*, 430.

one of the works of Rufinus' contemporary, Augustine.[6] Augustine was probably writing a few years after Rufinus, so may well be quoting him.

These precise words are not found in Scripture. Perhaps Rufinus had Isaiah 43:10 in mind: "you are . . . my servant whom I have chosen, that you may know and believe me, and understand that I am he." Here Isaiah mentions believing before understanding. Rufinus expounds this, very appropriately, to mean that believing comes chronologically prior to understanding, because believing is the necessary prerequisite for a right understanding.

Augustine develops this truth in greater detail. He writes: "If you have not understood, I say, believe. For understanding is the reward of faith. Therefore do not seek to understand in order to believe, but believe that you may understand." Augustine makes reference to John 7:17: "if anyone wants to do his will, he shall know concerning the doctrine whether it is from God." He equates knowing with understanding and wanting to do his will with believing. The latter equation he bases on John 6:29: "this is the work of God, that you believe in him whom he has sent."[7]

A few years before the end of the eleventh century an Italian monk called Anselm became Archbishop of Canterbury. In a book written fifteen years earlier he made a general statement about the believer's situation in words which very closely resemble those of Augustine: "The believer does not seek to understand that he may believe, but he believes that he may understand: for unless he believed he would not understand."

Later Anselm expressed the same truth in a personal way: "I long to understand in some degree your truth, which my heart believes and loves. For I do not seek to understand that I may believe, but I believe in order to understand. For this also I believe—that unless I believed I should not understand." Anselm recognizes that we were created to see God, but that, because of sin, we have lost this blessedness and brought misery upon ourselves. As a result, we can no longer seek God unless God first reaches out to us, and we cannot find God unless he reveals himself to us. Otherwise, Anselm says, we strive towards God, and

---

6. Augustine, *John*, Tractate 29, para. 6, 367–68. The language of patristic quotations has been updated.

7. Augustine, *John*, Tractate 29, para. 6, 368.

merely stumble on ourselves; we can only look downwards until God raises us up so that we can look upwards.[8]

This mighty, gracious divine initiative is what leads us to faith. Believing is responding to God's revelation, and without that believing response there is no possibility of understanding divine things. But that believing response cannot take place unless God first comes to us and makes himself known. Only then can we believe, and only in believing can we understand the truth.

Augustine makes the same point. He considers what it is to "believe in him": it is "by believing to love him, by believing to esteem highly, by believing to go into him and to be incorporated in his members. It is faith itself then that God exacts from us: and he does not find that which he exacts, unless he has bestowed what he may find."[9]

That is why the declaration "I believe" has to stand at the head of the credal statement. We do not learn the doctrines of the faith in order, having understood them, to be able to say, OK then, I am persuaded, I believe. We are led to believe by the grace of God in his self-revealing outreach to us, and the result is that we seek him more and more, and so our understanding of divine mysteries is formed and shaped and increased on the foundation of our God-given faith.

The words "I believe" can, therefore, only be said in a tone of wonder and adoration. They are my recognition that God has committed himself to me, and it is in response to that commitment that I make my commitment to him. I say "I believe" with amazement in my voice, as I acknowledge the heart-transforming miracle that has turned an incorrigible unbeliever into one who is now enabled to take God seriously, to love him, to trust him, to believe. I cannot say "I believe" except with baited breath, rejecting any sense that this is my achievement, and humbly rejoicing in the marvelous mercy of the one who has made me a believer. I understood nothing. I was a spiritual dim-wit. What an astonishing thing God has done in granting me faith and launching me on to the pathway to understanding!

The passionate commitment involved in believing is emphasized by the Latin wording of the Apostles' Creed, and by the presumed Greek original which lies behind the Latin version—and indeed by the regular phraseology of the New Testament. More literally the words "I believe

8. Anselm, *Proslogion*, 4.
9. Augustine, *John*, Tractate 29, para. 6, 368.

in" would be translated "I believe into". That is not an acceptable idiom in English, but we need to ponder the implications of the Greek and Latin wording, *eis* or *in* respectively, followed by the accusative. This usage is said to be "a striking departure from ordinary Greek."[10]

It has been suggested that the introduction of the phrase *believe* with *eis* followed by the accusative was important for stressing the vital distinction "between mere belief and personal trust," and that this wording emphasizes the bringing of the believer into union with Christ, with faith as the entry point.[11] Augustine has hinted at the significance of the phrase by his reference to "believing to go into him and to be incorporated in his members." To believe *into* God is to make such a commitment that one is identified with God. To say, "I believe into God" is to say, I have totally aligned my existence with God; I am nothing without my God; I depend upon God entirely; I view everything now in the light of this passionate relationship with himself into which God has graciously drawn me.

We can go further still. Alister McGrath points out that "I believe in God" could mean little more than *I am of the opinion that there is a God*. However, its real import is far stronger.[12] A Latin dictionary gives *to believe* as only the fourth possible meaning of the word *credo*. Meanings one to three are *to entrust, to have confidence in,* and *to give credence to*.[13] A secular Greek dictionary likewise suggests *to entrust* as one of the possible renderings of the Greek verb *pisteuō*.[14] To say, "I believe in God" means that I have entrusted myself to God. I have placed myself in his hands. I have given myself up to him to look after me. I have abandoned self-confidence and I am relying on him for everything in life, death and eternity. I have complete confidence that he will take care of me unfailingly in every time of need. On the basis of God's remarkable initiative of grace, I have willingly and gladly become his. The hymn-writer expresses it like this:

> I lift my heart to thee, Savior divine;
> For thou art all to me, and I am thine.
> Is there on earth a closer bond than this,
> That my Beloved's mine and I am his?

10. Michel, "*pistis*," 599.
11. Cf. Moulton, *Grammar*, 68.
12. McGrath, *I Believe*, 20.
13. Smith and Lockwood, *Dictionary*, 164.
14. Liddell and Scott, *Lexicon*, 561.

Thine am I by all ties; but chiefly thine
That through thy sacrifice, thou, Lord, art mine.
By thine own cords of love, so sweetly wound
Around me, I to thee am closely bound.[15]

That is what it means to say "I believe".

The Apostles' Creed can therefore never be a mere statement of academic theology. It can only be a summary of the whole way that I regard my entire life. To recite this creed is to voice a definition of who I am. It is to be a true Christian.

To some people the assertion that believing must precede understanding might arouse the suspicion that the Christian faith is unreasonable, that believing is not the activity of a rational mind. Rufinus replies to this pagan accusation by insisting that "nothing in life can be transacted if there be not first a readiness to believe. . . . Nothing can possibly be done or remain stable unless belief precede." This applies not just in spiritual matters, but, in a generalized way, to every aspect of human life and practice—to the extent that, without a faith of sorts "not even common life can be lived."

Rufinus gives a number of examples. You don't set out on a sea voyage, entrusting yourself to the deep, unless you believe that you will have a safe passage. You don't commit seed to the ground unless you believe that the showers and sunshine will come in the right balance so that the crop will ripen. People get married because they believe that children will be born. Parents send their children to school because they believe that the teachers' instruction will be transferred to their children. People seek political power in the belief that they will be obeyed by peoples, cities, and armies.

Rufinus concludes: "But if no one enters upon any one of these several undertakings except in the belief that the results spoken of will follow, must not belief be much more requisite if one would come to the knowledge of God?"[16]

To seek to understand a God in whom you do not believe is surely the true irrationality. That means that any so-called "theology" which has become detached from God's self-revelation in his word, and has wandered into mere speculation is ridiculous. It is only because God has revealed himself, and this revelation has given birth to faith in our

---

15. By Charles Edward Mudie (1818–1890).
16. Rufinus, *Commentary*, para. 3, 1099; Cf. Pannenberg, *Creed*, 3–4.

hearts that we can even begin to embark on a life of exploration into the mystery of this glorious and gracious God.

However, in placing believing before understanding we have to be careful not to wander off into mysticism. It is striking that Rufinus, even as he emphasizes the priority of faith, nevertheless repeatedly uses the phrase "believe that." Faith is not just some vague, contentless, indefinable, ethereal feeling.[17] It is, most emphatically, in response to God's self-revelation that we believe. We believe because he has told us something about himself. We believe in order to understand, but we cannot believe at all without at least an embryonic understanding. Believing and understanding are one of a piece. Believing precedes understanding because it is the first installment of understanding, and understanding is the outworking of faith.

There is some point in Cranfield's suggestion, although he does not carry it through (any more than I am doing!) that discussion of the words "I believe" should really be postponed until the rest of the creed has been considered, because "it is whom we believe in that is decisive about Christian faith. It is not our action of believing but the One in whom we believe, who he is and what he has done, is doing, and will do, God himself in his grace and his self-revelation, that is all-important."[18]

Pannenberg points out that faith understood as a leap of blind decision without substantial justification is degraded to a work of self-redemption. What we believe is in fact the solid foundation of our believing. The faith of the believer depends, not on his decision to believe, but "on the factual substance in whose reliability he can trust."[19]

There is a hymn which includes the lines:

> My faith, it is an oaken staff,
> O let me on it lean.[20]

This conveys a quite false picture of faith. If we lean on our faith, we shall quickly discover that the oak has gone rotten and, as we put our weight on it, it will simply disintegrate. Faith is not something on which we lean, it is the act of leaning upon the God who is so reliably strong that he will never cave in under any pressure that could possibly come

---

17. Cf. Barth, *Dogmatics*, 25.
18. Cranfield, *Creed*, 8.
19. Pannenberg, *Creed*, 10.
20. By Thomas Toke Lynch (1818–1871).

upon him. I believe, and in so doing I am safe, because the God who has revealed himself to me is the rock.

Most aptly Wolfhart Pannenberg points out that

> Isaiah told Ahaz, king of Judah: 'If you will not believe, surely you shall not be established' (Isa. 7:9). He meant that the man who is not anchored in what is unshakeable and enduring—that is to say in the God of Israel—cannot himself endure. For everything passes except the eternal God, and justifies no ultimate, unconditional trust.... The eternal God ... [is] the unshakeable foundation on which a man can unconditionally build.[21]

---

21. Pannenberg, *Creed*, 5.

3

In God

As soon as we see in the words "I believe" a passionate personal commitment we are led to the recognition that this God, with whom we have come into relationship and with whom our identity has been thoroughly bound up, is himself absolutely personal. How could we make a personal commitment to a God who was not personal? Our personal commitment to God is a response to a personal approach from God.

"I believe in God" can never, for the sincere believer, represent the vague awareness that there is some mysterious force, some inexplicable power, "out there" somewhere, or "in here" somehow. I do not believe in a philosophical idol who is nothing more than the end of an argument which leads, allegedly by a process of logic, to the conclusion that god must exist. "God" is not some kind of fall-back, because nothing else is as readily explained in the absence of the God hypothesis, and certainly not "a stop-gap for our embarrassments,"[1] one whom, in desperation, we drag in "when we are at the end of our resources."[2] Karl Barth goes so far as to say that the idea of a supreme being, which is as far as the human being can go by his own powers of reasoning, "has nothing to do with God."[3]

No—when I say "I believe in God" I am talking about my friend, one whom I trust, one whom I love, one whose mercy I have received, one who has been unimaginably good to me, one whom I dare to claim that I know. I am speaking of the personal God.

---

1. Bonhoeffer, *Letters*, 138.
2. Bonhoeffer, *Letters*, 107.
3. Barth, *Dogmatics*, 23.

Rufinus may put it untidily, but it is true, nonetheless, that "'God' . . . is the name of that nature or substance which is above all things."[4] However, the substantiality of God is not to be understood as if it is some sort of gas, or atmosphere, or vapor, or an electric current that secretly determines our fate in a mechanistic way. This divine nature is not a mere thing. The wonderful fact is that he who is above all things is the personality from whom all personhood derives its reality. The one who, as God, is over all, is the very one into whom I have placed my believing confidence because he has, in incalculable kindness, made himself known to me, not as a force or power, but as the lover of my soul.

Being personal, God is not remote and aloof. Despite the quaint feel of his language nowadays, Alexander Stewart well says,

> God is not abstract divinity, dwelling in
> 'heavens too high for our upreaching,
> Coldly sublime, intolerably just.'
> Nay, but the All-Great is the All-Loving too.[5]

This personal God of biblical revelation is a far cry from the Unmoved Mover, as the Greek philosopher, Aristotle, labeled his understanding of God. Aristotle pictured this world of time and matter as being in everlasting circular motion. But motion cannot begin unless something already there produces it. This "First Cause" is what makes everything else move and change, but in itself it must be free from the possibility of change, while ceaselessly exercising the power of causing motion. This power is not exercised by action, since that would involve motion on the part of the Mover, and yet it is said to be unmoved. Its only activity is that of self-contemplation, and it can have no knowledge of, or relationship with, anything outside itself.[6] It seems that the Unmoved Mover does not so much push things to get them moving, as sit there like a magnet, drawing everything into motion by the power of its pure lure.

But this is not the lure of love, not in any genuine definition of the word. There is no reciprocal relationship. Aristotle's god is totally impersonal. "This Eternal Mind enclosed in a sterile self-sufficiency, ev-

---

4. Rufinus, *Commentary*, para. 4, 1100.
5. Stewart, *Creeds*, 59.
6. See Armstrong, *Ancient Philosophy*, 87–88.

erlastingly contemplating its own thinking ... is not at all like anything we mean by the word 'God.'"[7]

But because the creed-affirming believer is passionately committed to a personal God, equally unacceptable is the reduction of God to the deepest, innermost depths of myself and the world. Such a definition of God is just as depersonalizing as the view that God is a transcendent force.

In the second half of the twentieth-century, it became quite popular to describe God as "the ground of being." This was a result of the influence of Paul Tillich. He uses the phrase many times in the first volume of his *Systematic Theology*. For example, he writes: "The religious word for what is called the ground of being is God."[8] Conversely, he claims that "many confusions in the doctrine of God and many apologetic weaknesses could be avoided if God were understood first of all as being-itself or as the ground of being."[9]

However, the phrase "ground of being" sounds depressingly impersonal as a title for the God in whom I have come to believe. The Bible does not describe God in such terms. It tells us that God is love (1 John 4:8). You cannot fall in love with the ground. You do not commit yourself passionately to a well-grounded argument. But the God who is so personal that he can only be portrayed as love in himself—there is one in whom I can believe with intense, intimate longing.

Schubert Ogden claims that, in a secularized society, "God" must be defined as the ground of the significance of human being and the world. God is "the very meaning of reality," to the extent that belief in "God" is really unavoidable.[10] However, in such a statement both the terms "belief" and "God" are drastically truncated. Neither is recognizable as being what the earnest believer who affirms the Apostles' Creed really means when he or she makes this passionate commitment to one who is greatly loved. Ogden maintains "that the primary use or function of 'God' is to refer to the objective ground in reality itself of our ineradicable confidence in the final worth of our existence."[11]

---

7. Armstrong, *Ancient Philosophy*, 90
8. Tillich, *Systematic Theology*, 156.
9. Tillich, *Systematic Theology*, 235.
10. Ogden, *Reality*, 39, 44–45.
11. Ogden, *Reality*, 37.

This statement is a give-away. For the passionate believer who voices commitment and longing in the words of the creed, to describe God as a function, as something of use, is already to betray the fact that we are not talking about the same God. Inter-personal relationships are never merely functional. Just as in human life, to seek to "use" another person is dehumanizingly tyrannical, so to imagine that God is there for our use is to treat him as less than personal.

Ogden may have a point in his argument that, pressed to its logical conclusion, all human discourse, thought, and behavior proceeds on the assumption that "God" exists. This, however, still raises the question, is the presupposed god of universal human confidence really the beloved one who has revealed himself to us and so invited us to engage, with all-consuming desire, in the quest for him? The faith of the creed is, as we have seen, a response to the God who has revealed himself to us, and whom otherwise we could not possibly know, not a mere affirmation of the opinion that the word "God" can be defined in such a way as to make it true by definition to say that God is real.

Ogden's comments would have a point if he spoke in terms of seeing God as the *source* of the meaningfulness of existence. But then he is the source of meaning because he is. To identify God with the meaningfulness of existence is too reductionistic. That is not the God of whom the creed leads me to say, I believe in him.

Ogden claims that traditional theism has depicted God in ways that entail the denial that he is really related to us. He mentions pure actuality, immutability, impassivity, aseity, and immateriality as examples.[12] However, as Ogden indeed admits,[13] these are not the perfections in which God reveals himself in Scripture. They are philosophically motivated speculations, some, at least, of which may be entirely wrong—at any rate as classically understood.

It is noteworthy that the Apostles' Creed does not portray God in these kind of terms, even though at certain points in the development of its wording some of these terms crept in.[14] However, it is to the credit of the early believers that they have passed down to us a creed which, in its final form, avoids turning God into a metaphysical, impersonal It.

---

12. Ogden, *Reality*, 48–49.
13. Ogden, *Reality*, 50.
14. See Kelly, *Creeds*, 174, 176; cf. Rufinus, *Commentary*, para. 5, 1102–3.

Ogden appears to believe that it is impossible to relate to a God who is not found in the depths of ordinary human experience. However, my contention is that a God of the depths who still falls short of being personal in a thoroughgoing way is also not one to whom we can "relate" in any ordinary understanding of the word. Relationship implies mutuality and conscious enjoyment of one another. It suggests communication and self-aware participation in one another's lives.

Admittedly, Ogden is attempting to portray God as "infinite personal existence,"[15] and speaks, intentionally paradoxically, of his "absolute relativity."[16] However, relativity and relationship are not the same thing. For Ogden, God's relativity is "his being related to all others" as the absolute ground of any and all relationships.[17] But I still get the sense from Ogden's terminology that there is nothing more to God than his being that ground—and that falls short of the intensely personal God revealed in Scripture.

To be able to say "I believe in God" requires a view of God as one to whom I can consciously relate, not as one with whom relating is an inevitable feature of mere existence. Relationship is something entered into voluntarily, happily, out of love, not something which simply happens automatically as part of the definition of what it is to exist. The Apostles' Creed is a satisfying statement of faith, because it implies that God is personal and has drawn me by grace into real relationship with himself.

I find myself in agreement with Richard Dawkins on this point. In his recent book, *The God Delusion*, he points out that the word "God" becomes completely useless if it is defined so broadly that it is inevitable that people find God wherever they look for him.[18] Dawkins quotes a telling comment by Carl Sagan: "If by 'God' one means the set of physical laws that govern the universe, then clearly there is such a 'god'. This God is emotionally unsatisfying. . . . It does not make much sense to pray to the law of gravity."[19]

As Winkie Pratney says, "Even a cursory reading of the Bible shows us a striking fact: God really *is* personal. . . . God's personality *is* alive

---

15. Ogden, *Reality*, 62.
16. Ogden, *Reality*, 66.
17. Ogden, *Reality*, 60.
18. Dawkins, *Delusion*, 12–13.
19. Dawkins, *Delusion*, 19.

in the Bible; he is constantly represented as one who sees, hears, acts, moves, reacts, and responds to a living, moving creation as its living, moving Creator."[20]

Having mentioned Richard Dawkins, it is worth observing that his aim is to demonstrate the improbability of the God-hypothesis. He considers various arguments for the existence of God, and attempts to debunk them. However, his rejection of some of these arguments is far from convincing. Take the cosmological argument, for example. Why is there anything at all and not nothing? Does existence itself not point to a Creator? Dawkins says not, preferring to appeal to "a big bang singularity."[21] This still leaves open the question, Why did the big bang happen?

Dawkins' arguments for the improbability of God are just as unprovable and no more cogent than arguments for the probability of God. Much of his book is assertion which is beyond proof. In the end it becomes a matter of faith, the difference between the theist and the atheist being where you place the emphasis.

Actually the Bible never tries to demonstrate God's reality. It simply takes it for granted. The grand opening statement, "In the beginning God," tells us that God is the ultimate assumption without which there is nothing. God is the precondition for all human exploration and discourse. It is only possible for Richard Dawkins to deny God's existence because God exists! All arguments for the existence of God start with us, and work towards God. The Bible starts with God and puts us in our place. The Bible does not try to prove God's existence, because God is personal, not a logical inference. It therefore calls us to meet him.

One currently fashionable evangelistic program, the Alpha Course, invites people to realize that "we were created to live in a relationship with God," and that it is through the experience of a relationship with God that the purpose and meaning of life become clear.[22] The closing paragraph of the Course textbook begins with these words: "How great God is and what a privilege it is to walk in a relationship with him, to be loved by him and to serve him all our lives."[23] Whatever its shortcomings, at this point the Alpha Course certainly throbs to the heartbeat

20. Pratney, *God*, 170–71.
21. Dawkins, *Delusion*, 78.
22. Gumbel, *Questions*, 15–16.
23. Gumbel, *Questions*, 250–51.

of the Biblical revelation of a God who is intensely personal, and with whom I can enjoy genuine personal relationship.

Not that the Bible ever refers to "relationship" with God. However, the Biblical language of knowing God may fairly be paraphrased in terms of relationship. To know God is not a mere intellectual knowledge. It is personal acquaintance with one who is living and personal. The Hebrew root *yāda'*, most often translated "to know", speaks of the experience of intimacy[24]—and, most startlingly, shows us that we can enjoy such intimacy with God. God is personal, and our personality reflects his, and answers to the call that comes from him.

In Exodus 33:13 Moses prays that he might know God. We have only just been told that "the Lord spoke to Moses face to face, as a man speaks to his friend" (v. 11). Moses knew what it was to enjoy personal relationship with God, and wanted to experience that relationship at a deeper level. In verse 12 Moses has reminded the Lord of a statement which he had made: "I know you by name, and you have also found grace in my sight."

Moses' prayer that he may know the Lord proceeds on the basis of the Lord's prior knowledge of Moses. The Lord knew Moses by name: he had a "personal affection" for Moses.[25] Relationship with God is possible because he has looked upon us with loving favor. As a personal God he takes the initiative of grace and draws unto into that relationship with himself where we can truly say "I believe in God" with passionate commitment.

But Moses' conversation with God indicates how we may know the Lord in his divine personality. In verse 12 the Lord's word assures Moses that he has found grace, but in verse 13 Moses prays that he may find grace in the Lord's sight. The starting point for relationship with God is his outreaching grace. It is by the same personal approach in grace that the Lord makes to us repeatedly, constantly, that our personal relationship with him is sustained. We cannot claim a relationship with God as a right. We do not deserve a relationship with God. Grace alone brings us, calls us, draws us, into personal relationship with him. A personal God invites us, woos us, and creates in our hearts the longing to know him.

---

24. Gesenius, *Lexicon*, 190.
25. Gill, *Exposition*, on Exod. 33:12.

The personal nature of God is brought out also in John's first letter. The possibility of genuine relationship with a God who must, therefore, be personal is indicated in 4:19, "we love him because he first loved us." This suggests a warm, emotional relationship. But the two-way experience of our love for God and God's love for us is rooted in God's loving approach to us. We relate to God with a depth of passion, only because we are responding to his prior love to us. "In loving, we do but reciprocate God's love and respond to it. For our love would be but a poor and sorry thing unless it were linked on to God's love, as the consequence, or as it were the continuation of it—the reflection or reproduction of it. Always, it must be ultimately, in the last resort, God's love on which we fall back."[26]

But to speak like this of God is to emphasize that when we say "I believe in God" we are talking about a God who is personal. On the words "God is love" (1 John 4:8) Stephen Smalley says that they reflect "the Jewish (OT) understanding of God as living, personal and active,"[27] while Howard Marshall rightly comments that "the statement stresses the personality of God to the fullest extent."[28]

The personal nature of a relational God has been emphasized recently in the approach which has become known as "Open Theism." It is certainly true that there is much about Open Theism which is questionable. However, it is rarely the case that everything said by a particular movement is bad, and we must be careful not to over react. It seems to me that those who are proposing this view of God have spotted some important Biblical emphases, which ought not to be dismissed out of hand.

Open Theism, as summarized by John Sanders, teaches that God's sovereignty over all is general, rather than a meticulous control of every minute detail. God created human beings with genuine freedom and invites us to collaborate with him towards the fulfillment of his goals. While there are certainly some things which God brings about unilaterally, there are other things which God has left open, depending on our requests and actions. There is no danger that God's eternal purpose will fail, but his purpose relates to the destination rather than the route, and God's strategies for achieving his purpose are flexible.[29]

---

26. Candlish, *1 John*, Vol. 2, 157.
27. Smalley, *1, 2, 3 John*, on 1 John 4:8.
28. Marshall, *Epistles of John*, 213.
29. Sanders, *Openness Theology*, paras. 1–5.

We may well want to question this limited view of God's sovereignty. However, the strength of Open Theism is that it takes the Bible seriously as a real revelation of what God is like. It recognizes that there are passages which speak of God's sovereign actions, such as Isaiah 46:9–10, "I am God, and there is none like me, declaring the end from the beginning, and from ancient times things that are not yet done, saying, 'My counsel shall stand, and I will do all my pleasure.'" Many such texts are definite predictive prophecies. One example would be Jeremiah 5:15–18, which begins, "'Behold, I will bring a nation against you from afar, O house of Israel,' says the Lord," and ends, "'Nevertheless in those days,' says the Lord, 'I will not make a complete end of you.'"[30]

However, there are other verses and passages which represent God as responding to human choices. It is worth noting a few examples of texts in the latter category. In the dying years of Judah's independent existence as a political entity, the Lord instructs Jeremiah to address the people from the temple court. He says, "Perhaps everyone will listen and turn from his evil way, that I may relent concerning the calamity which I purpose to bring on them because of the evil of their doings" (Jer. 26:3). The response of the people of Nineveh to Jonah's preaching had this result: "God saw their works, that they turned from their evil way; and God relented from the disaster that he had said he would bring upon them, and he did not do it" (Jonah 3:10).

The traditional explanation of such statements may be illustrated by Calvin's comments on the Jonah reference:

> Strictly speaking, no repentance can belong to God: and it ought not to be ascribed to his secret and hidden counsel. God then is in himself ever the same, and consistent with himself; but he is said to repent, when a regard is had to the comprehension of men: for as we conceive God to be angry, whenever he summons us to his tribunal, and shows to us our sins; so we also conceive him to be placable, when he offers the hope of pardon. But it is according to our perceptions that there is any change.[31]

There is, however, something unsatisfactory about the idea that certain Scriptures are accommodating God to our perception, and are not telling us about God as he is in himself. The danger of such an ap-

---

30. Other examples of texts in this category would include Num. 23:19; 1 Sam. 8:9; Ps. 139:2, 16; Jer. 1:5; Acts 15:18.

31. Calvin, *Minor Prophets*, Vol. 3, 115.

proach is that the nature of the Bible as a true and real revelation of God is undermined.

The advocates of Open Theism usually claim that God does not know in advance when human outcomes will generate a response on his part. That, surely, is to go too far. Even human beings can sometimes predict the future with considerable accuracy. How often do we hear the statement, I could see it coming! The book of Proverbs twice says, "a prudent man foresees evil and hides himself" (Prov. 22:3; 27:12). Nevertheless, the strength of Open Theism is this: rather than explaining one set of texts away on the basis of the other, it seeks to do justice to the entirety of God's revelation of himself as a personal, relational God.

In his book on Jonah R.T. Kendall takes a similar line. He points out that it is possible to quote some verses, such as Numbers 23:19 or 1 Samuel 15:29, which tell us that God does not change his mind, and another set, including Genesis 6:6, Exodus 32:14, and 2 Kings 20:1–6, which suggest the opposite. Kendall admits that our tendency is to embrace a particular view of the difficulty, and then force other verses to fit in to our preferred scheme. Kendall's advice on solving the problem is to empty ourselves before the Lord, to come to the Bible like a child, and to be open to the fact that we do not know the answer.[32] "God is not meant to be fully understood. He is meant to be worshipped."[33]

Within Open Theism's framework of understanding, God is dynamically personal. A few references will demonstrate this and clarify the implications of such a statement. Clark Pinnock finds the model of God as a caring parent decisive in the Bible. God has "qualities of love and responsiveness, generosity and sensitivity, openness and vulnerability." He is "a person (rather than a metaphysical principle) who experiences the world, responds to what happens, relates to us and interacts dynamically with humans."[34]

Elsewhere Pinnock describes the Biblical ideal of God as "a dynamic, relational person; vulnerable, sympathetic, accessible and committed to relationships."[35] He defines the view of God which is lifted up in the Bible as that of a personal God who desires loving relationships which are "mutual, reciprocal and give-and-take." Pinnock continues:

32. Kendall, *Jonah*, 202–4.
33. Kendall, *Jonah*, 210.
34. Pinnock, "Systematic Theology," 103.
35. Pinnock, *Mover*, 7.

"The Bible presents God as a personal agent who creates and acts, wills and plans, loves and values in relation to covenant partners. God is often presented as the husband of his people and father of children, who nurtures, raises, and calls them to participate with him dynamically in an open future."[36]

William Placher is right to say that "in writing of a God who is vulnerable in love, a God who freely chooses to suffer, Christian theologians are only reclaiming their own birthright, for it is just such a God that we encounter in the Bible."[37]

Important for our understanding of God as personal is the doctrine of the Trinity. The Apostles' Creed has a Trinitarian structure. It has three main sections, each affirming belief in one of the three persons of the triune God. The Heidelberg Catechism asks how the articles are divided, and the answer is: "Into three parts: The first concerns God *the Father* and our *creation*; the second God *the Son* and our *redemption*; and the third God *the Holy Spirit* and our *sanctification*."[38] It is true that Calvin divided the creed into four parts, treating the remaining clauses which follow the statement of faith in the Holy Spirit under the heading of the Church.[39] However, it is probably better to regard these as belonging with the affirmation of faith in the Holy Spirit, as depicting "the fruits of the Spirit in action."[40]

Although the doctrine of the Trinity is not spelt out in this creed, it is implied by this structure. Grant's contention that the creed does not support Trinitarian belief[41] may have some relevance to the original Roman Creed, but can hardly be true of the creed in its final form. The truth of the Trinity is not spelt out, because it is the creed's underlying assumption, without which it would not be possible to say "I believe" at all, since the one in whom I believe is the one who has revealed himself as the triune God.

Pinnock sees Trinitarian faith as pointing clearly to the personal nature of God: he "embodies a relational fullness and richness in himself. Given the fact that Father and Son are persons and that the Spirit is

36. Pinnock, *Mover*, 25–26.
37. Placher, "Vulnerability of God," 194.
38. *Heidelberg Catechism*, Q. 24.
39. Hesselink, *Catechism*, 110–11 ; Muller, *Unaccommodated*, 132–3.
40. Kelly, *Creeds*, 155.
41. Grant, *Gods*, 168.

spoken of in personal terms in the Scriptures, it is appropriate to speak of God as a community of persons."[42] Thus, personal relationships are intrinsic to the Godhead: "the tri-personal God is the very model of love, a community where each gives and receives love."[43] Augustine describes the Trinity as the "perpetual dearness of love."[44] The invitation which comes to us to enter into personal relationship with God is the gracious outflow and overflow of that inner Trinitarian love. Because God is personal, we may know, experience and enjoy "the friendship of the Lord," which is how Pinnock translates Psalm 25:14.[45]

The faithful believer in affirming the creed says "I believe in God." I do so with joy, knowing that this is not an abstract statement, but the heartbeat of my entire life. I believe in the God who has revealed himself. In revealing himself he has made himself known, he has declared himself to be personal, he has, by his powerfully gracious and graciously powerful call, summoned me into relationship with him. And that call of grace and power has opened my heart and wooed me to love the personal God.

The very first chapter of the Bible tells us that God made humankind in his own image. Often we ask, what do we know about God which might help us to explain what it is for us to exist as his image? For example, Robert Shaw, in his exposition of the Westminster Confession, argues that God is a spirit, and therefore "in immateriality and immortality the soul of man bears a resemblance to God." He goes on to see the dominion which reflects the divine sovereignty and the original moral rectitude which reflected the divine holiness as further aspects of the divine image.[46]

However, it is worth considering whether the order of argument should be reversed. If humankind is the image of God, what do we know about human beings which might throw light for us on the being of God? Then we would answer: we human beings are persons; since we reflect the nature of God, he must therefore indeed be personal.[47]

---

42. Pinnock, "Systematic Theology," 107–8.
43. Pinnock, *Mover*, 28.
44. Augustine, *Creed*, para. 13, 699.
45. Pinnock, *Mover*, 158.
46. Shaw, *Exposition*, 63–64 .
47. Cf. Rice, "Biblical Support," 39.

Harry Boer advocates this procedure,[48] and concludes: "The central characteristic of Man as image of God is the quality of personhood. It is characteristic of God as sole Deity, and it is equally and radically distinctive of the three members of the trinity."[49]

In Genesis 1:27 humankind is said to be created as the image of God male and female. Karl Barth saw this as the Bible's intended definition of the image. Human being as male and female is being made for relationship. The male-female relationship is, however, simply interpersonal relationship in its most basic form.[50] Although Berkouwer finds Barth's exegesis unconvincing,[51] it seems to me that it merits serious consideration. Moreover, the capacity for interpersonal human relationships is a pointer to our capacity for relationship with God.

Relationships are fascinatingly enjoyable. To be able to relate to a God who is excitingly personal is a high privilege. When we say "I believe in God" we are giving our testimony that we have found it to be so—and we worship at the footstool of our heavenly friend. "God then is essentially love and grace. His mercy unto man is not merely an accidental thing: it is the essence of the divine heart."[52]

---

48. Boer, *An Ember*, 5–6.
49. Boer, *An Ember*, 8
50. Cited by Berkouwer, *Image of God*, 72–73.
51. Berkouwer, *Image of God*, 73–74.
52. Barth, *Faith*, 31.

4

The Father

GIVEN THAT GOD IS personal, it is not surprising that the first descriptive title which the creed uses for him is Father. The paternal nature of God is the chief expression of his personality. This is the major emphasis in the Bible, evident already in the Old Testament, coming to the fore in the teaching of Jesus, and serving as an underlying assumption in the witness of the apostles. In the Old Testament there is a total of a dozen direct references to God as Father. We then find well over 150 references in the gospels, and about seventy-five in the rest of the New Testament.

It is true that the Bible uses other pictures, descriptions, and titles to convey the nature of God, but equally true that the model of God as Father is something of a "controlling metaphor."[1] God's Fatherhood is the basic primordial truth in which belief in God is proclaimed.[2]

In this respect Biblical revelation stands out against the background of the surrounding pagan world. With reference to the period of Jesus' incarnate life, Donald Guthrie says: "Whereas the contemporary pagan world held its gods in fear, the Christian view of God's fatherhood brings an unparalleled element of intimacy into man's relation with God."[3]

The first reference in Scripture to God as Father is found in Deuteronomy 32:6. The LORD is here portrayed as the Father of Israel[4] by virtue of his having bought them. The juxtapositioning of Fatherhood and purchase seems a strange combination of terms. It may draw attention to the fact that it was in their redemption from Egypt in the exodus

---

1. Fretheim, *Suffering of God*, 11.
2. Cf. Kelly, *Creeds*, 133.
3. Guthrie, *New Testament Theology*, 80–81.
4. See also 1 Chr. 29:10; Isa. 63:16; 64:8; Jer. 3:19.

that God became Israel's Father by adoption.⁵ However, the verb can have more than one meaning. It is interesting to see that the translation of the verb in its first Biblical occurrence (Gen. 4:1) has to do with birth: in giving birth and becoming a mother Eve 'acquired' a son. Perhaps in our text we have the parallel idea that God, as Israel's Father, acquired them by begetting them—he brought them into being as the people to whom he committed himself in this personal relationship. The reference may well be to the exodus, but the emphasis is not so much on the redeeming purchase as on the motivating love.

Another Scripture, Jeremiah 31:9, depicts God's Fatherhood of Israel in beautifully tender terms. The Father is portrayed as gently pleading with his weeping children, and then leading them into refreshment and stability. The setting is the return of Israel to her land after the decades spent as refugees in exile. The LORD "will renew with her the same fatherly love he displayed in centuries past."⁶

Four mentions of God's Fatherhood in the Old Testament⁷ relate, in the first instance at least, to Solomon. The emphasis in 2 Samuel 7:14 is on the Father's care for Solomon his son, expressed in "all affection and tenderness."⁸ This involves both chastening and merciful care. By omitting the reference to chastening, the parallel passage (1 Chr. 17:13) makes the point that, as in all father-son relationships, the chastening is an aspect of the merciful care. Both contexts stress that the Father's mercy is immune to all possibility of withdrawal.

However, there is a second reason why the Chronicler does not mention the chastening. The ultimate thrust of the LORD's promise to David is Messianic. This was recognized by Jewish interpreters.⁹ Christ is the authentic Davidic king, the true Son of the Father. The Chronicler is inspired to give voice to the fact that the total fulfillment of this promise depends upon there coming a Davidic king of whom it will never be

---

5. So Gill, *Exposition*, on Deut. 32:6. The verb is translated 'redeemed' in the NKJV of Neh. 5:8.

6. Thompson, *Jeremiah*, 570.

7. In addition to the two texts mentioned, see 1 Chr. 22:10; 28:6; cf. also Ps. 89:26, where the reference is as much to David himself as to his 'seed' (v. 4).

8. Poole, *Annotations*, 718.

9. See Youngblood, *1 and 2 Samuel*, on 2 Sam. 7:14.

necessary to say, "if he commits iniquity." So "the Chronicler... tends to see Nathan's oracle in the light of the ideal king."[10]

In addition to those Scriptures which call God Father, there are two passages where the LORD is compared with a human father.[11] They bring out the same twin emphases which we have seen in connection with the LORD's Fatherhood of Solomon—his pity (Ps. 103:13), and his chastening (Prov. 3:12). Underlying the latter verse is the assumption that the father who exercises necessary discipline is motivated by his delight in his son.

In the former verse Derek Kidner finds "affection as well as compassion" in the word "pities"—a "warmly emotional word". This warmth of affection is "the mark of a true parent."[12] Calvin comments: "God is compared to earthly fathers, not because he is in every respect like them, but because there is no earthly image by which his unparalleled love towards us can be better expressed."[13]

Spurgeon brings out that unparalleled love in these vivid words: "Fathers feel for their children, especially when they are in pain, they would like to suffer in their stead, their sighs and groans cut them to the quick: thus sensitive, towards us is our heavenly Father. We do not adore a god of stone, but the living God, who is tenderness itself."[14]

When we turn to the New Testament we find that the same emphases are present as in the Old Testament. The first thing which strikes us as we begin to read the Synoptic Gospels is the frequency with which Jesus speaks to his disciples of God as their "Father in heaven" or their "heavenly Father."[15] That there is no need to try to make any kind of distinction between these phrases is obvious from the fact that one Gospel may use one phrase, and another Gospel the other in a parallel passage.[16] In presenting to the disciples the model prayer, Jesus encourages us to address God as "Our Father in heaven" (Matt. 6:9).

---

10. Anderson, *2 Samuel*, on 2 Sam. 7:14.
11. Or possibly three, if Ps 68:5 is included.
12. Kidner, *Psalms*, 366.
13. Calvin, *Psalms*, Vol. 4, 137.
14. Spurgeon, *Treasury of David*, Vol. 4, 280.
15. The first instance is Matt. 5:16.
16. Cf. Matt. 6:14 with Mark 11:25.

However, there is another phrase which occurs with equal frequency: Jesus often speaks of God as "my Father in heaven."[17] This points to the uniqueness and intimacy of relationship with God which Jesus enjoyed, and into which believers are drawn through him.[18]

In Matthew 11:27 (parallel Luke 10:22) Jesus claims an incomparable knowledge of the Father, but indicates that this knowledge is shared by those to whom he reveals his Father. John Nolland links this dominical saying with Exodus 33:12–13, and the mutual knowledge postulated between God and Moses. Here, clearly, the knowledge goes deeper, but Nolland rightly recognizes that the nuance of the Hebrew verb *yāda'* is present here too: this knowledge is not merely theoretical, but is "the intimacy of family relationship."[19] Dick France also notes that know "is much more than a mental acquaintance; it is an intimate relationship."[20] Hagner speaks of an intimate reciprocal knowledge between Father and Son, implying intimacy of relationship.[21] But the amazing thing is that those to whom the Son wills to reveal the Father also know him as the Son does. The disciples of Jesus share in intimate relationship with their heavenly Father. Hence the parallel phrases, "your Father in heaven" and "my Father in heaven."

The intimacy of Jesus' experience of the Father is seen in his use of "the everyday word *'abba* as a form of address to God" (Mark 14:36). Joachim Jeremias describes this as "the most important linguistic innovation on the part of Jesus."[22] *'Abba* was a colloquialism. It was used within the family setting, first by young children, but also by adult sons and daughters, as a form of address to the father whom they loved and respected. It had a "warm, familiar ring."[23] For Jesus to use *'abba* as a way of addressing God speaks of the indescribable depth of his sense of intimacy with the Father—the one whom in a special, unique, and unfathomable way, he loved and respected. Jeremias puts it well: "It expresses the heart of Jesus' relationship to God. He spoke to God as a child to its

---

17. The first occurrence is Matt. 7:21.
18. Hagner, *Matthew 1–13*, on Matt. 7:21.
19. Nolland, *Luke 9:21–18:34*, on Luke 10:22.
20. France, *Matthew*, 200.
21. Hagner, *Matthew 1–13*, on Matt. 11:27.
22. Jeremias, *New Testament Theology*, 36.
23. Hofius, "Father," 614.

father: confidently and securely, and yet at the same time reverently and obediently."[24]

And it is into this same reverent obedience, within the same context of confidence and security, that believers come to know God as our Father. Several texts highlight aspects of his fatherly care. He knows our needs (Matt. 6:8, 32), and on the basis of this awareness he provides for us (Matt. 6:26), giving us only what is good (Luke 11:13). Confident in this fatherly commitment, we may live without fear, even in a world of uncertainty (Matt. 10:29–31; Luke 12:32).

Donald Guthrie rightly says that "it is in John's Gospel that the Fatherhood of God is seen most clearly in relation to Jesus."[25] This is, indeed, "one of the major themes in John's Gospel,"[26] where "Jesus speaks of God as Father 106 times."[27] I want to home in on those texts which bring out the relational nature of God's Fatherhood and Jesus' Sonship.

We turn first to John 1:18, where Jesus is said to have his being in the Father's bosom. Merrill Tenney sees this phrase as showing intimate association, close fellowship, and constant relationship.[28] Leon Morris speaks of "its overtones of affection."[29] Westcott speaks of the closeness and tenderness implied by the image.[30] Jesus is the Father's "bosom companion."[31]

There are several verses which highlight the Father's love for the Son,[32] and the Son is said to abide in this love (John 15:10). Conversely, the Son loves the Father, and it is this love which drives him to obey the Father's will (John 14:31).

Into this mutual love of Father and Son, believers are caught up. The possibility of coming to God as Father lies in Jesus (John 14:6). Those who do come are loved by the Father (John 14:21, 23; 16:27), such that Jesus can refer to the Father as "my Father and your Father" (John 20:17). There is a clear particularity about this love: it is specifically directed to

---

24. Jeremias, *New Testament Theology*, 67.
25. Guthrie, *New Testament Theology*, 83.
26. Liefeld, *Luke*, on Luke 10:21.
27. Ladd, *Theology*, 247.
28. Tenney, *John*, on John 1:18.
29. Morris, *John*, 114.
30. Westcott, *John*, 15.
31. Lindars, *John*, 99.
32. John 3:35; 5:20; 10:17; 15:9; 17:24.

those who belong to Christ. Tenney suggests that the phrase "my Father and your Father" indicates the difference between his relationship to God and ours: he is the eternal Son of the Father, whereas his disciples must become members of his family.[33] More probably, I suggest, Jesus is stressing the wonderful fact that through faith in him we have been embraced by that very same Fatherhood which has been his portion eternally. This seems to be Calvin's understanding when he writes:

> Christ declares that we have this in common with himself, that he who is *his God and Father* is also *our God and Father*.... In other passages we learn that we are made partakers of all the blessings of Christ; but this is the foundation of the privilege, that he imparts to us the very fountain of blessings. It is, unquestionably, an invaluable blessing, that believers can safely and firmly believe, that he who is the God of Christ is *their God*, and that he who is the Father of Christ is *their Father*.[34]

Beasley-Murray links the disciples' experience of the Father's love with Moses' request that God would show him his glory (Exod. 33:13, 18).[35] The glory of God is seen in his Fatherhood. His glory *is* his Fatherhood. That is what sets him apart from all other claimants to deity. The true God alone is characterized essentially by this tender care for the people who belong to him. He is the only God with whom it is truly possible to enjoy relationship.

In the rest of the New Testament the theme of God's Fatherhood is not greatly elaborated, though it is assumed. A reference to God as Father is standard at the beginning of an epistle, and occasionally at the end as well.[36] On several occasions God is described as the Father of Jesus Christ.[37] 1 Corinthians 8:6 teaches that God the Father is the only God and that all things are from him.

However, there is a cluster of texts which emphasize the Father as the personal God whom believers know (1 John 2:13), and who loves

---

33. Tenney, *John*, on John 20:17; see also Tasker, *John*, 225–26; Morris, *John*, 842; Westcott, *John*, 293.

34. Calvin, *John*, Vol. 2, 262.

35. Beasley-Murray, *John*, on John 14:21.

36. Rom. 1:7; 1 Cor. 1:3; 2 Cor. 1:2; Gal. 1:3; Eph. 1:2; 6:23; Phil. 1:2; 4:20; Col. 1:2; 1 Thess. 1:1; 2 Thess. 1:1–2; 1 Tim 1:2; 2 Tim. 1:2; Titus 1:4; Phlm. 3; 1 Pet. 1:2; 2 John 3; Jude 1; Rev. 1:6.

37. Rom. 15:6; 2 Cor. 11:31; Eph. 3:14; Col. 1:3; cf. Rev. 2:27; 3:5, 21.

them (2 Thess. 2:16) enough to exercise discipline when appropriate (Heb. 12:9[38]). Paul describes God as "the Father of mercies" (2 Cor. 1:3)—the fountain and source of mercy,[39] the one whose entire character is mercy.[40] In his first letter the apostle John has "an outburst of wonder"[41] as he stresses that the Father's love is astonishingly lavish[42] in that it constitutes us his children (1 John 3:1). Professor Blaiklock tries to capture the etymology of the word *potapos* (literally *how and where*, usually rendered *from which country?*) by translating *what unearthly love*. He draws out its significance in these words: "There could be no conceivable method or device whereby sinful human beings attain such a state or such a privilege save by the exercise of a power unimaginable in its strength and its unearthliness. It is all of love and grace."[43]

This is the Father with whom the believer has fellowship (1 John 1:3). This entails a relationship in which the believer cries out to the Father as *'Abba* (Rom. 8:15; Gal. 4:6), a form of address which indicates that the believer is caught up into the same intimate closeness with the Father enjoyed by the Son of God himself.

To speak of God as Father, therefore, points to the tender love of God towards his children. However, it also highlights the fact that the Father is related primarily to his only-begotten Son, and that this tenderness towards us as his children is a wonderful, gracious conferment upon us of the very same intimate and affectionate love which he has eternally for the Son.

Kelly suggests that the earliest understanding of the word *Father* in the era of the creed's origin had to do with neither of these emphases, but was an alternative term for God as Creator.[44] This may well be right. The quotations which Kelly includes certainly back up his claim. However, the fact that the creed as we have received it contains an additional reference to God as Creator seems to imply that, by the sixth century at any rate, the identification of Fatherhood and Creatorship was no longer current.

38. Referring to Prov. 3:12.
39. Martin, *2 Corinthians*, on 2 Cor. 1:3.
40. Hodge, *Corinthians*, 381.
41. Stott, *Epistles of John*, 118.
42. G. W. Barker, *1, 2, 3 John*, on 1 John 3:1; Smalley, *1, 2, 3 John*, on 1 John 3:1.
43. Blaiklock, *Children of Light*, 58–59.
44. Kelly, *Creeds*, 135–36; see also McGiffert, *Creed*, 14, 108–9.

Kelly acknowledges that, by the fourth century, the creed's affirmation of God's Fatherhood was generally taken as a reference to the special relationship of Father and Son within the Trinity.[45] He cites Cyril of Jerusalem, who pointed out that the word *father* inevitably suggests to the mind the idea of a son.[46] The doctrine of the Trinity is, admittedly, a mystery to our understanding. Rufinus, therefore cautions, "that God then is the Father of his only Son our Lord is to be believed, not discussed."[47]

However, the word "Father" stresses, not merely the fact of God's relationship with his only Son, but also the warmth of paternal affection which God feels for him, and, through him, for us as well. Clement of Rome exhorts us to love "our gracious and merciful Father," whom we have come to know through his electing grace.[48] The Christological basis of God's Fatherhood of believers is emphasized by the Heidelberg Catechism: "The eternal Father of our Lord Jesus Christ . . . is for the sake of Christ his Son my God and my Father; in whom I so trust as to have no doubt that he will provide me with all things necessary for body and soul."[49]

Karl Barth sums it up well: "God is Father because he has a Son and we can be his children because this Son stands for us before him."[50] But as Professor Cranfield reminds us, "This fatherhood of God in relation to us is not at all natural or necessary. It is, rather, a matter of sheer grace, the stupendous grace of the eternal God, who adopts human beings as his sons and daughters for the sake of his own dear Son and gives them the right to call him 'Father.'"[51]

In his two catechisms, Martin Luther draws out the implications of the statement, "I believe in God the Father." In the Small Catechism he says, "He provides me richly and daily with all the necessaries of life, protects me from all danger, and preserves and guards me against all evil; and all this out of pure paternal, divine goodness and mercy."[52] As the

---

45. Cf. Witsius, *Creed*, who devotes Vol. 1, 146–66 to this theme.
46. Kelly, *Creeds*, 134.
47. Rufinus, *Commentary*, para. 4, 1101.
48. Clement, *Corinthians*, 29.1, 57.
49. *Heidelberg Catechism*, Q.26.
50. Barth, *Faith*, 45.
51. Cranfield, *Creed*, 13.
52. Luther, *Enchiridion*, 78.

Large Catechism explains, "he does all this out of pure love and goodness, without our merit, as a benevolent Father."[53] Luther then makes this application of the truth that God is our Father:

> We ought, therefore, daily to practise this article, impress it upon our mind, and to remember it in all that meets our eyes, and in all good that falls to our lot, and wherever we escape from calamity or danger, that it is God who gives and does all these things, that therein we sense and see His paternal heart and His transcendent love toward us. Thereby the heart would be warmed and kindled to be thankful, and to employ all such good things to the honor and praise of God.[54]

---

53. Luther, *Larger Catechism*, 59.
54. Luther, *Larger Catechism*, 60.

5

Almighty

In the English translations of the New Testament the word "almighty" translates the Greek term *pantokratōr*.[1] In the Old Testament "almighty" translates the Hebrew word *šadday*, often found in the divine title El Shaddai.[2] This word is also translated *pantokratōr* by the LXX on fifteen of its forty-eight occurrences, all in the Book of Job.[3] More commonly (118 times) in the LXX *pantokratōr* translates *ṣāḇā'*, familiar in the description of God as the "Lord of hosts."[4]

The rendering "almighty" has rather crept into the English versions via Jerome's Latin translation, which uses *omnipotens* for *pantokratōr* in the New Testament and *šadday* in the Old. This is a pity, because it conveys the wrong impression. "Almighty" suggests that the point is that God has the ability to do absolutely everything. Whether or not that is as a matter of fact true, it is certainly not what is implied by the Greek and Hebrew terms.

Pantokratōr means "ruler over everything," while *šadday* is thought to be connected with a word for mountain,[5] suggesting the loftiness of God's throne from which he surveys and rules the world. The other Hebrew term, *ṣāḇā'*, represents the armies of God, a figurative description of the forces by which he exercises his sovereignty. "Hosts has reference to any group, human or divine, called upon by God to mediate a divine objective."[6]

---

1. 2 Cor. 6:18; Rev. 1:8; 4:8; 11:17; 15:3; 16:7, 14; 19:6, 15; 21:22.
2. Gen. 17:1; 28:3; 35:11; 43:14; 48:3; Exod. 6:3; Ezek. 10:5.
3. Job 5:17; 8:5; 11:7; 15:25; 22:17, 25; 23:16; 27:2, 11, 13; 32:8; 33:4; 34:10, 12; 35:13.
4. E.g., 2 Sam. 7:8; 1 Chr. 11:9; Jer. 23:16; Mic. 4:4.
5. So *Theological Wordbook of the Old Testament*, 2333.
6. Fretheim, "Yahweh," 1298.

The Biblical terminology is therefore far more dynamic than the Latin and English translations suggest. God's almightiness is not a static concept of a latent ability, but a description of the actual activity of God in his providential and universal rule.[7] As Rufinus puts it: "God is called almighty because he possesses rule and dominion over all things"[8]—and not merely possesses, but actually exercises that dominion and rule.

This is much in keeping with the personal nature of God which we have already highlighted. Our Father is also the universal ruler. The universal rule is in the hands of the one who is our Father. God's absolute sovereignty is not a cold determinism, but the outworking of passionate love. That fact is calculated to bring us comfort and confidence amidst all the ups and downs of our often mysterious course through life. Kelly expresses this fact splendidly, noting that the Christian catechumen who declared his faith in the words of the creed knew "that the eternal Father of the universe was also the Father of Jesus the Christ, and had even vouchsafed to adopt him as his son by grace; and he knew that the sovereign power which God possessed by right had been signally manifested in the resurrection of his Son and in the redemption of his chosen people."[9]

The Heidelberg Catechism rightly recognizes that to say "I believe in God . . . almighty" is not to state an abstract philosophical principle. In answer to the question about the first clause of the creed the providence of God is briefly mentioned. The next question elaborates on the meaning of God's providence, which it defines as "the almighty and everywhere present power of God, whereby, as it were by his hand, he still upholds heaven, earth and all creatures, and so governs them that herbs and grass, rain and drought, fruitful and barren years, food and drink, health and sickness, riches and poverty, yes, all things, come not by chance but by his fatherly hand." This is followed by an application of the truth that God in providence rules over everything. The knowledge of this truth means "that we may be patient in adversity, thankful in prosperity, and with a view to the future may have good confidence in our faithful God and Father that no creature shall separate us from his

---

7. See Kelly, *Creeds*, 137; McGiffert, *Creed*, 110.
8. Rufinus, *Commentary*, para. 5, 1102.
9. Kelly, *Creeds*, 139.

love, since all creatures are so in his hand that without his will they cannot so much as move."[10]

This exactly captures the Biblical meaning of the fact that God is almighty. Commenting on this section of the Heidelberg Catechism, Louis Praamsma says: "providence . . . means that God takes care of all things. They do not slip out of his control. He holds everything in his hand." He goes on to enlarge on this: "All things in creation, nothing excepted, are in God's hand. There is nothing too big, not even the largest star, nor too small, not even the tiniest atom, that is not in God's care."[11]

Calvin also is right in tune with the Scriptures in his explanation of God's omnipotence: "Omnipotence is attributed to him, by which is signified both that he administers all things by his providence, governs by his will, and directs by his power and his hand."[12] Similarly, Novatian, writing in the middle of the third century, says that God's "care will consequently extend to every individual thing, since his providence reaches to the whole."[13]

I like those references to God's care of all things. God's providential control, his sovereign rule over absolutely everything, is not a heartless, tyrannical dictatorship. It is genuine care. It is motivated by the same love with which the Father has adopted us as his children, the same love with which the Father carries his children through "the changes and chances of this mortal life,"[14] the same love with which the Father is passionately committed to his eternal, beloved Son. And that caring love rules over all things for the glory of the only Son and the ultimate good of the family adopted in him.

It is true that there are times when the Bible seems to speak of God's unrestricted ability as a more abstract notion. For example, the LORD asks Abraham, "Is anything too hard for the LORD?" (Gen. 18:14). In prayer, Jeremiah affirms, "There is nothing too hard for you," and the LORD replies, "Behold, I am the LORD, the God of all flesh. Is there anything too hard for me?" (Jer. 32:17, 27). The angel assures Mary that "with God nothing will be impossible" (Luke 1:37). Jesus told his dis-

---

10. *Heidelberg Catechism*, Qs. 27–28.
11. Praamsma, *Before the Face*, 41–42.
12. Calvin, *Catechism, 1538*, 20.i, 22.
13. Novatian, *Trinity*, 1241.
14. *Book of Common Prayer*, Prayers for use after the Collects of Morning or Evening Prayer or separately, 60, 832.

ciples that "the things which are impossible with men are possible with God" (Luke 18:27), and indeed that "with God all things are possible" (Matt. 19:26; Mark 10:27).

However, it is necessary to say two things about this.

First, these questions and statements arise in the course of the LORD's outworking of his grand redemptive purpose. It is not too hard for the LORD to enable Sarah to give birth, because his sovereign rule requires that Abraham have his seed, the seed from which the Christ must come, Christ who is the true Seed of Abraham, as Galatians 3:16 teaches. It is not too hard for the LORD to restore his exiled people to their land, because their renewed presence there is vital in view of the coming of Jesus Christ, who, according to the prophet, must be born in Bethlehem (Mic. 5:2). It is not impossible for God to enable Elizabeth and Mary to give birth, because their respective sons, John the Baptist, and, supremely, Jesus, stand at the very center of God's saving purpose. Jesus' words followed his disappointing conversation with the rich young ruler who declined to follow the Lord, preferring to keep his material wealth. Nevertheless, the universal sinful human "trust in riches" (Mark 10:24) is no obstacle to God's sovereign, saving power. All these texts refer to divine possibilities in the sphere of the outworking of his eternal purpose of salvation in Christ, which is precisely what God's providential government over all things is directed towards.

Second, the word translated "too hard" in the Old Testament passages really means marvellous or wonderful. The LORD's question to Abraham really amounts to the declaration that nothing is a marvel where the LORD is concerned. The things which to us seem astonishing miracles are all simply part of the sovereign outworking of his purpose. In fact, using exactly the same word, Psalm 72:18 indicates that the only things which God is capable of doing are wonders.[15] To translate *almightiness* or *omnipotence* as the ability to do absolutely anything is in fact an insult to God. It says too little, for God is quite incapable of doing anything except those things which are wonderful marvels or marvellous wonders!

Perhaps one of the most marvellous and wonderful things about the almighty God is the truth which we have already highlighted—that his providential care over all things is directed towards the well-being of his children. He is indeed our Father as well as being the almighty, and

15. Cf. Ps. 136:4.

it is specifically as our Father that he exercises his sovereign rule. His rule over all things is an expression of his fatherly care for us. We see this from the two occasions when the Lord introduces himself to the patriarchs as El Shaddai.

The first such occasion is in Genesis 17:1–2. Having said to Abram, "I am Almighty God," the Lord soon says, "I will make my covenant between me and you." In this covenant the Lord pledges himself to give Abram descendants, and then to multiply their numbers and establish them in their homeland. However, at the very heart of the covenant stands the Lord's commitment "to be God to you and your descendants after you" (Gen. 17:7); "I will be their God," he says (Gen. 17:8). The God who sits on his exalted throne is the very God who comes down to be the Father of his people, and, as their Father, to exercise his universal rule with a view to their increase and security in the land, under his blessing.

The other occasion on which the Lord introduces himself as El Shaddai is in conversation with Jacob on his return to Bethel after twenty years away from home (Gen. 35:11). Having declared his name, the Lord immediately continues, "Be fruitful and multiply; a nation and a company of nations shall proceed from you, and kings shall come from your body. The land which I gave Abraham and Isaac I give to you; and to your descendants after you I give this land" (Gen. 35:11–12). Here again is a commitment to apply his universal, sovereign rule to the welfare of his people throughout the generations to come.

F. B. Meyer points out that prior to Genesis 17:1 Abram had known God by other names, but never before had God introduced himself as El Shaddai. Meyer suggests that every new revelation of the divine name preceded a new departure in God's dealings with his people.[16] Here, as God pledges himself in covenant to his chosen race he declares that his universal sovereignty will be directed towards their preservation, establishment and blessing.

Gordon Wenham notes that the title El Shaddai "is always used in connection with promises of descendants: Shaddai evokes the idea that God is able to make the barren fertile and to fulfill his promises."[17] Derek

---

16. Meyer, *Abraham*, 79.
17. Wenham, *Genesis 16–50*, on Gen. 17:1b.

Kidner finds the name in Genesis "matched to situations where God's servants are hard-pressed and in need of reassurance."[18]

We may cling to the same reassurance. God sits on the throne of the universe. But his sovereign rule is not self-seeking and deterministic, it is not aloof and tyrannical. It is as Father that God rules. His sovereignty is ever slanted towards the good of his people. But he is first of all the Father of our Lord Jesus Christ, and his sovereign rule has as its final and all-embracing aim the ultimate good, the greatest possible glory, of his beloved Son. And in the beloved Son, the Lord Jesus Christ, God has become our Father. As the almighty God he rules with a view to our preservation, our establishment, our blessing. Where we are hard-pressed, God turns barren situations to fruitfulness for us, so that we press on in the confidence that our Father who loves us passionately rules over all things wisely, and therefore, in the end, all must be well.

This, surely, is brought out by 2 Corinthians 6:18. It is the Lord Almighty who announces, "I will be a Father to you." His almighty rule is fatherly in nature and is for us, his "sons and daughters." The apostle has here adapted an Old Testament citation. It is generally recognized that the first line of the verse is taking up the promise to Solomon of the Davidic covenant in 2 Samuel 7:14.[19] Earlier in that chapter God had identified himself as "the Lord of hosts" (2 Sam. 7:8), a title which David later takes up in prayer (2 Sam. 7:26–27). This may be the source of Paul's use of "Lord Almighty." The reference to sons and daughters is a natural corollary of the description of God as Father. It may well be Paul's own elaboration on the description of Solomon as God's son, recognizing that in the New Testament church, male and female have an equal standing before the God who is Father of all.

And for the people to whom he has made himself knowable and known as Father, God, as El Shaddai, the highly exalted ruler, in providential sovereignty, is working out his Christ-centered purpose of salvation and glory.

---

18. Kidner, *Genesis*, 129.
19. Although Hodge, *Corinthians*, 548, disputes this.

6

Creator of heaven and earth

THE REASON WHY GOD rules over all things is that all things in heaven and on earth belong to him by virtue of the fact that he created them all. Indeed, as Calvin maintains, "this term [Creator] does not merely imply that God so created his works once, that afterwards he took no care of them."[1] The notion of God's permanent, constant, incessant preservation and sustenance of all things is included within the concept of God as Creator.

Kelly comments that the truth that God created the universe was one "which marked Christianity off from all other religions."[2] Anthony Flew once made a distinction between the layman's and the theologian's sense of creation: "In the layman's sense to say that the universe is a or the creation entails that it must have had a beginning. . . . In the theologian's sense the heart of the matter is not a beginning out of nothing but a constant and absolute dependence. In this interpretation it would not be inconsistent to say both that the universe is God's creation and that it had no beginning."[3]

On his terms the early Christians who developed the statements of the Apostles' Creed were laymen. Theirs was not the supposedly sophisticated, unbiblical approach of the modern theologian. When they said that God was the Creator of heaven and earth they meant that only God is eternal and that this universe to which we belong was initiated by him at a particular moment in time. And that view certainly was a distinctive of Christianity in the prevailing pagan worldview of the time, where the

---

1. Calvin, *Catechism, 1545*, Q. 27.
2. Kelly, *Creeds*, 372.
3. Flew, *Western Philosophy*, 65–66.

Middle Platonists by and large read their ancient creation myths symbolically "and so held to the eternity of the world."[4]

Flew's caricature of the layman's view of creation as a beginning out of nothing is precisely what the early church taught. Tertullian, for example defined the rule of faith as prescribing the belief "that there is only one God, and that he is none other than the Creator of the world, who produced all things out of nothing by his own Word."[5]

This has remained the orthodox Christian view throughout the centuries. "The doctrine of creation *ex nihilo* (out of nothing) is an essential Christian teaching."[6] The seventeenth-century Heidelberg Catechism says that the eternal Father of our Lord Jesus Christ "of nothing made heaven and earth with all that is in them."[7] And a modern theologian (in the true sense of the word!), Professor Cranfield, writes: "By calling God the Father 'creator of heaven and earth' we are affirming that he is the sole originator of all reality other than himself. He has not, like a craftsman, fashioned it out of some already existing material, but has created all things out of nothing."[8]

Witsius spells this fact out in some detail. He writes: "Before the creation, nothing at all existed, excepting God," and then proceeds to explain the full extent of the word "nothing": no world, no shapeless matter from which other substances were formed, no spirits distinct from God, "but absolutely nothing."[9]

This remains a Christian distinctive even in our postmodern world. Richard Dawkins admits that his alternative idol—Natural Selection—is irrelevant beyond the sphere of biology. He does, however, cling to the hope that it might be a "consciousness raiser" outside its original territory, and that, in the area of cosmology, the improbability of creation by an outside intelligence will become clearer with the progress of scientific research.[10] However, Karl Barth rightly points out that, in speaking of God as Creator and his work as the creation, we are in a realm which is completely inaccessible to human view or human thought. All that

---

4. Armstrong, *Ancient Philosophy*, 152.
5. Tertullian, *Prescription*, 448.
6. G. I. Williamson, *Heidelberg*, 46.
7. *Heidelberg Catechism*, Q. 26.
8. Cranfield, *Creed*, 17.
9. Witsius, *Creed*, Vol. 1, 181.
10. Dawkins, *Delusion*, 114.

natural science can do is to trace the world's development. But it cannot penetrate the question of origins. "The Bible speaks in Genesis 1 and 2 of events which lie outside of our historical knowledge."[11]

This means that we are utterly dependent on the Creator's revelation to know that the heaven and earth to which we belong had a beginning. Indeed, as Wolfhart Pannenberg has said, "if God's being God means that he is the origin of everything real, and that without him there is nothing at all, then without him nothing real can be understood in depth, either; it can at most be superficially described."[12]

I have just one quibble with these words. It seems to me that, if God is the origin of everything real, then without him nothing real can be properly understood *at all*. Even the superficial descriptions which human research can put forward can only have any validity because they spring from his common grace, which gives even ungodly people a measure of true insight into the nature of things. Strictly speaking, nobody is ever in the position of studying creation without God, because, as the apostle Paul acknowledged, it is in him that we (all of us, the entire human race) live and move and have our being (Acts 17:28).

To describe God as the Creator "of heaven and earth" reminds us that there are two parts of God's creation. The Nicene Creed added to this distinction another one, "things visible and invisible." These two distinctions are not identical,[13] but cut across one another. There are in our human experience on earth invisible things (such as the wind and the sun's warmth, not to mention such intangible realities as love and joy, or pain, or wonder), in addition to the visible fabric of *terra firma* on which we exist. The heavens may include visible things (stars, clouds, the colors in the sky), as well as the spiritual heavenly realities which are unseen, including angelic spirits, and all the spiritual blessings which are ours in the heavenly places in Christ.

Barth paraphrases the words "visible and invisible" in terms of things "conceivable and inconceivable."[14] This emphasizes the point that in the creation there are things of which we can achieve some understanding, things which we can manipulate and use, but also things

---

11. Barth, *Dogmatics*, 51.
12. Pannenberg, *Creed*, 35–36.
13. *Pace* Seitz, "Our Help," 26.
14. Barth, *Dogmatics*, 61.

which must inevitably remain for all time beyond our understanding, things which are out of reach.

It is true that the boundaries of human research and understanding are constantly being pushed outwards—and rightly so. That is part of what is involved in our existence in God's image for dominion in which we tend and keep the earth (Gen. 1:28; 2:15). As scientific possibilities enlarge, ethical challenges arise. Nevertheless, we should not react, and complain that man is playing at being God. Rather we should rejoice that man is fulfilling his God-given role as the image of divine dominion. However, the further science advances, the more conscious we human beings become of our ignorance. Dawkins is right when he says that ignorance is a challenge and a spur to further investigation,[15] but it is also an invitation and a stimulus to deeper humility before the Creator whose marvellous works must always remain a source of awe and wonder, of breath-taking amazement.

That sense of awe and wonder really comes through in Novatian's description of God's creation. It is worth quoting at some length. He describes God the Father almighty as "the absolutely perfect Founder of all things," and says that he

> has suspended the heavens in lofty sublimity, has established the earth with its lower mass, has diffused the seas with their fluent moisture, and has distributed all these things, both adorned and supplied with their appropriate and fitting instruments. For in the solid vault of heaven he has both awakened the light-bringing sunrisings; he has filled up the white globe of the moon in its monthly waxings as a solace for the night; he, moreover, kindles the starry rays with the varied splendors of glistening light; and he has willed all these things in their legitimate tracks to circle the entire compass of the world, so as to cause days, months, years, signs, and seasons, and benefits of other kinds for the human race. On the earth, moreover, he has lifted up the loftiest mountains to a peak, he has thrown down valleys into the depths, he has smoothly leveled the plains, he has ordained the animal herds usefully for the various services of men. He has also established the oak trees of the woods for the future benefit of human uses. He has developed the harvests into food. He has unlocked the mouths of the springs, and has poured them into the flowing rivers. And after these things, lest he should not also provide for the very delights of the eyes, he has clothed all things with the

---

15. Dawkins, *Delusion*, 126.

various colors of the flowers for the pleasure of the beholders. Even in the sea itself, moreover, although it was in itself marvelous both for its extent and its utility, he has made manifold creatures, sometimes of moderate, sometimes of vast bodily size, testifying by the variety of his appointment to the intelligence of the Artificer. And, not content with these things, lest perchance the roaring and rushing waters should seize upon a foreign element at the expense of its human possessor, he has enclosed its limits with shores; so that when the raving billow and the foaming water should come from its deep bosom, it should return again unto itself, and not transgress its concealed bounds, but keep its prescribed laws.

Having spoken so eloquently of creation's splendor, Novatian concludes this chapter with the words, "And thus considering the greatness of the works, we should worthily admire the Artificer of such a structure."[16]

Two things are noteworthy in Novatian's account. First, the object of his adoration is God. God is the subject of every statement which Novatian makes about the creation. It is not creation which Novatian wishes to admire. Rather, through the creation his worship is directed upwards to the Creator. J. I. Packer points out that the main question addressed by Genesis 1 and 2 is not "how?" but "who?"[17] It is tragic if we become preoccupied with the grandeur of creation to the extent that we lose sight of the Creator. It is sad that Richard Dawkins can speak of "a quasi-mystical response to nature and the universe" and of "transcendent wonder,"[18] without bowing to give glory to the wonderful Creator, without whom there would be no nature, no universe. Unless we can say "I believe in God . . . Creator of heaven and earth," then our admiration of nature becomes idolatry. It is the lie to which Paul refers in Romans 1:25.

The second thing which stands out in Novatian's doctrine of the Creator is the way in which creation is intended for the service of the human race. We are reminded of Paul's words to Timothy, "Every creature of God is good" (1 Tim. 4:4), words which echo the refrain of Genesis 1, culminating in the grand summary of verse 31, "And God saw everything that he had made, and indeed it was very good."[19] The context

---

16. Novatian, *Trinity*, 1228–29.
17. Packer, *Christian*, 32.
18. Dawkins, *Delusion*, 11, 12.
19. Cf. Gen. 1:4, 10, 12, 18, 21, 25. The LXX uses *kalos* consistently throughout these

of 1 Timothy 4:3-4 specifies marriage and food as examples of created things which are good—good, that is, for us. The Greek word here, *kalos*, implies that creation is good in the sense that it does us good, that it enhances our experience of life, that it makes of our existence something of beauty: creation serves to confer a nobility upon us in our thankful enjoyment of it. To speak of the goodness of the creature, therefore, is to speak of the Creator's goodness and kindness, which he has so splendidly and generously deposited for us in the works of his hands from which we benefit and profit.

I referred earlier to Anthony Flew's distinction between the theologian and the layman, the "layman's" view of creation hinging on its having had a beginning, the "theologian's" emphasizing "creation's" dependence upon God. Actually, it is a false dichotomy. For the true believer, whether a layman or a theologian, the doctrine that God is Creator means both these things at once: there was a moment in time when the eternal God brought into being for the first time ever something other than himself, and, from that moment on, that something has existed in total, unbroken dependence upon him.

This is Isaiah's message to a people facing the sorry prospect of defeat and exile. Their impending refugee status could lead them to despair even of God. Isaiah 40 affirms that the very God who created the ends of the earth (v. 28) is the one who as Creator is still at work in his creation in the present tense (v. 26). "The earth, nature, and the universe are put in their places and kept in their ways by the sovereign will of the Creator."[20] All things, all people are dependent on him. Before him the status of the human race is akin to that of a grasshopper (v. 22). It is God who nullifies human power (v. 23-24), and it is God who overcomes human weakness (vv. 29-31). No one can defy him, and no success is achievable independently of his grace. "His absolute control over all human life is quite unchallenged."[21]

In a stimulating article on this phrase as it occurs in the Nicene Creed, Christopher Seitz points out that the phrase "the maker of heaven and earth" is "a fixed formula" which "appears again and again in the Old Testament" (actually, the precise Biblical wording uses the verb, "made," rather than the noun, "maker"). Seitz cites Psalm 124:8 as

---

verses, the word used by Paul in 1 Tim. 4:4.

20. Watts, *Isaiah 34–66*, on Isa. 40:21.
21. Grogan, *Isaiah*, on Isa. 40:21–24.

one example: "Our help is in the name of the LORD, who made heaven and earth." For Seitz, the juxtaposing of these two clauses indicates "that more is at stake in the creed's use of this phrase than a metaphysical description about creation."[22]

Examining the Biblical contexts of this phrase suggests that Seitz is right. Disregarding one occurrence in a statement by Hiram, King of Tyre (2 Chr. 2:12), the phrase is found seven times in the Old Testament and twice in the New. The affirmation that the LORD "who made heaven and earth" is his people's helper, already noted in Psalm 124:8, is found also in Psalm 121:2. In Psalm 146:5–6 the happiness of the person who has this God for his help is declared. Additionally, on two occasions the Psalmist links this description of the LORD with a prayer for blessing (Pss. 115:15; 134:3). Hezekiah proclaimed that the LORD God of Israel "made heaven and earth" as he cried out to the LORD to save Judah from the hand of the Assyrians (2 Kgs. 19:15, 19; Isa. 37:16, 20). In Acts 4:24 the Jerusalem church takes up this Old Testament title for God in praying for his enablement for the apostles as their ministry faced the threats of a hostile community (cf. Acts 4:29–30). In the end the intervention of the God "who made heaven and earth" will bring the gospel to "every nation, tribe, tongue and people" on earth (Rev. 14:17).

A variant on the exact phrase is found in Jeremiah 32:17, where the plural with the article "the heavens" replaces the anarthrous singular "heaven." Jeremiah uses the words in an implicit cry for the LORD's intervention in the days of Chaldean supremacy (cf. Jer. 32: 24–25).[23]

There are also texts which elaborate on the basic description. The LORD "made heaven, the heaven of heavens, with all their host, the earth and everything on it" (Neh. 9:6). Similar elaborations come four times in Isaiah.[24] In Jeremiah 10:12 and 51:15 the positions of "earth" and "heaven" are reversed in elaborations of the basic phrase. What all seven of these contexts share in common is that they are seeking, acknowledging, or anticipating the LORD's help in difficulty—his deliverance of his people from exile.

All these texts, then, connect the fact that the LORD is the "Creator of heaven and earth" with the assurance that he is for his people, to help,

---

22. Seitz, "Our Help," 19–20.

23. This variant also occurs in the context of the Sabbath commandment in Exod. 20:11 and 31:17; these texts are not relevant for the present discussion.

24. Isa. 44:24; 45:12, 18; 51:13.

to bless, to save, to deliver. And the outcome of his gracious intervention on his people's behalf will be their happiness. It is a wonderfully uplifting statement, and once again it points to the personal nature of our God.

"I believe in God . . . , Creator of heaven and earth." But, as Luther rightly saw, this truth is not to be held at a distance. It is not merely a truth for the people of God as a corporate entity. It is an expression which is also deeply personal. "What is the force of this," Luther asks, "or what do you mean by these words?" He answers:

> This is what I mean and believe, that *I* am a creature of God; that is, that he has given and constantly preserves to *me my* body, soul, and life, members great and small, all *my* senses, reason, and understanding, and so on, food and drink, clothing and support, wife and children, domestics, house and home, etc. . . . Thus we learn from this article that none of us has of himself, nor can preserve, his life nor anything that is here enumerated or can be enumerated, however small and unimportant a thing it might be, for all is comprehended in the word *Creator*.[25]

And since I am a creature and God is my Creator, I must remember that "there is no creature hidden from his sight, but all things are naked and open to the eyes of him to whom we must give account" (Heb. 4:13). I am accountable to my Creator, and he is the one "unto whom all hearts are open, all desires known, and from whom no secrets are hid."[26] From him *I* cannot hide. I must therefore "remember my creator" (cf. Eccl. 12:1) before I am a day older. I must remember him every day, and commit my soul to him "as to a faithful Creator" (1 Pet. 4:19), as to the God of grace to whom I can turn with confidence, the Father almighty whose grace will keep me now and for ever.

---

25. Luther, *Larger Catechism*, 59 [emphases added].
26. *Book of Common Prayer*, The Holy Eucharist, Rite One, 323.

7

And in Jesus Christ, his only Son, our Lord

At this point we reach "the heart of the Christian confession."[1] It is the fact that in Jesus Christ the eternal Son of God has become flesh which sets Christianity apart from every other religious outlook. It is, quite obviously, the centrality of *Christ* which makes Biblical theism *Christian*. McGrath rightly points out too that Christianity differs from other ideologies and religions in that "they are essentially abstract systems."[2] Christianity, by contrast, entails being in living relationship with the person, Jesus Christ.

We thus see the continuity between the strands of the Apostles' Creed so far. To say "I believe" means that I am making my passionate personal commitment to God. To say "I believe in God" is to acknowledge the personal nature of the God to whose personal self-revelation my personal commitment is a response. To speak of him as "Father" is to define the nature of his personhood. To describe him as the "almighty, Creator of heaven and earth" is to recognize that, being personal he is unceasingly active and relational in his providential care of the world. Now we learn further that we are brought into relationship with this personal God by the human person, "Jesus Christ," in whom God has himself become human.

We consider these introductory words to the creed's account of the life and work of Jesus under three headings.

THE NAME THAT DEFINES HIS PURPOSE

We believe in Jesus. When a new baby is on the way the parents often draw up a short list of potential names to give their new child. If it is a

---

1. Barth, *Dogmatics*, 65; cf. Pannenberg, *Creed*, 44.
2. McGrath, *I Believe*, 37.

boy, will he be James, John, or Justin? Whichever choice wins the day, whether it's Mum or Dad who gets first preference, the lad will still be the same person.

But in the case of Jesus the name is not a mere label. His parents could not have selected some other name without fundamentally altering the character of their child. In fact, Jesus' name was not given to him by his parents, but by his heavenly Father, even "before he was conceived in the womb" (Luke 2:21). "It is a name which, like him who bears it, has come down from heaven."[3] God's angel instructed Mary, "you will . . . bring forth a son, and shall call his name JESUS" (Luke 1:31). To ensure that obedience to God's command did not become a matter for negotiation, an angel repeated the instruction to Joseph, along with a statement of the reason, "you shall call his name JESUS, for he will save his people from their sins" (Matt. 1:21). Jesus had to be so named, because his name defines his purpose. He was born into the world to be the Savior.

Strictly speaking, *Jesus* means "the LORD saves." It is the Greek equivalent of the Hebrew name *Yĕšuaʿ* (Joshua),[4] which "is the oldest name containing the divine name Yahweh"[5] or Jehovah. Usually, the name points away from its bearer to the saving grace and power which belongs to the LORD alone. However, in giving this name to this child God is telling the world that he has deposited his saving power uniquely in this one person. The angel's words to Joseph "attribute to Jesus what was formerly reserved for God."[6] It is not, therefore, inappropriate to define the name more briefly in the single word "Savior,"[7] and to recognize the profound Christological implications of the name. As if to stress this, the word "he" (*autos*) is emphatic, indeed, "peculiarly so"[8]: he—Jesus, and Jesus alone—"he and none other"[9] is the LORD who saves. Witsius points out that the name "Jesus" includes a glory proper to God alone. He cites Isaiah 43:11, "I, even I, am the LORD, and besides me there is no Savior."[10]

3. Spurgeon, *New Testament*, Vol. 1, 1.
4. The name Joshua is always translated *Iēsous* in the LXX.
5. Rengstorf, "*Iēsous*," 331.
6. Rengstorf, "*Iēsous*," 332.
7. See Acts 13:23.
8. Bengel, *Gnomon*, Vol. 1, 114.
9. Slater, *Matthew*, 121.
10. Witsius, *Creed*, Vol. 1, 237.

Karl Barth rightly observes that "when a Savior is spoken of, the necessity of salvation is thereby implied."[11] Calvin makes a similar point: commenting on the angel's statement, "he shall save his people from their sins," he writes, "The first truth taught us by these words is, that those whom Christ is sent to save are in themselves lost."[12] Luther, in the course of expounding the second section of the creed, elaborates on our lostness at some length. He refers to our captivity under the power of sin, the devil, death, and all evil.[13] Jesus comes as the embodiment of the LORD's salvation, because we human beings need to be saved. What it is that we need to be saved from is clearly spelt out in the angel's message to Joseph—it is our sins from which we are in dire need of rescue.

Don Carson points out that there is more to the salvation which God provides in Christ than just the rescue of people from their sins: it "refers to the comprehensive salvation inaugurated by Jesus that will be consummated at his return." However, in this initial declaration of the LORD's salvation in Jesus the word "focuses on what is central, viz., salvation from sins; for in the biblical perspective sin is the basic (if not always the immediate) cause of all other calamities."[14]

To understand something of the significance of Jesus as our Savior from sin it is instructive to look at what is said in the Old Testament about Joshua, and so to see the typological relevance which lies behind the divine allocation of this particular name to his Son. Don Sinnema raises a needed caution about typology. He notes that "Jesus fulfilled Joshua's calling," that "his work brought Joshua's to completion." However, if we only view Joshua as a type of Christ, we are in danger of inverting the proper relationship.[15] It is in the light of Jesus that we see the true meaning of Joshua's role. As Praamsma puts it, Joshua "performed deeds that foreshadowed work that would later be done perfectly by Jesus himself."[16]

The distinctive work of Joshua was to cause Israel to inherit the land (Deut. 1:38; 31:7), which he did by crossing over before the people (Deut. 31:3). According to Deuteronomy 6:23, God's redemptive work for Israel

---

11. Barth, *Faith*, 59.
12. Calvin, *Evangelists*, Vol. 1, 98.
13. Luther, *Larger Catechism*, 61.
14. Carson, *Matthew*, on Matt. 1:21.
15. Sinnema, *Reclaiming the Land*, 110.
16. Praamsma, *Before the Face*, 45.

consisted in two parts: he brought them out from Egyptian bondage, in order to bring them in to the promised land. Whereas Moses' role was connected with the bringing out, Joshua's calling related to the bringing in. The settlement of the people in the land is described as their "rest,"[17] which is elaborated to mean dwelling in safety (Deut. 12:10), and, in the LXX translation of Deuteronomy 5:33, where the word "rest" replaces the allusion to life in the Hebrew text, to be in a position where all goes well with the people—which is, indeed, true life. This was the LORD's achievement through Joshua.[18]

However, the New Testament observes that Joshua did not give the people rest (Heb. 4:8), because the true meaning of the promise was "something better" (Heb. 11:40), namely "a heavenly country" (Heb. 11: 16). It has been pointed out that Isaiah had already used the concept of rest with reference to the messianic age.[19] I agree with E.A. Martens that the New Testament spiritualisation of the concept of land should not be turned into something ethereal: it symbolizes the fact that life with God takes place here and now, that discipleship is all-embracing.[20] The "heavenly country" has come down to earth in Jesus Christ.

What, then, is his work of saving his people from their sins? If salvation is equivalent to rest, and rest means safety, well-being, and genuine life, then the emphasis in the name Jesus must be his purpose to rescue us from the danger, ill-being, and death into which our sins have plunged us as a result of our losing touch with heaven while we live on earth. As the true Joshua, Jesus goes before us to bring us into the living experience of heavenly realities, so that, even now during our earthly life, we enjoy security in God, true welfare from God, and real life with God.

But part of what that means for us is discovered in what it meant for him. As well as the definition "Savior," the name Jesus is also powerfully linked in the New Testament with the function of servant. It comes out most clearly in Peter's preaching in Acts 3:26: "God, having raised up his Servant Jesus, sent him to bless you, in turning every one of you away from your iniquities."[21] That Jesus was God's servant *par excellence*

17. Exod. 33:14; Deut. 3:20; 12:9; 25:19; Josh. 1:13.
18. Josh. 21:44; 22:4; 23:1.
19. Kalland, *Deuteronomy*, on Deut. 12:1–14.
20. Martens, *Plot and purpose*, 115.
21. See also Acts 3:13; 4:27, 30.

is stressed by Matthew's perception that the Servant prophecies of Isaiah are realized in his life and ministry (Matt. 12:18). And Jesus saw himself as "one who serves" (Luke 22:27), as one whose service would involve the ultimate, but the ultimately purposive, sacrifice (Matt. 20:28; Mark 10:45).

But Peter's words indicate that as God's Servant Jesus turns his people away from their sins. As Savior, he rescues us from the deadly consequences of our sins, but his saving work and his serving work come together, because in saving us from the danger, ill-being, and death which result from our sinful loss of touch with heaven, he also turns us away from our sins themselves. The result is that, as Servant, he becomes the model for our renewed human life. We become God's willing servants, turning our back on our sins, and turning our face towards heaven, so that here on earth we not only enjoy heavenly realities, but also live out the costly challenge of heavenly priorities.

THE TITLE THAT EXPLAINS HIS POSITION

Jesus is the Christ. That was the message of the earliest Christian preachers.[22] Their point was that he is the fulfilment of the implicit Old Testament expectation of the one who was to come as the LORD's anointed. For "Christ" is not a surname, but a title, translating the Hebrew term *māšîaḥ*, familiarly rendered "Messiah," and meaning "anointed one."

McGiffert's claim that *Christos* in the creed functions not as a title, but merely as part of the name of the historical figure, Jesus Christ, and that the apostle Paul in his letters uses the term in just such a way[23] is unconvincing. McGiffert's own comment counts against it when he acknowledges that Paul "as a Jew would always be conscious of the original meaning of *Christos* if anyone was,"[24] especially in view of Luke's account of Paul's preaching, in which he set out to prove (Acts 9:22), explain and demonstrate (Acts 17:3), and testify (Acts 18:5) that Jesus is the Christ.

I have described the Old Testament messianic hope as implicit. Rengstorf points out that the Old Testament "exhibits no clear developments of the messianic expectation."[25] It was only in the intertestamental

---

22. Acts 5:42; 9:22; 17:3; 18:5, 28.
23. McGiffert, *Creed*, 112–14.
24. McGiffert, *Creed*, 113.
25. Rengstorf, "*Christos*," 337.

period that the anticipation of the arrival of a definite Messiah figure became highly focussed. It was "a product of later Judaism,"[26] though it may be true that there are just "two unambiguous references to this figure" in Daniel 9:25 and 26.[27]

Nevertheless, it is clear that, by the time of Jesus, a concrete messianic expectation was widespread. The words of the Samaritan woman, "I know that Messiah is coming" (John 4:25), are proof of this. Given the prevalence by then of this certain hope, we can imagine the tone of excitement in which Andrew said to Simon Peter, "we have found the Messiah" (John 1:41). That Jesus accepted the designation "Messiah" or "Christ" is clear from his reply to the Samaritan woman, "I who speak to you am he" (John 4:26), as well as from his enthusiastic response when Peter confesses, "You are the Christ, the Son of the living God." Jesus replied, "Blessed are you, Simon Bar-Jonah, for flesh and blood has not revealed this to you, but my Father who is in heaven" (Matt. 16:16–17).

What, then, does this title tell us about Jesus our Savior?

In the Old Testament we read of three categories of men who were anointed for office—priests, kings, and prophets. On the basis of this fact, some interpreters of the Apostles' Creed have seen in the title Christ a declaration that Jesus is the true and final holder of the threefold office. Calvin asks, "What force then has the name Christ?" His answer says, "It signifies that he is anointed by his Father to be King, Priest and Prophet."[28]

However, a close examination of the Old Testament data suggests that this may be making too much of the word. Limiting our consideration to the presence in the LXX of the substantive *Christos* as applied to human persons, we discover that it is used only three times of an anointed priest,[29] just twice of anointed prophets,[30] but that it refers twenty-nine times to an anointed king.[31]

---

26. Motyer, "Messiah," 987.

27. Oswalt, "*Mšh*," 1126.

28. Calvin, *Catechism, 1545*, Q. 34; so also *Heidelberg Catechism*, Q. 31; Witsius, *Creed*, Vol. 1, 264–65.

29. Lev. 4:5, 16; 6:22.

30. 1 Chr. 16:22; Ps. 105:15.

31. 1 Sam. 2:10, 35; 12:3, 5; 16:6; 24:6, 10; 26:9, 11, 16, 23; 2 Sam. 1:14, 16; 2:5; 19:21; 22:51; 23:1; 2 Chr. 6:42; 22:7; Ps. 2:2; 18:50; 20:6; 84:9; 89:38, 51; 132:10, 17; Isa. 45:1; Lam. 4:20. There are a further four instances of *Christos* in the LXX. Dan. 9:25 has already been mentioned as a prophecy of the true Messiah. In Ps. 28:8, the allusion

It seems, therefore, that Rengstorf is right to say that "only the figure of the king has to be reckoned as messianic in the sense of specific messianic expectation," and that "the dominant motif in the idea of the messiah is the kingly one."[32] To speak of Jesus as "the Christ," then, is to say, "Jesus is King."

Rengstorf also makes the point that "the [messianic] expectation is ultimately related to the idea of the kingship and the sovereign kingly rule of God."[33] This indicates that there is a smooth transition within the Apostles' Creed from the idea of God the Father as the "almighty, Creator of heaven and earth," to the fact that Jesus is the Christ—the anointed one in whom the sovereign providential rule of God has been brought down from heaven to earth, is now being exercised on earth from his heavenly throne, and will be finalized ultimately in the new heavens and the new earth.

It is a valid insight, I am sure, which Karl Barth puts forward when he stresses that "Jesus," a Hebrew name, is linked with the title "Christ," a Greek word. He finds it significant that Jesus "was not named Jesus Messiah by the first community, but Jesus Christ," and traces in this combination the progress from Israel to the whole world.[34] The God of Israel is the God of all the earth. Jesus, the Jew, came into the world when Greek culture and language dominated the scene. The Greek title Christ declares that his kingship, which is the revelation of the sovereign providential rule of God, is for every tribe and tongue and people and nation (Rev. 5:9).

Jim Packer is therefore right to say that, for the compilers of the creed, "to call Jesus *Christ* was to claim for him a decisive place in history and a universal dominion which all men everywhere must acknowledge."[35] Because our Savior is the Christ, Christianity is inevitably a missionary faith. As the men of Samaria recognized, the Christ is the Savior of the world (John 4:42). As the apostle Paul says, God was in Christ reconciling the world to himself (2 Cor. 5:19).

---

appears to be (unusually) to the people as a whole, while in Hab. 3:13, it seems to mean Moses (see Armerding, *Obadiah, Nahum, Habakkuk*, on Hab. 3:13). The referent in Amos 4:13 is unclear, and in any case *Christos* is a mistranslation of the Hebrew.

32. Rengstorf, "*Christos*," 335, 336.
33. Rengstorf, "*Christos*," 335.
34. Barth, *Dogmatics*, 72–73.
35. Packer, *Christian*, 36.

And in Jesus Christ, his only Son, our Lord 55

THE DESCRIPTIONS THAT CLARIFY HIS RELATIONSHIPS

In the remaining two phrases of our present study we learn how Jesus is related, first to the Father as "his only Son," and then to us—to the world, indeed—as "our Lord."[36] As I hope to show, in both cases Jesus is related both as God and as a human being.

His only Son

In considering this phrase we are confronted with another fascinating translation issue. The Latin text of the creed uses the word *unicus* for "only." This word is found three times in Jerome's Latin version of the New Testament, in each case referring to a person who was the one and only child of his or her mother or father. The dead man whom Jesus raised was "the only son of his mother" (Luke 7:12); it was Jairus' "only daughter" who was dying (Luke 8:42); after Jesus had descended from the Mount of Transfiguration a man implored his help on behalf of his "only child" (Luke 9:38). In every instance the Greek word translated *unicus* is *monogenēs*.

This Greek word appears five times with reference to Jesus (John 1:14, 18; 3:16, 18; 1 John 4:9). In these instances Jerome preferred to translate by *unigenitus*, so highlighting the fact that Jesus was more than merely the only Son of God: he was God's Son by generation, as distinct from creation. The Greek text of the creed supposed to underlie the Latin version also uses *monogenēs*, so it is presumably significant that the Latin text opted for *unicus* rather than *unigenitus*. Howard Marshall and K. H. Bartels both suggest that Jerome probably departed from the older tradition from anti-Arian motives.[37]

It is a matter of debate amongst New Testament scholars whether *monogenēs* is best translated "only-begotten" or simply "only." Merrill Tenney, for example, finds *monogenēs* derived from *genos* (meaning "kind" or "species"). He concludes that *monogenēs* means "one of a kind," "only," "unique," and not "only-begotten." He believes, therefore, that *unicus* is the best Latin translation, and that the emphasis is on the thought that, as the "only" Son of God, Jesus has no equal.[38] On the other hand, Barnabas Lindars finds the context and the Old Testament

---

36. See Pannenberg, *Creed*, 70.
37. Marshall, *Epistles of John*, 214, n. 8; Bartels, "*monos*," 725.
38. Tenney, *John*, on John 1:14.

background decisive for the meaning "only-begotten" in John 1:14.[39] The fact that the term can stand alone as a substantive in that context does suggest that it means more than merely "only" there, whereas its use elsewhere of ordinary human sole children would point in the other direction. It is perhaps true that either nuance may be present, depending on the context and the subject. What is clear, though, is that the early Latin translators understood *monogenēs* straightforwardly, as meaning no more than "only."

Jesus Christ, then, is related to God as his only Son. This is true in the first place as regards his divine nature.

God's Son in his divine nature

Even if the creed does not give the word "only" the fuller meaning of "only-begotten," the fact that the Scriptures can speak of angels (Job 38:7) and of other human beings as God's sons, whether by creation (Luke 3:38), by election (Exod. 4:22), or by resurrection (Luke 20:36), necessarily confers upon the word "only" a deeper significance. Whereas Christians become God's spiritual sons (Rom. 8:14) by adoption (Eph. 1:5) and by faith (Gal. 3:26), Jesus is God's Son "by verity of nature,"[40] eternally pre-existent.[41] This distinction between Jesus' Sonship by nature and ours by the adoption of grace is emphasized by Calvin and by the Heidelberg Catechism.[42]

Even though the word *unicus* does not mean "only-begotten," the distinction between Jesus as God's only Son, and angels and people as other sons of God inevitably points to uniqueness, not only of relationship, but also of being. McGrath rightly notes that the word *unicus* entails the rejection of adoptionist Christology.[43] Augustine cites the creed as "his only Son," but goes on to stress the implication that the Son is as fully divine as his Father: "for it could not be that God's only Son should not be God." Augustine points to human analogies: "What each is, that it engenders. Man does not beget an ox, sheep does not beget dog, nor dog sheep. Whatever it is that begets, that which it is, it begets."[44]

39. Lindars, *John*, 96.
40. Rufinus, *Commentary*, para. 8, 1105.
41. See Luther, *Enchiridion*, 79; Kelly, *Creeds*, 143.
42. Calvin, *Catechism, 1545*, Qs. 46–47; *Heidelberg Catechism*, Q. 33.
43. McGrath, *I believe*, 45.
44. Augustine, *Creed*, para. 3, 691.

The significance of "Son of God" as indicative of Jesus' relationship as divine to the Father is spelt out superbly by George Hendry. He notes that "*Son of God* points to the relation of this man to God in his being," and explains its significance for Christian faith:

> What Christians believe is not merely that God acted in this man, even if the action was decisive and conclusive. This would leave only a difference of degree, and not of kind, between Christ and others in whom God also acted in the course of saving-history. For such men who served as instruments of God's action in history the descriptive category is "man of God," and the paradigm is Moses (Deut. 33:1). But Christ is more than the man of God; he is the Son of God. His relation to God is more than functional; it is ontological. There is more than divine action in him; there is divine being.[45]

This truth is vital for the integrity of the Apostles' Creed, and for the truth of the gospel.[46] "This is what makes his coming definitive."[47] If Jesus is not true God, then nothing else which the creed goes on to tells us about him has any relevance whatever. This brief phrase is the key to the interpretation of all the rest of the information which the creed gives us about Jesus.

But Jesus Christ is related to God as his only Son also as regards his human nature.

GOD'S SON IN HIS HUMAN NATURE

This fact is emphasized by Wolfhart Pannenberg, who says that it is both possible and necessary "to understand the title 'Son of God' as being the interpretation of Jesus' *human* appearance."[48] Pannenberg is, admittedly, too one-sided about this. Nevertheless, the point is well made, provided the twin truths of Jesus' Sonship as God the Son, and his Sonship in his human role are held in better balance than Pannenberg seems to achieve.

Pannenberg argues that the Old Testament was familiar with "son of God" as a designation of the king of Judah. Although he does not state this, it is presumably the promise of the Davidic covenant which

---

45. Hendry, "Christology," 55.
46. Cf. Cranfield, *Creed*, 23.
47. Hendry, "Christology," 55.
48. Pannenberg, *Creed*, 62; cf. McGiffert, *Creed*, 115.

Pannenberg has in mind. He concludes that "in the Jewish sphere of tradition the title Son of God merely characterized Jesus' function—that he had been appointed to exercise God's rule over the world."[49] Apart from the fact that the word "merely" is somewhat unnecessary, this is a valid comment, and draws out the implication of the title "Christ" against the background of the creed's description of God as almighty Creator.

This aspect of Jesus' Sonship comes out most clearly at two points in Jesus' earthly life—in the baptism-temptation narratives, and at the resurrection.

Having been endorsed by the Father's voice from heaven, accompanied by the descent of the Spirit in the form of a dove, as the beloved and well-pleasing Son (Matt. 3:17), Jesus is immediately led out into the desert where the tempter twice mocks him with the words, "If you are the Son of God" (Matt. 4:3, 6). His challenge now is whether he will remain true to his calling as the man whom God has appointed to that Sonship in which his divine purpose is delegated to his earthly representative. The alternative would be to use his divinely endowed powers to satisfy himself. We may be very grateful that Jesus did rise to the challenge of that Sonship: it means that we are saved.

It was his resurrection which conclusively sealed Jesus' Sonship as a man. This is clear from Acts 13:33, where Paul cites Psalm 2:7 in connection with the resurrection. The *today* when the Son was begotten is clearly the day of his resurrection. We have to be careful here, for Jesus was very evidently God's Son as a man before his resurrection from the dead. That is obvious from the gospel accounts.

Alexander's attempt to understand the raising up of Jesus in this verse as his incarnation, the resurrection only coming into view in the following verse,[50] is unconvincing, first because the resurrection has already been the theme from verse 30, and second because back in verse 23, where Jesus is said to have been raised up by God in what clearly is a reference to the incarnation, a different Greek verb is used. Charles Knapp seems to be right in reading Paul as regarding the resurrection "as the final and divine assurance of the Sonship of Jesus." He compares Romans 1:4.[51]

---

49. Pannenberg, *Creed*, 64.
50. J. A. Alexander, *Acts*, Vol. 2, 29; so also Blunt, *Acts*, 192.
51. Knapp, *Acts*, 187.

Perhaps we can go a little further, and see the resurrection of Jesus as the first stage of his installation as the *exalted* Son of God. Previously he had been the Son in the humiliation and hiddenness of his incarnate earthly life. Now, for the first time a human being begins his ascent to heaven as the Son of God in glory.

It is the hiddenness of his earthly Sonship which accounts for the failure of many of his contemporaries to discern the full truth about him (cf. Mark 6:3). As the Son of God on earth Jesus did not throw his weight around. Clement of Rome writes: "The scepter of the greatness of God, the Lord Jesus Christ, came not with the noise of bragging or extravagance, in spite of the power that was his, but in lowliness of mind."[52] He refused to put "the insignia of majesty"[53] on display. To do that was precisely the temptation which enticed him in the desert. In his resurrection he was begotten Son of God as the man in glory in all the fullness of heavenly splendor.

The mysterious hiddenness of Jesus' earthly Sonship becomes the model for our lives as the Father's adopted sons in him. Christian commitment should never be seen as a route to power, prestige, applause, kudos, influence, admiration, fame, wealth, glory. Our calling in this world is to be the followers of a man of sorrows, a suffering servant. The challenge is that we should have "this mind . . . which was in Christ Jesus" (Phil. 2:5). The way of discipleship, the way of sonship, is the way of pain, suffering, misunderstanding, persecution, the way of death. But through the tears we look forward in hope to reward and glory.

The hymn writer puts it like this:

> Go, labor on; spend and be spent,
> Thy joy to do the Father's will;
> It is the way the Master went;
> Should not the servant tread it still?[54]

This hymn goes on to remind us that our fellow human beings may well heed us not, love us not, praise us not, that we must expect to labor on in weakness, sometimes fainting and cast down, that the Christian life is a life of toil. It must be so, because we follow the Son of God.

---

52. Clement, *Corinthians*, 16.2.
53. Kent, *Philippians*, on Phil. 2:7, quoting J. B. Lightfoot.
54. By Horatius Bonar (1808–89).

Our Lord

This title too has both a divine and a human aspect as it pinpoints Jesus' relationship to us. Calvin recognized this dual thrust when he said, "He is, moreover, our Lord, not only according to the divinity which he holds together with the Father from eternity, but also in that flesh in which he was set forth to us."[55]

OUR LORD IN HIS DIVINITY

It is frequently recognized by students of the Apostles' Creed that the LXX sets the context for the first way in which the title Lord must be understood. In God's providence the title *kurios* had become the regular Greek translation for the Biblical name for God, now rendered in English versions as LORD (in capitals). Cranfield explains succinctly: "The most important part of the background of Paul's and the earliest church's use of 'Lord' in reference to Jesus was use of the same title in the Greek version of the Old Testament to represent the Hebrew divine name Yahweh (Jehovah)."[56] The result of this use of LORD meant that when the confession "Jesus is Lord"[57] became current, it had the unmistakable implication, "Jesus is God."

Amongst early Christian writers, one who was aware in a particularly acute way that Jesus as "our Lord" is our God was Ignatius of Antioch. Phrases such as "Jesus Christ our God," or "our God, Jesus Christ," occur with some frequency in his letters,[58] and there are, according to R.M. Grant,[59] a further three passages where Ignatius certainly speaks of Christ as God.[60]

It has sometimes been claimed that this amounts to little more than the assertion that Jesus has the value of God in relation to us, but that Ignatius stops short of an absolute identification of Jesus Christ with

---

55. Calvin, *Catechism, 1538*, 20.ii, 22.
56. Cranfield, *Creed*, 24.
57. See Rom. 10:9; 1 Cor. 12:3; Phil. 2:11.
58. Ignatius, Ephesians, inscr.; 18.1; Trallians, 7.1; Romans, inscr.; 3.3; To Polycarp, 8.3.
59. Grant, *Apostolic Fathers*, 7.
60. Ignatius, Ephesians, 15.3; 19.3; Smyrnaeans, 1.1. There are another three places (Ignatius, Trallians, 7.1; Smyrnaeans, 6.1; 10.1) in which Christ is spoken of as God in only some MSS of Ignatius' letters, and both Lightfoot, *Apostolic Fathers*, 169, 316, and Schoedel, *Ignatius*, 147-8, 248, doubt that the identification is original in these contexts.

God.⁶¹ However, more recent studies of Ignatius' letters have questioned this.⁶² When Ignatius calls Jesus "our God," he does not merely mean that Jesus might as well be God as far as we are concerned. Neither does he mean that Jesus is the one whom we happen to choose to be God for us out of the dazzling choice of divine possibilities presented to us by the religions of the world. What he means is that Jesus Christ is the one true God, our God, the God for all of us, for every human being, for all the world, simply because there is no other God than the Trinity of Father, Son and Spirit, who has made himself known in the human person, Jesus.

Our Lord in his humanity

He is Lord over us because he is the most senior of all people; he is indeed, the one and only true human being, for he is "without sin" (Heb. 4:15), and sin is a detraction, a fall, from real humanness. As Lord of the world, Jesus bears the world's government on his shoulders (Isa. 9:6), and this places the world under the obligation of submission and obedience towards him. But we are not talking of submission under the thumb of a tyrant, nor of reluctant obedience to a dictator. We are talking about glad allegiance to the one who is able to "sympathize with our weaknesses" (Heb. 4:15), and whose Lordship is the reign of grace and love.

As usual, Luther brings out the practical application of this truth:

> I believe that Jesus Christ . . . is my Lord; who has redeemed me, a lost and condemned man, secured and delivered me even from all sins, from death, and from the power of the devil, not with gold or silver, but with his holy, precious blood, and with his innocent sufferings and death; in order that I might be his own, live under him in his kingdom, and serve him in everlasting righteousness, innocence and blessedness.⁶³

Jesus said, "You call me Teacher and Lord, and you say well, for so I am." He then pointed out what follows: he sets the example, and we must do as he has done (John 13:13, 15).

---

61. So, e.g., Lightfoot, *Apostolic Fathers*, 26, 29, 169; von Harnack, *History of Dogma*, 188.

62. So, e.g., Corwin, *Ignatius*, 132; Grant, *Apostolic Fathers*, 8; Schoedel, *Ignatius*, 39.

63. Luther, *Enchiridion*, 79.

Karl Barth draws attention to Luther's use of the singular, "my Lord," whereas the creed says "our Lord" in the plural.[64] Luther is echoing Thomas's words to Jesus in John 20:28, "My Lord and my God." Jim Packer poses the challenge, "how can you say 'our Lord' in church until you have first said 'my Lord' in your heart?"[65]

It is interesting to observe that this creed, which begins with words of personal, passionate, individual commitment, now introduces a corporate element in the words "our Lord." It is true that I must believe for myself, but equally true that I cannot believe on my own. In believing I am one with all those who believe, across time and across the world. We are "called to be saints, with all who in every place call on the name of Jesus Christ our Lord, both theirs and ours" (1 Cor. 1:2).

Christianity requires personal faith, but this is a faith which implants the believer into the body of all those who ever have believed, who do now believe, wherever they may be, and who ever will believe in future generations, in Jesus Christ our Lord. There is no such phenomenon as a Christian in isolation. Even if, in exceptional times, circumstances may isolate a Christian physically from fellow believers, we are always inescapably united spiritually to the entire company of God's elect. And because that spiritual unity is inescapable, there is no excuse in normal circumstances if we willfully isolate ourselves from other believers. That applies equally to the local congregation and to the individual believer.

Moreover, the ultimate goal of the word "our" in the phrase "our Lord" is that "the world might taste and see the wonders of his grace," remembering that "the arms of love that compass me would all mankind embrace."[66]

Those who sincerely mean the Apostles' Creed cannot, therefore, avoid having a missionary heart. Any Christian congregation which is rooted in these realities of Christian orthodoxy will inevitably have a missionary vision. The world has got to be our parish, because Jesus Christ truly is the only Lord over all the earth.

---

64. Barth, *Dogmatics*, 92.
65. Packer, *Christian*, 38.
66. From the hymn, *Jesus! the name high over all*, by Charles Wesley (1707–88).

8

He was conceived by the Holy Spirit, and born of the virgin Mary

KARL BARTH GIVES A happily apt title to his chapter on this section of the creed: "The Mystery and the Miracle of Christmas."[1] The virgin birth was certainly a miracle, and the incarnation as a human being of the Son of God is truly a mystery beyond our ability to understand.

Louis Praamsma suggests that "the most beautiful story in the Bible is the Christmas story. Even though we have heard it innumerable times," he goes on, "it continues to hold us spellbound."[2]

The Apostles' Creed does not recount the whole story. It just homes in on the central fact, that fact which makes the story not merely beautiful, but vitally meaningful for every man and woman, boy and girl who has ever lived. It homes in on that central fact which transports us through and beyond our sense of being spellbound, to compel us to realize that we are bound to take this story seriously for its inner, urgent depths of challenge and relevance for our true welfare.

Two things are said in this clause, though it is hard to separate them one from the other. To the extent that the two things can be distinguished, we may say that Jesus' being conceived by the Holy Spirit is the reality, of which the virgin birth is the sign, as is indicated prophetically by Isaiah 7:14.

It is certainly not the case that the Spirit-conception was dependent upon the virgin birth, as if it were the physical fact of the virgin birth which made Jesus divine, a point stressed by Robert Reymond.[3] Rather, the virgin birth was the divinely appointed indicator as to which of the

---

1. Barth, *Dogmatics*, 95.
2. Praamsma, *Before the Face*, 57.
3. Reymond, *New Systematic Theology*, 550.

many babies "born of a woman" (Gal. 4:4) was the Christ, the Son of God, our Lord. It was the signpost erected by God to direct us to the location of the incarnate God in human life.

As to the precise physical method by which the Spirit enabled the virgin to conceive we can only speculate. In December, 2006 the Daily Mail carried an item headed "Stem cell scientists create 'virgin birth' breakthrough in mice." It reported that scientists in Boston, USA, had successfully stimulated the eggs of female mice to enable them to develop into embryos without the introduction of male sperm.[4] It is often assumed that it was some such technique which God used to bring about the virgin birth of Jesus. If so, it should be no surprise to a believer to know that God was capable of doing millennia ago something that twenty-first century scientists are only just beginning to be able to contemplate.

However, in my view it is worth considering the possibility that the Holy Spirit created an embryo and then implanted it into Mary's womb.[5] With the progress of medical science, the implantation of an embryo produced through fertilization *in vitro* into the womb of a woman, whether the biological mother or a surrogate, is now possible. "The human uterus is able to receive young embryos [and] insure their growth and implantation."[6] There is no medical reason why an embryo cannot be implanted in the womb of a woman who is a virgin. Again, why should we doubt that God was able to achieve centuries ago what scientists can do today?

Of course, God's achievement was a miracle, however he did it. Scientists may be able to implant an embryo, but they still need to obtain an egg from a woman and a sperm from a man in order to carry out the fertilization technique in a test tube. No such limitations restricted God's ability. If it is true that the Spirit-conception and virgin birth were the result of embryo implantation, then that human embryo was a direct

---

4. See http://www.dailymail.co.uk/pages/live/articles/news/news.html?in_article_id=422767&in_page_id=1770.

5. I am indebted to Mrs. Anne Wintersgill, a member of my former congregation in Stockton-on-Tees, for first putting this suggestion to me back in the mid 1990's. The more that I have though about it since, the more I have become persuaded that hers is most likely to be a correct insight.

6. From the abstract of Mandelbaum et al., "Moment de la transplantation," lines 2–3.

creation, and God's achievement was a totally new act of creation out of nothing.[7]

The suggestion that the conception of Jesus was an implanted embryo would avoid having to explain how, if an egg had been taken from Mary's ovary, the sinful nature inherent in all human beings other than Jesus was not passed on. It would also avoid the unlikely idea that the sinful nature is contained only in the male seed.[8] It might be objected to this view that Jesus would not then have been genuinely human. It might lead to a Valentinian understanding of Christ, which McGiffert explains "as meaning only the passage of a pre-existent being through the womb of the Virgin, without actually becoming man or assuming human flesh."[9] However, God created Adam from nothing as a genuine human being in the beginning; it would have been no problem for him to repeat the exercise in the case of the last Adam.

Indeed, such a fresh act of special creation *ex nihilo* would have been entirely appropriate. It accords well with the truth of the new creation in Christ. It emphasizes the radically new beginning which took place in the incarnation, a new beginning which Cranfield explains in fine terms:

> God himself made a new beginning in the course of the history of his creation by coming himself in person and becoming part of that history. He himself originated this particular human life by a new act of creation. Jesus Christ is not a Savior arising out of the continuity of our human history, but God in person intervening in it, coming to the rescue.[10]

The different preposition in each half of this clause may well point towards an understanding of conception in which Mary herself contributed nothing genetic. Jesus was conceived by (*de/dia*) the Holy Spirit: he was the sole agent. He was born of (*ex/ek*) Mary. She was the receptacle into which the Holy Spirit placed his new creation, and out of which the miraculously created child emerged.

---

7. Pace Barth, *Dogmatics*, 97.

8. Grudem, *Systematic Theology*, 531, has to address both these issues in the context of his understanding of the virgin birth, and concludes that prevention of the transmission of sin from Mary to Jesus was itself miraculous.

9. McGiffert, *Creed*, 123.

10. Cranfield, "Virgin Birth," 189.

It has become fashionable in some circles to deny that the virgin birth is a historical fact. Karl Barth, strongly asserts the need to maintain belief in the historicity of the virgin birth. He considers the argument that, since the virgin birth is the sign and the incarnation the reality, we can dispense with the sign and still hold on to the reality. "Let me warn you against this," he writes. "It is rare in life to be able to separate form and content."[11] Barth fears the danger "that, by eliminating the sign, we thereby eliminate the thing signified," and points out that "exactly this seems to have happened"—that "those who have wanted to get rid of the miraculous birth . . . have lost the incarnation along with it."[12]

Cranfield lists and answers seven arguments which are put forward against the historicity of the virgin birth of Jesus. The arguments are these: (1) there is actually very little space in the New Testament devoted to the virgin birth; (2) the genealogies of Jesus trace his descent through Joseph, which puts a question mark against the virgin birth; (3) the fact that Jesus' family did not believe in him during his earthly life is inconsistent with a virgin birth; (4) the origin of the idea of a virgin birth is claimed as Isaiah 7:14, but this passage was not interpreted Messianically in Judaism; (5) there are parallels in Greek mythology in the myths about the offspring of gods and women, and these may have inspired the idea of a virgin birth; (6) it is alleged that much in the infancy narratives is unhistorical, and the virgin birth is part of the same mythological package; (7) underlying all arguments against the virgin birth is the assumption that a miracle is impossible.

In response to each argument Cranfield makes the following points: (1) he highlights probable allusions to Jesus' miraculous conception throughout the New Testament; (2) he notes that Joseph was Jesus' legal father, even though he was not his biological father; (3) he reckons that Mary and Joseph would have been naturally reticent about the circumstances of Jesus' birth, even at home; (4) he suggests that Isaiah 7:14 would not have been read as a Messianic prophecy of virgin birth unless the fact of a virgin birth was already assumed; (5) he dismisses the alleged parallels with Greek mythology, since not one of them contains the idea of a virgin birth; (6) he demonstrates that skepticism about the historicity of the birth narratives in general is unfounded; (7) he insists

---

11. Barth, *Dogmatics*, 96.
12. Barth, *Faith*, 86.

that it is not possible for a believer to assert with logical consistency the impossibility of miracles.[13]

But what is the value of the virgin birth for us? What is the message conveyed by this part of the Apostles' Creed? Two main truths may be stressed.

JESUS IS REALLY DIVINE AND GENUINELY HUMAN

That is the mystery of the incarnation. In this one person, God

> deigns in flesh to appear,
> widest extremes to join.[14]

The statement that Jesus was conceived by the Holy Spirit indicates that he was unique from that very moment.[15] "Since he had been actually conceived by the Holy Spirit, it was plain that he had never at any moment of his earthly existence been anything else than God."[16] Jesus "was God, with no reservation and no ambiguity."[17]

Hans Urs von Balthasar makes a pertinent observation about the passive voice of the word "conceived." The eternal Son of God "does not incarnate himself." Von Balthasar goes on, "the Creed describes not a 'taking of something to oneself,' but an 'acquiescing in something that happens to one.'" Here von Balthasar discerns, even pre-natally, the obedience of God the Son to the Father's will in the covenant of redemption. "The Son permits, in full consciousness and with full consent to the divine plan for redemption, himself to be used as the Father wishes."[18] But the creed insists that the obedient Son who was thus conceived was indeed the eternal Son of the Father, himself possessed of unqualified divinity.

However, Packer points out that the early church fathers appealed to the virgin birth as proof of Jesus' true humanity.[19] Very early in the history of the church the heresy known as "Docetism" arose. This term is derived from a Greek word meaning "to seem." Those who put forward

---

13. Cranfield, "Virgin Birth," 178–85.
14. From the hymn, *Let earth and heaven combine*, by Charles Wesley (1707–88).
15. McGrath, *I Believe*, 45
16. Kelly, *Creeds*, 377.
17. Barth, *Faith*, 80.
18. Von Balthasar, *Credo*, 45–46.
19. Packer, *Christian*, 42.

this view were well motivated, in that they desired to proclaim Jesus' full divinity as eloquently as possible, but it resulted in the undermining of his genuine humanity. It taught that Jesus only seemed to be human, but that he was not exactly as human as we are. He was human in appearance, but the reality is that he was God, God in human form, but only God inside.

This error was in the background when the apostle John wrote his letters. That is why he stresses three times that "Jesus Christ has come in the flesh," and labels the rejection of this truth as deception in the spirit of antichrist (1 John 4:2, 3; 2 John 7). While it may sound plausibly exalting to the Lord to emphasize his divinity to the extent that the full authenticity of his human nature is undermined, it is actually to set oneself in direct opposition to him. "Our Lord's deity is not enhanced when men, thinking to do him honor, detract from the completeness of his manhood."[20]

In response the orthodox believers pointed to Jesus' virgin birth. Look, they said, he began life just as we do, emerging from a mother's womb. He was really human, not just a phantom of humanity, not just "a divine being who masqueraded as a human being,"[21] not "an intermediate being," but "a man like us, a man without reservation."[22] McGiffert sees in the creed's identification of Mary by name a further example of the desire to make the reference to Jesus' birth definite and explicit.[23]

Ignatius of Antioch had to face the heresy of Docetism, and it is in his letters to the Trallians and the Smyrnaeans that he confronts this error head-on, while making some indirect allusions to it in his Ephesian and Magnesian letters.[24] In answer to those who claimed that the experiences of Christ's humanity were "merely in semblance,"[25] Ignatius insists, amongst other things, on the reality of his human birth: as he says, Jesus Christ was "truly born."[26] It is in such a context that mentions of Mary or

---

20. F. F. Bruce, "Humanity," 10.

21. McGrath, *I Believe*, 46.

22. Barth, *Dogmatics*, 97.

23. McGiffert, *Creed*, 125. Although I think that McGiffert overdoes the polemical purpose of the Apostles' Creed (see below, ch. 9), at this point I think he is correct in seeing an anti-Docetic motive.

24. See Lightfoot, *Apostolic Fathers*, 173.

25. Ignatius, Smyrnaeans, 2.1; 4.2; cf. Trallians, 10.1.

26. Ignatius, Trallians, 9.1; Smyrnaeans, 1.1; cf. Ephesians, 18.2; Magnesians, 11.1.

"the virgin" appear in Ignatius' letters.[27] It has been well said, in response to Roman Catholic extremes that the creed's statement "he was conceived by the Holy Spirit, and born of the virgin Mary" " bears witness "to the reality of the Incarnation, not the glory of Jesus' mother."[28] The same would apply to Ignatius' references to Mary. His great emphasis was that Jesus Christ was "the complete human being."[29]

Of all the ancient heresies Docetism is the one which crops up most often within the ranks of Evangelicalism. Roy Coad acknowledges that "a tendency to Docetism has always been a serious flaw in Darbyite thinking,"[30] which has "invariably" been "shy of the full implications of the incarnation."[31] John Nelson Darby was one of the early leaders of the Brethren, and through his influence "a weakness on the doctrine of our Lord's humanity, verging at times on Docetism, has been endemic in certain phases of the Brethren movement."[32]

This stemmed from Darby's assertion that "the Lord, having been rejected by the Jewish people, is become a wholly heavenly person."[33] Darby himself was not guilty of Docetism in an absolute sense. Nevertheless, by teaching that the earthly life of the Lord had relevance exclusively to the Jews, and that the church is associated with Christ only "while he is there at the right hand of God,"[34] that is, only in his exaltation, Darby effectively taught a *de facto* Docetism with reference to the church.

Later Brethren writers veered more explicitly towards an inadequate doctrine of the incarnation. Having documented this, F. F. Bruce concludes: "views subversive of our Lord's manhood find a measure of acquiescence such as would never be extended to views subversive of his deity."[35]

However, because of the spread of Dispensationalism beyond the confines of Brethrenism as a result of the influence of the Scofield Reference Bible, twentieth-century Evangelicalism as a whole became

27. Ignatius, Ephesians, 7.2; 18.2; 19.1; Trallians, 9.1; Smyrnaeans, 1.1.
28. Packer, *Christian*, 43.
29. Ignatius, Smyrnaeans, 4.2.
30. Coad, *Brethren Movement*, 135.
31. Coad, *Brethren Movement*, 152.
32. F. F. Bruce, "Humanity," 5.
33. Darby, "Hopes of the Church," 376.
34. Darby, "Second Coming," 225.
35. F. F. Bruce, "Humanity," 9.

tolerant of views which failed to do full justice to Christ's humanity, while remaining rigidly intolerant of deviation from a strict affirmation of his perfect deity. As F. F. Bruce comments, Apollinarianism (the view that Christ had no human mind, soul, will, or emotions, because the human psyche was replaced by his divine nature) is "the besetting heresy of evangelical Christians."[36]

When William Hendriksen asks, "Was it possible for the Savior to succumb to temptation?" and answers, "Definitely not,"[37] are we not at least dangerously close to Docetism? If it was not even possible for the Savior to fall into sin, then his humanity was not the same humanity as Adam's, and therefore not the same humanity as ours. In that case he is not the Savior of our humanity. The wonder of Jesus' sinlessness was not that the temptations were a mere charade, the outcome fixed in advance, but rather that, despite being tested to the limit, the possibility of failure on his part being very real, he did in fact resist every temptation of the devil. "Without sin" (Heb. 4:15) is more gloriously read as a celebration of the outcome of his life, not as the characteristic of his starting-point.

One writer interprets Mark 13:32 to mean that that the Lord could not have known the timing of the end of the world had he only been a man, but that he did in fact know it because he was also divine.[38] However, this does not appear to be the plain meaning of the text, and again seems perilously close to being a Docetic Christology. Herman Witsius reads this verse more competently when he sees in Jesus "a finite and limited understanding."[39]

In contrast to such views, the Apostles' Creed clearly states that Jesus Christ our Lord, God's Son, was born. He entered our world in the same way that we do, and shared our human experiences as one of us.

Two things follow from all this. The first is that we have a Savior and Lord who understands us. It is a wonderful text in Isaiah 63:9, which characterizes the relationship of the God of Israel to his people like this: "In all their affliction he was afflicted."[40] This is rightly described as "one of the most moving expressions of the compassionate love of God" in the

---

36. F. F. Bruce, "Humanity," 9.
37. Hendriksen, *Matthew*, 223.
38. Masters, *The Faith*, 118.
39. Witsius, *Creed*, Vol. 2, 6.

40. It is beyond the scope of this work to discuss the translation problems in this text.

Old Testament.⁴¹ Calvin sees in these words God's goodness and incomparable love towards his people: "he himself bore their distresses and afflictions."⁴² Calvin rather plays down the significance of this by adding, "not that he can in any way endure anguish, but, by a very customary figure of speech, he assumes and applies to himself human passions."⁴³ However, such a comment risks treating God's word as less than a real revelation of God. It is better to acknowledge the great "theological significance" of passages like this which "indicate that God himself suffers whenever his people are in the throes of affliction."⁴⁴

Now, in the coming of Jesus Christ, we see that this is God's relationship, not just to Israel, but to Israel as the paradigm of his relationship to all people groups, to the whole world, to every human being. Truly, we have a high priest who can sympathise with our weaknesses (Heb. 4:15), and not a God afar off, not a Savior who offers telephone consultations, but one who comes to see us; not a Lord who bosses us about from a remote palace, but one who shares our pain, our sufferings, our struggles, our griefs, our trials, and whose presence in the midst as "God with us" (Matt. 1:23) is the redeeming reality. As Robert Candlish has put it: "His coming in the flesh, accepted as a reality, implies his really putting himself alongside of those in whose flesh he comes, and serving himself heir to all the ills to which their flesh is heir." It is true that Jesus was in his person a sinless human being, but nevertheless he embraced our human nature "with all the liabilities which our sin has entailed upon it."⁴⁵

Alister McGrath brings out the comforting significance of these truths for us in all the sufferings of our life:

> Many of us feel low at points. We find resisting temptation difficult. We are frightened by the thought of suffering and death. It is here that the doctrine of the incarnation has a vital contribution to make. Through Christ, God knows what it is like to be tempted. He knows what it is like to suffer. When we pray in such situations, we don't have to explain to God what it is like—he already knows. He has been through it himself. He has experienced

41. Grogan, *Isaiah*, on Isa. 63:9.
42. Calvin, *Isaiah*, Vol. 4, 346.
43. Calvin, *Isaiah*, Vol. 4, 347.
44. Swart and Wakely, "Ṣrr," 855.
45. Candlish, *1 John*, Vol. 2, 81.

it firsthand. This is a deeply consoling thought: we have a God who knows and understands our weaknesses. He is someone we can approach in trust.[46]

The second thing which follows from the truth that Jesus is both divine and human is that we have to look at him to know what real humanity is. "If there is genuine humanity, here it is, where God makes himself a man."[47] We have, then, to come to Jesus, taking him as our personal Lord and Savior, if we are to begin to live an authentically human life. In sin, we are fallen from the glory of God (Rom. 3:23); the image of God in human existence has become like a tarnished mirror. Jesus is our restoration to reality as human creatures.

SALVATION IS BY GRACE ALONE

This may be seen in two ways. Barth finds in the exclusion of the male a symbol of the ruling out of human action and initiative. Underlying these observations is the assumption of male headship as the divinely instituted creation order. "The male, says Barth, "as the specific agent of human action and history, with his responsibility for directing the human species, must now retire into the background as the powerless figure of Joseph."[48]

Cranfield goes a step further, pointing out that even Mary's involvement as a virgin in the birth of Jesus "attests that God's redemption is 'by grace alone.'" Mary here represents humanity as a whole, and it "does nothing more than accept, than submit to being simply the object of God's grace." Our humanity in the person of Mary "is simply to be made the receptacle of God's gift, the object of God's mercy."[49] Elsewhere Cranfield adds that even Mary's acceptance of her role is God's gracious gift. In that sense she is the "highly favored one" (Luke 1:28).[50]

Mary is therefore the model for all of us in relation to God's salvation in Jesus. Barth and Cranfield both point out that by nature we are full of pride, but each of them combines that word with a different part-

---

46. McGrath, *I Believe*, 51.
47. Barth, *Dogmatics*, 97.
48. Barth, *Dogmatics*, 99.
49. Cranfield, *Creed*, 30.
50. Cranfield, "Virgin Birth," 189.

ner. Barth speaks of our "pride and defiance,"[51] Cranfield of our "pride and self-reliant initiative."[52] Whether our pride takes the form of defying God in a brazen fashion, or whether it takes the form of imagining that we can impress God on our own initiative, that we can rely on ourselves to achieve the salvation of the world, either way the gospel of Jesus Christ our Lord demolishes our pride. As Augustine said, he was "born lowly, that thereby he might heal the proud."[53]

The gospel tells us plainly that we are helpless until God comes to save us, but then it assures that in Jesus he does come. The gospel mocks every human attempt to set the world to rights, but then it points us to the amazing mercy of an astonishingly gracious God, who rescues us entirely on his own initiative. The gospel warns us that we can contribute absolutely nothing to the experience of being saved, but then it invites us to receive what God freely gives in Jesus Christ his Son.

As we receive that grace, we find ourselves again in the position of Mary, accepting that we are inevitably the Lord's slaves.[54] In Bible times a slave existed in absolute dependence on his owner and master. Slavery "involved the abrogation of one's own autonomy."[55] As our Savior, the Lord Jesus Christ cancels out our supposed autonomy, and redefines our existence entirely as the passive recipients of God's grace. We find ourselves willingly recognizing that we are totally dependent on the God of grace to save us.

Von Balthasar notes that "the miracle that the 'barren' woman will have more children that the fertile one is a stock symbol of God's power to reverse things."[56] It is in the context of this recurring symbol that the virgin birth occurs, a still greater miracle in the ongoing pattern of God's saving power.

The miracle births of Isaac and John from the ageing mothers Sarah and Elizabeth, the delayed conceptions of Rebekah, Rachel, Manoah's wife, and Hannah, testify to the truth that the LORD "grants the bar-

---

51. Barth, *Dogmatics*, 99.
52. Cranfield, "Virgin Birth," 189.
53. Augustine, *Creed*, para. 6, 693.
54. The word "maidservant" in Luke 1:38 is *doulē*, the feminine equivalent of *doulos*, slave.
55. Tuente, "*doulos*," 593.'
56. Von Balthasar, *Credo*, 47.

ren woman a home, like a joyful mother of children" (Ps. 113:9[57]). This Psalm uses the reversal of barrenness as a symbol of salvation. Our dull, fruitless, worthless, ruined, barren lives become purposeful only when God raises us, poor and needy as we are, from the dust and the ash heap (Ps. 113: 7). He has done that by humbling himself (Ps. 113:6), by coming to earth in the person of his Son as a human being via the womb of Mary, in order to experience life on the ash heap, life on the rubbish dump of our ruined world. In this divine self-humbling we see that glory of God which is above the heavens (Ps. 113: 4). And the result is that in Jesus Christ we are lifted out of the pit, and seated amongst princes (Ps. 113:8).

Princely humanity is found in Jesus Christ and in him alone. It is what we were made for. We were not created for misery and gloom. We were not created for rebellion and sin. We were not created for judgment and hell. We were created for royal dominion, for the knowledge of God. And what we lost is given back to us in Jesus Christ, God and man. What we lost is given back to us by the amazing initiative of divine grace. And so we hear Augustine's exhortation: "Man exalted himself and fell; God humbled himself and raised us up. Christ's lowliness, what is it? God has stretched out a hand to man laid low. We fell, he descended; we lay low, he stooped. Let us lay hold and rise."[58]

---

57. Cf. 1 Sam. 2:5; Isa.54:1.
58. Augustine, *Creed*, para. 6, 693.

9

He suffered under Pontius Pilate, was crucified, died and was buried

It is a striking thing about the Apostles' Creed that we have no sooner finished considering the mystery and the miracle of Christmas than we immediately find ourselves already at Good Friday. We are reminded that Jesus "suffered," and the nature and the result of his suffering are indicated by the words "crucified" and "died."

McGrath rightly speaks of the change of pace at this point in the creed, as it "rapidly takes us through the events of Christmas, Holy Week, Good Friday and Easter Day."[1] The creed says nothing about the life of Jesus between Bethlehem and Calvary. It is silent on the subject of his baptism, the temptations, his miracles, his teaching, the calling of the disciples, his disputes with the Pharisees, the events of Palm Sunday and the final week of his life before his trial and crucifixion.

How do we account for this? Is it a good thing that this summary of the Christian faith should have such a glaring omission at this point?

McGiffert's view that the creed is content "to repudiate certain false views which were causing particular trouble at the time," and that everything not immediately related to that concern was duly omitted[2] falls foul of the likely baptismal origin of the creed. Its function was more probably catechetical than polemical.[3]

Another approach is to say that the life of Jesus does not belong to the substance of our redemption. This appears to be Calvin's view. He asks the reason for the immediate transition from Jesus' birth to his death and for the omission of the story of his life. He suggests the follow-

---

1. McGrath, *I Believe*, 44–45.
2. McGiffert, *Creed*, 122.
3. See Kelly, *Creeds*, 30–52.

ing answer: "Because nothing is dealt with here except what so pertains to our redemption as in some degree to contain the substance of it."[4]

Karl Barth, rightly, objects to this approach. Calvin's explanation is vulnerable to the accusation that Jesus' ministry was ultimately unnecessary if it is his death alone which pertains substantially to redemption. Such a view merits the scathing challenge that "we can't embrace a theology in which Jesus' entire thirty-three-year incarnation could be reduced to a long weekend's activity."[5]

Barth, by contrast, takes the creed to have "remarkably compressed" the entire work of Christ into the word "suffered."[6] Our gaze is focussed on the cross, but all of Jesus' preceding experience comes into its purview: "the whole life of Jesus comes under the heading 'suffered.'" Barth presents a catalog of Jesus' sufferings: his birth in a stable, the skepticism of his own family, his rejection by his nation, the lack of obvious success attending his ministry, his betrayal and denial by men from his inner circle: "this man is persecuted all his life."[7]

In this way of reading the creed Barth is following the Heidelberg Catechism, which states its understanding of the word "suffered" like this: "That throughout his life on earth, but especially at the end of it, he bore in body and soul the wrath of God against the sin of the whole human race."[8]

Louis Praamsma comments on this part of the Catechism as follows:

> Throughout his entire life Jesus bore the burden of sin on his shoulders. That was his constant suffering. The sin of the world was already on his shoulders in the manger in Bethlehem. Contact with sinful people who unwittingly made him suffer without understanding or accepting him, hurt him time and again. Sin confronted him daily in the temptations and challenges of the devil.[9]

Witsius categorizes Christ's sufferings under four periods: the commencement of his life, his private life, his public life, and the end of his life.

4. Calvin, *Catechism, 1545*, Q. 55.
5. Chalke, "Cross Purposes," para. 18.
6. Barth, *Dogmatics*, 95.
7. Barth, *Dogmatics*, 102–3.
8. *Heidelberg Catechism*, Q. 37.
9. Praamsma, *Before the Face*, 61.

He subdivides the sufferings at the end of his life into those endured in Gethsemane, those experienced in his trial before the Jews, the sufferings of his trials in the houses of Pilate and Herod, as well as his death itself.[10]

I certainly would not wish to contradict the suggestion that Jesus' suffering began long before Calvary, and that the word "suffered" can be seen as an apt description of his entire life as the "man of sorrows," who was "acquainted with grief" because he was "despised and rejected by men" (Isa. 53:3). Jesus the Son of God came into a world in rebellion against God. Not surprisingly, therefore, God suffers in his world, and the experience of Jesus became the focus of that perennial rebellion. "Here there is an unveiling of man's rebellion against God."[11]

Nevertheless, it seems to me that Barth's well-motivated attempt to find the whole life of Jesus subsumed under the word "suffered" reads into the creed more than its composers intended. The immediate reference to Pontius Pilate seems to me to define the suffering of Jesus very particularly.

It is, of course, true that the whole of Jesus' ministry was lived under the governorship of Pontius Pilate. Luke 3:1–2 informs us that it was while Pontius Pilate was governor of Judea that the word of God came to John the Baptist, launching him into his preparatory role as the one who went before the Lord. In a general way, therefore, Jesus' entire ministry, seen as a time of suffering, could be said to have taken place "under Pontius Pilate."

However, the creed's mention of Jesus' suffering under Pontius Pilate is clearly very specific. It is difficult grammatically to separate the word "suffered" from the phrase "under Pontius Pilate," and to make the former stand alone. It was not the case that the whole of Jesus' life took place within the time parameters of Pilate's governorship,[12] as would seem to be necessary on Barth's reading of this clause. The entire clause "suffered under Pontius Pilate" refers quite obviously to Jesus' trial and sentence. All the allusions to Pilate in the later parts of the New Testament are thus specific.[13]

The reason, then, for the jump from Christmas to Passiontide in the Apostles' Creed is the profound awareness on the part of the church,

---

10. Witsius, *Creed*, Vol. 2, 45–46.
11. Barth, *Dogmatics*, 104.
12. Cranfield, *Creed*, 31–32.
13. Acts 3:13; 4:27; 13:38; 1 Tim. 6:13.

and, indeed, of Christ himself,[14] that the chief reason for the incarnation was the cross. This is not to be understood in such a way that Jesus' life and ministry become substantially and ultimately irrelevant, but as the recognition that the culminating purpose for which this particular life was lived was the final experience of suffering under Pontius Pilate. The wording of the creed bears witness to the conviction of the early Christians that their Lord and ours was not primarily a mere miracle-worker, nor a great teacher. It was by his suffering that he achieved the real objective of his life.

When a new baby is born, we hope for a purposeful life to follow. We would speak of the new human arrival as being born to live. Jesus was different. He was born to live, certainly. He was like all of us in that respect. But we have to say of Jesus Christ something that we would never say of any other human being: he was born to die. Every human being who is born will inevitably die at length. With Jesus alone we couch the connection in purposive terms. Jesus himself declared, as the cross began to loom, "For this purpose I came to this hour" (John 12:27). As the events leading directly to his crucifixion started to take place with his arrest in the garden, Jesus acknowledged the imperative that the prophecies of Scripture be fulfilled in this very way (Matt. 26:54). It is this vital priority in the existence of the Christ which the creed picks up.

The phrase "under Pontius Pilate" merits consideration for its own sake. It is perhaps surprising that the name of a brutal[15] Roman governor should find a place in a summary of the Christian faith.[16] However, the presence of this name serves a vitally important purpose. It marks the suffering of Jesus as a datable event,[17] and thus anchors Christian believing in historical fact. Witsius understands the purpose of the mention of the name of the Roman governor as being "to facilitate the comparing of the epoch of Christ's suffering with the Roman histories."[18] The date brings out the fact "that these events did not happen [just] anywhere or at [just] any time, and that the gospel is not simply a system of ideas."[19]

---

14. See von Balthasar, *Credo*, 51.

15. Pilate's brutality is well attested in secular histories, and is indicated in Luke 13:1.

16. See Kelly, *Creeds*, 149.

17. See Augustine, *Creed*, para. 7, 694.

18. Witsius, *Creed*, Vol. 2, 51.

19. Kelly, *Creeds*, 150.

Rufinus emphasizes this point very clearly: "They who have handed down the Creed to us have with much forethought specified the time when these things were done—'under Pontius Pilate'—lest in any respect the tradition should falter, as though vague and uncertain."[20]

Ignatius of Antioch refers several times in his writings to Pontius Pilate, in each case to stress the reality of the sufferings of Christ, and to remind the recipients of his letters that their Savior's suffering is a datable event, an established fact of history. In his letter to the Trallians he states that Jesus Christ was truly persecuted during Pontius Pilate's time.[21] Writing to the Magnesians, Ignatius dates Christ's birth, passion, and resurrection, "which happened within the period of Pontius Pilate's governorship"; he then urges his hearers to be fully persuaded of these realities, since they were "truly and surely done by Jesus Christ."[22]

In Christian thinking about the role of Pontius Pilate in Jesus' sufferings another emphasis has figured fairly regularly. It is represented by Louis Praamsma in his study on the Heidelberg Catechism, although it is not actually the point made by the Catechism. Praamsma writes: "Jesus' innocence was clearly proven in the best court available at the time."[23] In the providence of God, Pilate's part in the proceedings was to establish and declare that Jesus was indeed an innocent victim, that Judas' acknowledgement that he had betrayed "innocent blood" (Matt 27:4) was in fact correct.

All four evangelists emphasize this point. Matthew tells us that it was Pilate's wife who urged her husband to recognize that Jesus was a just (*dikaios*) man (Matt. 27:19), an assertion which Pilate later repeats (Matt. 27:24). Matthew, Mark and Luke all report Pilate's rhetorical question to the crowd, "What evil has he done?" (Matt. 27:23; Mark 15:14; Luke 23:22). Luke and John both cite his categorical statement that he found no fault in Jesus (Luke 23:4, 14; John 18:38; 19:4, 6). David Senior helpfully translates Pilate's words at this point as "I find no case against him."[24] Luke adds Pilate's observation that Herod agreed with this assessment (Luke 23:15).

---

20. Rufinus, *Commentary*, para. 18, 1113.
21. Ignatius, Trallians, 9.1; cf. Smyrnaeans, 1.2.
22. Ignatius, Magnesians, 11.1.
23. Praamsma, *Before the Face*, 62.
24. Senior, *John*, 72–73.

On the basis of this conviction that Jesus was innocent, the Scriptures build their understanding of the reason and purpose of Jesus' suffering. "The judge bears testimony to his innocence, so that there may be evidence that he suffered not for his own misdeeds but for ours."[25] Even though the creed does not spell out a theology of the atonement, it is obvious from the very jump from the birth to the death of Jesus that its compilers understood that his death was the crucial event with saving significance: "that Christ died is a simple matter of history; that Christ died *for our sins* is the gospel itself."[26] Therefore, "the cross of Jesus is the center-piece of the Creed."[27]

Pannenberg claims that the idea that Jesus' sufferings were vicarious "is only indirectly referred to in the Apostles' Creed, simply through the especial stress which is laid on Jesus' death."[28] True, though, this may be, the indirect allusion is no less significant, and no less powerful: the "especial stress" is most marked, and blatantly obvious.

Jesus' sufferings took the form of death by crucifixion. In this fact the Heidelberg Catechism finds a reference to God's curse, and rejoices in the transfer to the Savior of the curse which lay upon us.[29] Behind this understanding of events lies the statement of Deuteronomy 21:23 that "he who is hanged is accursed of God." The apostle Paul applied this text to the cross of Christ, and saw, in his being cursed, redemption for us (Gal. 3:13).

The original import of Galatians 3:13 had to do with the release of the Jews into the fullness of justification in Christ, a justification merely foreshadowed by the interim era of the law.[30] Paul is more concerned at that stage in his letter with the manner of Christ's death, rather than its meaning. Nevertheless, it is true that the hanged man of Deuteronomy 21:23 was hanging because he was accursed, not *vice versa*. He was accursed because of the reason for his death—execution for "a sin worthy of death" (Deut. 21:22). In a similar way, in the case of Jesus Christ, "the manner of his death, crucifixion, symbolized dramatically the meaning of his death."[31]

25. Calvin, *Catechism, 1545*, Q. 58.
26. McGrath, *I Believe*, 61.
27. Packer, *Christian*, 44.
28. Pannenberg, *Creed*, 79.
29. *Heidelberg Catechism*, Q. 39.
30. Bayes, *Weakness*, 155–6.
31. Craigie, *Deuteronomy*, 285–6.

The Heidelberg Catechism explains the meaning of Christ's death in terms of satisfaction: only the death of the Son of God could make satisfaction to divine justice for our sins.[32] Luther likewise says that everything included in the creed's article on God the Son serves the sole purpose of explaining our redemption: Jesus Christ came to suffer death "that he might make satisfaction for me, and pay what I owe, not with silver and gold, but with his own precious blood."[33]

Several facts are stated or presupposed here. The first is that we owe God a debt which is beyond our ability to pay. The second is that we deserve the sentence of death for our failure. The third is that the death of Jesus on the cross was in our place: he served our sentence instead of us. The final fact is that, by the shedding of his blood, Jesus paid off the debt that we owe to God: we are in the clear, justified, as far as God is concerned, because of the one who substituted himself for us. Calvin sums all this up: "He died so that the penalty owed by us might be discharged, and he might exempt us from it."[34] Hence we can sing the praise of our God of mercy in these words:

> Because the sinless Savior died,
> My sinful soul is counted free;
> For God, the just, is satisfied
> To look on him and pardon me.[35]

As Jesus breathed his last he cried out with a loud voice,[36] "It is finished" (John 19:30)—a single word in Greek. Praamsma suggests that this was the word that would have been written in those days on a bill when it was paid.[37] Because of Jesus, we owe God nothing, and God gives us everything. As the old chorus puts it:

> I owed a debt I could not pay,
> He paid a price he did not owe;
> I needed someone to wash my sins away;
> And now I sing a brand new song,
> "Amazing Grace," the whole day long.
> Christ paid a debt that I could never pay.[38]

---

32. *Heidelberg Catechism*, Q. 40.
33. Luther, *Larger Catechism*, 61.
34. Calvin, *Catechism, 1545*, Q. 57.
35. From the hymn, *Beneath the throne of God above*, by Charitie Lees Bancroft (1841–1923).
36. Matt. 27:50; Mark 15:37.
37. Praamsma, *Before the Face*, 63.
38. Anonymous.

Because Jesus in his death achieved this vicarious settlement and so fulfilled his life-purpose, it is an apt way of describing the cry, "It is finished," when David Senior says that "Jesus dies with majestic assurance."[39]

Perhaps the loveliest prophetic picture of what Jesus did for us is found in the substitution of the ram for Isaac on the altar of burnt offering (Gen. 22:13). Isaac is facing death. He is to be a burnt offering (Gen. 22:2), and the thing about a burnt offering was that it was total (Lev. 1:9, 13). Isaac was facing total extermination. That is our predicament in sin: eternal death hangs over us. However, as the knife of slaughter is about to fall, that knife which would terminate Isaac's existence once and for all, the voice of divine grace intervenes from heaven. A ram is seen in a nearby thicket. "So Abraham went and took the ram, and offered it up for a burnt offering instead of his son."

The Bible was not written for an intellectual elite. It does not use terminology designed to baffle or merely to impress. One of the key words for understanding the heart of Biblical faith is that simple, everyday word "instead." The ram's existence was decisively terminated instead of Isaac's. It was an either-or situation. It was one or the other. One of them had to die on that altar, and the other one would live. In "this divinely-provided substitute, the vicarious curse-bearing of God's own unspared Son was prefigured."[40]

Jesus died instead of us. It was either-or. It was us or him. He is the word of divine grace. He was punished instead of us, and we are forgiven. He paid the debt instead of us, and we are exonerated. He went to the cross, and we go on our way, free, truly alive. As Matthew Henry explains it: "Christ was sacrificed in our stead, as this ram instead of Isaac, and his death was our discharge."[41]

This Biblical explanation of Jesus' death is called penal substitution. Jesus suffered our penalty, so that we will never have to face it. Hallelujah!

There has been a recent attempt from within the broad evangelical community to deny the penal and substitutionary nature of Christ's atoning death. In their book *The Lost Message of Jesus* Steve Chalke and Alan Mann devote a five-page section to the subject of the atonement.[42]

---

39. Senior, *John*, 118.
40. Kline, "Genesis," 99.
41. Henry, *Commentary*, 41.
42. Chalke and Mann, *Lost Message*, 180–5.

Quoting John 3:16, they ask, "How then, have we come to believe that at the cross this God of love suddenly decides to vent his anger and wrath on his own Son?" They distance themselves explicitly from the doctrine of penal substitution by describing the idea of "a vengeful Father punishing his Son for an offence he has not even committed" as a form of cosmic child abuse, a twisted and morally dubious version of events, a contradiction of the statement "God is love," and a mockery of Jesus' teaching to love our enemies and to refuse to repay evil with evil.

The cross, for Chalke and Mann, is a symbol of love, which proves that God is here with us in this messy world. What, then, did Jesus do when he died? Chalke and Mann reply: "He absorbed all the pain, all the suffering caused by the breakdown in our relationship with God and in doing so demonstrated the lengths to which a God who is love will go to restore it."

Steve Chalke followed up this book with an article in the September 2004 issue of *Christianity Today*. Here he cites Joel Green and Mark Baker to the effect that penal substitution is not the one, correct, all-encompassing explanation of the cross—for there is no such thing, and that it distorts key Biblical concepts.[43] He claims that neither the Bible nor patristic writers teach penal substitution, that the doctrine is really a theological novelty dating from the nineteenth-century, and that its roots are to be found in pre-Christian paganism.[44]

Chalke's main problem with penal substitution is clearly his sense that it is inconsistent with the fundamental truth that "God is love": "it presents us with a God who is first and foremost concerned with retribution flowing from his wrath against sinners. The only way for his anger to be placated is in receiving recompense from those who have wronged him; and although his great love motivates him to send his Son, his wrath remains the driving force behind the need for the cross."

Chalke finds this inconsistent with Jesus' teaching about God. The God illustrated by the father in the parable of the prodigal son is not angry: "there is no theme of retribution"; rather, "the story is one of outstanding grace, of scandalous love and mercy." Besides, adds Chalke, Jesus' teachings on anger, retaliation, and loving one's enemies would turn God into someone who does not practise what he preaches if he looks for appeasement before he forgives.

43. Cf. Green and Baker, *Recovering*, 147–48.
44. Chalke, "Cross Purposes," paras. 10–11, 21.

Chalke then articulates what might be called his theory of absorption which replaces the doctrine of penal substitution: "On the cross Jesus does not placate God's anger in taking the punishment for sin, but rather absorbs its consequences and, in his resurrection, defeats death."

I think we can summarize Chalke's position in two statements: (1) love and retributive wrath are incompatible, and therefore penal substitution is incompatible with the fundamental fact that God is love; (2) the cross is the divine absorption of the world's suffering, as a result of which all the powers that inflict suffering are defeated and divine love triumphs.

In an excellent paper delivered to the Evangelical Alliance Symposium on the Atonement in 2005, Garry Williams engages directly with Chalke's arguments. He highlights, on the basis of Romans 12:19, the fallacy of arguing that we must be required to act precisely as God does. He works out the Trinitarian context for the doctrine of penal substitution: if we deny that the Father can punish the Son or that the Son can propitiate the Father we have effectively embraced modalism.[45]

Earlier I quoted Chalke and Mann's caricature of penal substitution as "this God of love suddenly decides to vent his anger and wrath on his own Son." This comment suggests that they are weak on the doctrine of the eternal decree of the triune God. It was no sudden decision on the Father's part to punish a reluctant Son for the sins of the world. The cross was an event eternally prepared for and worked towards in Trinitarian agreement.

Chalke sees the cross as a demonstration of divine love. This raises the question, How? Unless there is a purpose to the cross it demonstrates nothing; it is simply pointless. Chalke and Mann are quite wrong to see the concept of penal substitution as totally contradicting the love of God. It is rather the elucidation of what it means to say "God is love." It is the explanation which gives the doctrine of the atonement logical coherence.

Chalke says that "no single theory can capture the breadth and profundity of the cross." He may well be right as regards the breadth: it is certainly not necessary in defending penal substitution to deny that there is truth in other models of atonement. However, the profundity, the depth, of the cross demands penal substitution. Without that expla-

---

45. Williams, "Justice, Law, and Guilt," 8.

He suffered under Pontius Pilate, was crucified, died and was buried

nation all the other models lack coherence. Jim Packer recognized this over thirty years ago.[46]

Chalke tries to enlist George Eldon Ladd as a supporter. He quotes the following passage from Ladd: "In pagan Greek thought the gods often became angry with men, but their anger could be placated and the good will of the gods obtained by some kind of propitiatory sacrifice. Even in the Old Testament, the idea of atonement as the propitiating of an angry deity and transmuting his anger into benevolence is not to be found."[47]

However, in defence of Ladd, we have to accuse Chalke of being disingenuous at this point. Ladd is not denying that the Biblical doctrine of the atonement is propitiatory, only that the initiative is not with man to force God's hand. Ladd's very next sentence reads: "It was the very love of God that accomplished the atonement wrought by Jesus' death." A few pages later Ladd says: "The death of Christ has to do not only with man and his sin; it also looks Godward, and as such it is propitiatory."[48] The immediately preceding sentence, which ended a section advocating the substitutionary nature of Christ's death, said: "God visited upon sin its just doom and penalty in him who is not only the sinner's representative, but also his substitute."[49]

The Bible does view atonement in several different ways, but penal substitution is the logical knot which holds them all together. There may be more to atonement than penal substitution alone, but there certainly cannot be less. The believer will always rejoice with trembling to be able to say,

> Bearing shame and scoffing rude,
> In my place condemned he stood;
> Sealed my pardon with his blood:
> Hallelujah! What a Savior![50]

Finally, we need to make a brief comment on the presence in the creed of the word "buried." The burial of Jesus already found a mention in the Pauline confessional passage in 1 Corinthians 15:4. "Why was he

---

46. Packer, *What did the Cross Achieve?*
47. Ladd, *Theology*, 424.
48. Ladd, *Theology*, 429.
49. Ladd, *Theology*, 428.
50. From the hymn *Man of sorrows what a name*, by Philip Paul Bliss (1838–76).

buried?" The Heidelberg Catechism asks this question, and replies, "To show thereby that he was really dead."[51] "Burial emphasizes the finality of death."[52]

Mark's gospel connects Jesus' burial with the reality of his death by emphasizing that Pilate verified that Jesus was actually dead before giving permission to Joseph of Arimathea to remove the body for burial. Mark notes that Pilate was surprised to hear that Jesus was already dead, evidence that Jesus' death occurred unusually quickly for a crucifixion, a testimony to the paradoxical fact that he retained sovereign control even as he came under the control of his enemies. Pilate therefore sent for the centurion to check out the details. On discovering that the death had indeed taken place, "he granted the body to Joseph" (Mark 15:44–45). "Confirmation of death through burial . . . helped counterattack views which insisted that Jesus had not died but had been spirited away by his disciples."[53]

We may take immense comfort from the fact that Jesus really was dead. It means that every person who relies on him for salvation really is saved.

---

51. *Heidelberg Catechism*, Q. 41; see also Calvin, *Catechism, 1545*, Q. 62.
52. F. F. Bruce, *Corinthians*, 139.
53. Senior, *Mark*, 134.

10

He descended to hell

WILLIAM CUNNINGHAM TAKES A rather negative view of this clause of the creed, which was indeed a late addition. He writes: "In so far as the statement that Christ descended into hell is merely to be found in the creed, we are under no obligation to explain or to believe it." Having said that, he does, nevertheless, go on to consider what it might mean, and his discussion fills up two whole pages![1]

It is true that "there is no phrase in the Apostles' Creed that has caused so much difficulty as this."[2] The Formula of Concord clearly sets out the issues at stake, at least as they had surfaced in disagreements within the Lutheran Churches in the middle years of the sixteenth-century:

> There has been a dispute touching this article among certain divines who profess the Augsburg Confession: when and how our Lord Jesus Christ, as our Catholic Faith attests, descended into hell? Whether this came to pass before or after his death? Moreover, it has been asked whether he descended in soul only or in divinity only, or indeed in soul and body, and whether this came to pass spiritually or corporally? It has also been disputed whether this article is to be referred to the passion, or to the glorious victory and triumph of Christ.[3]

Of this catalog of interpretative options, only three, or so it seems to me, are of great concern. First, what was the timing of Christ's descent to hell relative to his death? Second, how did the descent to hell affect him in the interrelationship of bodily and spiritual experience? Third, was the descent to hell part of his passion or the commencement of his

1. Cunningham, *Historical Theology*, 90–92.
2. G. I. Williamson, *Heidelberg*, 76.
3. *Formula of Concord*, Art. 9, 159.

victory? Intricate debate about the role of his two natures in the descent to hell does not appear to have much point.

To raise these questions presupposes that, Cunningham's protest notwithstanding, there is validity in the statement that "he descended to hell." Although Grudem questions whether these words really have a rightful place in the creed,[4] Williamson points out that, despite the difficulties attending them, the church has never been willing to remove them.[5] We therefore take as our starting point the assumption that this phrase, though not in itself found in the Scriptures, does articulate something which is true, and we follow the lead of Herman Witsius, who recommends that our concern be less what various ideas people have held of this clause "as what, in conformity with the analogy of faith and the language of Scripture, they ought to have understood."[6]

It is not easy to address the three problems raised by the Lutherans separately in a satisfactory way, since they are very much intertwined with each other. The various combinations of solutions will become clear in the course of our examination of the phrase.

This clause first entered the creed in a Greek version in the year AD 359, where the word now rendered "hell" was *katachthonia*.[7] This term occurs just once in Scripture, at Philippians 2:10, where it is translated by the NKJV as "those under the earth." This is generally taken to mean "the satanic hosts and lost humanity in hell,"[8] although some read it, in conjunction with its two parallel phrases "those in heaven," and "those on earth," as referring to the entirety of created reality, celestial, terrestrial, and subterranean.[9]

If that verse is the source of this statement of the creed, then Christ's descent to hell may mean either of two things.

CHRIST'S DESCENT TO HELL AS HIS BURIAL

Taking the term *katachthonia* to refer to the underground level of created existence, then for Christ to have descended to that level would

---

4. Grudem, *Systematic Theology*, 587.
5. G. I. Williamson, *Heidelberg*, 76.
6. Witsius, *Creed*, Vol. 2, 141.
7. Kelly, *Creeds*, 378.
8. So Kent, *Philippians*, on Phil. 2:10.
9. So Moule, *Philippian Studies*, 96.

simply be an elaborate way of repeating, and of adding vividness to, the previous clause that he "was buried," "a colorful equivalent of 'dead' and 'buried,'" as Kelly puts it.[10]

This was, indeed, the way in which some early commentators on the creed understood these words. Rufinus, for example, notes the absence of the clause from older versions of the creed, but adds: "It seems to be implied, however, when it is said that he 'was buried.'"[11] Stewart interprets this to mean that "Rufinus considers it a roundabout way of saying 'buried.'"[12]

Some who have understood the clause as an elaboration of the reference to Jesus' burial have seen greater significance to it than merely the vividness and color which it adds. Cunningham, acknowledging that the creed is at this point making a statement which is sanctioned by Scripture, takes it to mean that Jesus "was really and truly dead in the same sense which other men die, by the actual separation of the soul from the body, and that he really continued under the power of death for a time."[13] The Westminster divines understood the descent into hell to describe Christ's "being buried, and continuing in the state of the dead, and under the power of death till the third day."[14] Jesus' death was "a genuine death, not a simulated one."[15]

However, I think Calvin is right to object to this interpretation of the phrase "he descended to hell" on two grounds. First, he points out that it would be odd to follow an unambiguous statement that Jesus was buried by an alleged equivalent phrase, which actually adds obscurity, rather than clarification, to the previous words. Second, he suggests that a summary of the Christian faith is not likely to include a mere tautology, and that it is to be expected that this phrase will be saying something additional.[16]

The Church of England devotes one of its articles to this part of the creed, and appears to follow Calvin in rejecting the identification of the descent with the burial. The article reads: "As Christ died for us, and

---

10. Kelly, *Creeds*, 383.
11. Rufinus, *Commentary*, para. 18, 1113.
12. Stewart, *Creeds*, 53.
13. Cunningham, *Historical Theology*, 91.
14. *Westminster Larger Catechism*, Q. 50, 152–53.
15. Packer, *Christian*, 49.
16. Calvin, *Institutes*, 2.16.8.

was buried, so also it is to be believed that he went down into hell."[17] The words "so also" imply that a distinction is being made between Jesus' death and burial on the one hand, and the descent to hell on the other, although the article does not go on to elaborate on what the meaning of the phrase might be.

Further evidence that more than a repetition of the allusion to Jesus' burial is intended may be found in an examination of the Latin term used. The English phrase "he descended to hell" translates *descendit ad inferna*. It is this word, *infernus*, which Jerome used to translate *katachthonia* in Philippians 2:10.

On all but three[18] of its Old Testament occurrences *infernus* in the Vulgate translates the Hebrew word *šeʾôl*. It is true that *šeʾôl* is used quite often as equivalent to "grave," or at least the NKJV interprets the Hebrew original to mean "grave."[19] However, there are rather more texts where "grave" would seem not to be the most appropriate rendering, where something more than the burial-place of a corpse, something more sinister, is in view.[20] Eugene Merrill noting that *šeʾôl* may designate both the grave and the "netherworld," adds the comment that it is "particularly the latter" which is meant.[21]

Turning to the New Testament, in addition to its use in Philippians 2:10, *infernus* translates *hadēs* five times,[22] *thanatos*[23] and *tartaroō*[24] once each, and is once inserted with the sense of "grave" where there is no Greek equivalent.[25] Don Carson finds it impossible to sustain a distinction between *hadēs* and *gehenna* (the Jewish term of which *tartaros* was

---

17. *Thirty-Nine Articles*, Art. 3, 488.

18. Pss. 94:17; 115:17; Isa. 7:11.

19. Gen. 37:35; 1 Sam. 2:6; 1 Kgs. 2:9; Job 14:13; 17:13; 21:13; Pss. 6:5; 30:3; 31:17; 49:14; 88:3; 141:7; Prov. 30:16; Hos. 13:14.

20. Num. 16:30, 31; Deut. 32:22; Job 11:8; Pss. 55:15; 86:13; 116:3; Prov. 1:12; 9:18; 15:11, 24; 23:14; 27:20; Isa. 5:14; 14:9, 15; Ezek. 31:16, 17; 32:21; Amos 9:2; Jonah 2:2; there is another cluster of texts where it is a moot point whether one should opt for "grave" or for a less physical rendering (so Job 17:16; Pss. 9:17; 16:10; 18:5; 139:8; Isa. 28:15, 18; 38:18; Ezek. 32:27; Hab. 2:5).

21. Merrill, "*šeʾôl*," 6; contrast, however, *Theological Wordbook of the Old Testament*, 2303, which argues for "grave" as the invariable meaning of *šeʾôl*.

22. Matt. 11:23; Luke 10:15; Acts 2:27, 31; Rev. 1:18.

23. Acts 2:24.

24. 2 Pet. 2:4.

25. Luke 16:22.

the Greek equivalent[26]), and concludes that they are synonyms meaning "hell."[27] Richard Bauckham, too, notes that *tartaros* is regularly used in Jewish Greek literature of the place of divine punishment.[28]

This linguistic evidence seems to point to a deeper significance in the phrase "he descended to hell" than merely an additional reference to Jesus' burial.

CHRIST'S DESCENT TO HELL AS AN EXPERIENCE OF HIS SOUL

For those for whom talk of a descent to hell is simply an elaboration on Jesus' burial, its primary reference is to his body. However, if *katachthonia* is read as the abode of fallen and lost angels and people, then the reference to Christ's descent there must pertain primarily to the spiritual aspect of his being. It is "the inward explanation of what is outwardly happening in his death and tomb."[29] Stewart perceives the need for the early Church, over against Docetic teachings which denied to the Son of God a human soul, "to account in the creed not only for the body, which was 'crucified, dead and buried,' but also for the soul."[30]

On this alternative understanding of *katachthonia* the significance of Christ's descent into hell can be read in two main ways. This is where the question as to the timing of the descent relative to Jesus' death arises.

Christ's descent to hell as an event following his burial

The order of the phrases in the creed could be read as suggesting that the descent to hell came chronologically later than the crucifixion and the act of burial. There have been those who have taken these words to mean that Christ's soul went to hell during (at least part of) the three days and three nights that the Son of Man was in the heart of the earth (Matt. 12:40), that this phrase is an account of what transpired during the period between the cross and the resurrection. Where the clause has been understood in this way, several different explanations of the

---

26. So Thayer, *Lexicon*, 615.
27. Carson, *Matthew*, on Matt. 5:22; see also Hendriksen, *Matthew*, 496.
28. Bauckham, *Jude, 2 Peter*, 249.
29. Barth, *Faith*, 95.
30. Stewart, *Creeds*, 53.

purpose of the descent have been offered, and the question whether the descent pertained to the passion or the victory comes into view.

Christ's Descent to Hell as the Experience of Torment

It has sometimes been claimed that during the interval between his death and his resurrection Christ's soul went to hell and experienced its torments, the torments due eternally to sinners. This experience was, then, the consummation of the Savior's passion. Karl Barth understands it in this way: "As soon as the body is buried, the soul goes to hell, that is, into remoteness from God, into that place where God can only be the Adversary, the enemy."[31]

Cunningham credits this view to Calvin,[32] though I am not persuaded that he reads the Reformer correctly, as I shall demonstrate later.

The main obstacle to this view would seem to be the Lord's words to the penitent thief on the cross, "Today you shall be with me in paradise" (Luke 23:43). If Jesus and this saved sinner were to be together in paradise that very day, it is hard to see how it can be construed that Jesus went from the cross to hell to suffer the torments of condemnation. Liefeld rightly observes that these words seem to "preclude the idea that Jesus descended into hell after his death."[33] Wayne Grudem notes that the cry, "It is finished" (John 19:30), and the words, "Father, into your hands I commend my spirit" (Luke 23:46), equally count against the notion of a post-crucifixion descent to hell.[34]

Christ's Descent to Hell as a Step En Route to Paradise

An alternative approach sees a descent to hell in the interval between the crucifixion and the resurrection as the first step on the route to the Savior's triumphant victory. In this sense the descent to hell may be understood as having taken the form of a brief visit on the way to paradise. This interpretation may take two forms.

---

31. Barth, *Faith*, 95.
32. Cunningham, *Historical Theology*, 82.
33. Liefeld, *Luke*, on Luke 23:43.
34. Grudem, *Systematic Theology*, 593.

Christ's descent to hell as the proclamation of his victory

One way is to understand Christ's purpose in descending to hell as proclamatory and celebratory. This can be construed in either of two ways.

Christ's descent to hell as the declaration to his foes of their defeat

First, Christ's proclamation in hell may be seen as the conclusive declaration to the evil spirits and to the lost souls of former generations of the sealing of their ultimate defeat. Packer sees this as one aspect of Christ's activity in hell, and reads 1 Peter 3:18–19 as the evidence: Christ was "put to death in the flesh but made alive by the Spirit, by whom also he went and preached to the spirits in prison."[35]

Cunningham is right to describe 1 Peter 3:19 as a "very obscure and difficult passage."[36] Several different interpretations have been put forward. Cunningham himself mentions two, first, that Christ by the Spirit preached to Noah's contemporaries through the patriarch's instrumentality, while they were still alive, albeit imprisoned in their sin and unbelief,[37] and second, that Christ's preaching by the Spirit to this world, locked up in the prison of its sinfulness, took place after his resurrection through the instrumentality of apostolic evangelism.[38] Yet a third interpretation of the 1 Peter text sees the spirits in prison as the fallen angels, and understands Christ's resurrection by the power of the Spirit to have been the decisive declaration to them of their defeat. The preaching is not then understood as evangelistic, but as declamatory.[39] A variation on this last reading sees the proclamation as taking place after the ascension.[40]

On any of these interpretations of this verse, it has nothing to do with a descent to hell in the period between the cross and Easter Day. Calvin rejects the view "that Christ's descent to hell is here referred to" on the grounds that "there is no mention made of the soul of Christ, but only that he went by the spirit: and these are very different things, that Christ's soul went, and that Christ preached by the power of the Spirit."[41]

---

35. Packer, *Christian*, 49–50; so also Stibbs, *1 Peter*, 142.
36. Cunningham, *Historical Theology*, 92.
37. Grudem, *1 Peter*, 158, 204–39, defends this view.
38. So Brown, *1 Peter*, Vol. 2, 203–7.
39. So Blum, *Peter*, on 1 Pet. 3:19.
40. Kelly, *Peter*, 154–56.
41. Calvin, *Catholic Epistles*, 113.

Christ's descent to hell as the liberation of his people

The second way of reading the statement of the Apostles' Creed that "he descended to hell," understood as part of his journey to paradise, takes it as an allusion to the victory of Christ, regarding his descent as "a triumphant act of liberation,"[42] akin to the visit of the revived Aslan to the home of the white witch to breathe new life into the creatures whom she had turned to stone.[43] This entails understanding *katachthonia* not as the abode of the souls of the lost only, but the interim location of all the departed, the primary reference being to those who in every age died in the faith.

On this understanding the purpose of Christ's descent to hell is seen as the joyful announcement of his victory to the saints of Old Testament times, a victory in which they were to share. This reading is represented by Irenaeus, who writes:

> the Lord descended into the regions beneath the earth, preaching his advent there also, and declaring the remission of sins received by those who believe in him. Now all those believed in him who had hope towards him, that is, those who proclaimed his advent, and submitted to his dispensations, the righteous men, the prophets, and the patriarchs, to whom he remitted sins in the same way as he did to us.[44]

Packer combines with the previous approach two things which belong more to this interpretation. He suggests that Christ's presence turned Hades into paradise for all who had earlier died in faith, and that he perfected the spirits of departed believers, bringing them out of the gloom of Sheol into the experience of paradise.

He bases these claims on a reading of Psalm 88:3–6 and 10–12 as expressing the darkness of the pit for the souls of believers who had died before the time of Christ, contrasted with his words to the penitent thief in Luke 23:43, and on Hebrews 11:39–40 and 12:23, as allegedly teaching that the souls of the just of Old Testament times were not made perfect until the New Testament age.[45] Hebrews 11:39–40 asserts that Old Testament believers "did not receive the promise, God having provided

---

42. Kelly, *Creeds*, 380.

43. Lewis, *The Lion, the Witch and the Wardrobe*, ch. 16.

44. Irenaeus, *Against Heresies*, 4.27.2, 993 (cf. Tertullian, *Treatise on the Soul*, 55, 422).

45. Packer, *Christian*, 49.

something better for us, that they should not be made perfect apart from us." Hebrews 12:23, then speaks of "the spirits of just men made perfect."

It seems to me that Packer is building a rather over-elaborate theory on somewhat slender evidence. I am not persuaded that his understanding of the Hebrews texts is correct. John Brown's reading of Hebrews 11:40 seems more probable: "The whole body of the saved are together to be introduced into the full possession of the 'salvation which is in Christ Jesus with eternal glory.' There is to be 'a gathering together unto the Lord Jesus at his coming.'"[46]

In other words, the perfection anticipated is the ultimate eschatological goal which as yet awaits believers of both dispensations, and which all shall attain simultaneously, for, as Guthrie rightly says, "No part of the true Christian community can be complete without the rest."[47]

Wilson applies Hebrews 12:23 to believers of all ages,[48] not only those of the pre-Christian epoch.[49] It is perhaps significant that Hebrews 11:40 does not limit its reference to spirits as does 12:23. Taken together the two texts suggest that there is an interim perfection of spirit which is enjoyed by believers after death, pending that total perfection which awaits the entire people of God at the Lord's return.

Moreover, there is pertinence in the observation that, since the New Testament clearly does not teach that after death all people (unbelievers and believers alike) go to a dark and dismal place, then it is probable that any such construction of Old Testament teaching is a misreading.[50] The perfection of spirit into which departed believers enter has always been enjoyed from the moment of death by men and women of faith since the beginning of time.

A further argument against this interpretation is the fact that "hell" has to be understood in a positive sense, as the place where the faithful departed are at peace. This, in itself, makes it improbable that it was the intended meaning of those who first inserted these words into the creed, given that the Latin word *infernus* never has such a positive meaning in the Vulgate.

46. Brown, *Hebrews*, 597.
47. Guthrie, *Hebrews*, 247.
48. Wilson, *Hebrews*, 231.
49. So also Guthrie, *Hebrews*, 263; against F. F. Bruce, *Hebrews*, 378.
50. *Theological Wordbook of the Old Testament*, 2303.

Christ's descent to hell as the evangelization of the dead

The second main version of the approach which places the descent to hell after the burial involves seeing Christ's descent as an occasion of gospel proclamation and invitation to those who had not been believers during their earthly lifetime. 1 Peter 4:6 ("the gospel was preached also to those who are dead") is sometimes cited in support of this theory.

Pannenberg champions this line of interpretation. He argues that in the underworld Jesus continued to preach the gospel of repentance, and that this means "that those who are already dead are also still reached by the Christian message." This was true not only for those already dead at the time of Jesus' visit to the abode of the souls of the dead, but his descent to hell is reckoned to be a symbol of a perennial reality, namely that "salvation from future judgment is still made available in the realm of the dead to those who during their lifetime encountered neither Jesus nor the Christian message."[51]

Pannenberg argues that this doctrine tends towards a universalistic understanding of salvation. He raises an "urgent question":

> If God was revealed in Jesus for the first time, and if salvation for mankind only appeared in Jesus, what is to happen to the multitude who lived before Jesus' ministry? And what will become of the many who never came into contact with the Christian message? What, finally, is to happen to the people who certainly have heard the message of Christ but who—perhaps through the fault of those very Christians who have been charged with its proclamation—have never come face to face with its truth? Are all these people delivered over to damnation? Do they remain shut out for ever from the presence of God which has been made accessible to mankind through Jesus?

Pannenberg believes that the statement that "he descended to hell," understood not so much literally, but as a powerful symbol of Jesus' conquest of hell and its hold on the human race, means that the answer of the Christian faith to this vital question must be No.[52]

While universalism has to be an attractive possibility to a sensitive Christian conscience, it is hard to interpret the Scriptures as teaching unequivocally universal salvation. Although texts such as 1 Corinthians 15:22, "As in Adam all die, even so in Christ all shall be made alive,"

---

51. Pannenberg, *Creed*, 93; see also Jowett, *Peter*, 144.
52. Pannenberg, *Creed*, 94.

and Romans 11:32, "God has committed them all to disobedience, that he might have mercy on all," seem at first sight to be susceptible of the meaning that ultimately salvation will be universal, isolated verses such as these have to be read in the total context of Biblical revelation, and it is impossible to make an unqualified assertion that universalism has Biblical warrant.

Nevertheless, the Reformed doctrine of predestination does leave the impetus for salvation with God and the power of his grace. It is impossible for us to set limits on God's sovereign, irresistible grace. Many of our Reformed forefathers were quite clear that God's lavish mercy would ultimately embrace the vast majority of human beings, even if not absolutely all human beings.

Charles Hodge puts it particularly powerfully. He is commenting on Romans 5:18: "As through one man's offence judgment came to all men, resulting in condemnation, even so through one man's righteous act the free gift came to all men, resulting in justification of life":

> We have no right to put any limit on these general terms, except what the Bible itself places upon them. The Scriptures nowhere exclude any class of infants, baptized or unbaptized, born in Christian or in heathen lands, of believing or unbelieving parents, from the benefits of the redemption of Christ. All the descendants of Adam, except Christ, are under condemnation; all the descendants of Adam, except those of whom it is expressly revealed that they cannot inherit the kingdom of God, are saved. This appears to be the clear meaning of the Apostle, and therefore he does not hesitate to say that where sin abounded, grace has much more abounded, that the benefits of redemption far exceed the evils of the fall; that the number of the saved far exceeds the number of the lost.[53]

In similar vein, Lorraine Boettner writes:

> God is free in election to choose as many as he pleases, and we believe that he who is infinitely merciful and benevolent and holy will elect the great majority to life. There is no good reason why he should be limited to only a few. We are told that Christ is to have the preeminence in all things, and we do not believe that the Devil will be permitted to emerge victor even in numbers.[54]

---

53. Hodge, *Systematic Theology*, Vol. 1, 26.
54. Boettner, *Predestination*, 130.

It is only a small step from there to the hope that our entire race will finally share in the blessings of salvation, freely bestowed by a God of generous kindness. Boettner acknowledges that the Reformed faith provides the only logical basis for such a step to be taken. He writes: "So far as the principles of sovereignty and personal election are concerned there is no reason why a Calvinist might not hold that all men will finally be saved; and some Calvinists have actually held this view."[55] Nevertheless, as Boettner concedes,[56] we would be going beyond the evidence of Scripture to argue definitively that every individual person will at last be saved by the immense grace of God expressed in the all-sufficient atonement of Christ. It is, however, perhaps a possibility which we should be reluctant to rule out altogether as we bow before the inscrutable wisdom and lavish grace of an all-merciful God.

I would, however, question whether Pannenberg is right to couch this in terms of an opportunity for salvation after death. Such a theory seems incompatible both with Hebrews 9:27, "It is appointed for men to die once, but after this the judgment," and with the story of the rich man and Lazarus (cf. Luke 16:26).

On the former text, Pink comments, "As death leaves men, so shall judgment find them,"[57] while John Wesley writes, "At the moment of death every man's final state is determined."[58] Similarly Albert Barnes says that if people "neglect to avail themselves of the benefits of the atonement here, the opportunity will be lost for ever," and, describing the condition of people after death as a "changeless state," that then "there will be no opportunity to embrace the Savior who was rejected here on earth."[59]

Again, Luke 16:26 "means that in the afterlife there is no passing from one state to the other."[60] It graphically symbolizes "the irreversibility of a person's lot after death."[61] "After death the time of grace is past."[62]

Furthermore, it is improbable that 1 Peter 4:6 is referring to gospel preaching to the souls of people who have already died. It is more likely

---

55. Boettner, *Predestination*, 131.
56. Boettner, *Predestination*, 132.
57. Pink, *Hebrews*, 525.
58. Wesley, *Notes*, 837.
59. Barnes, *New Testament*, Vol. 9, 216–17.
60. Morris, *Luke*, 254.
61. Hendriksen, *Luke*, 786.
62. Geldenhuys, *Luke*, 426.

that Peter is talking about the righteous of Israel's past,[63] who are dead now, but who heard and believed the gospel while they were alive, as it was preached to them in its anticipatory and prophetic form prior to the coming of the age of fulfillment in Christ.

Nevertheless, Pannenberg's open-hearted desire to see in Christ's descent to hell a symbolic signal of universal salvation does drive us back to our Reformed roots, and to the recognition that God's saving grace may be vastly wider than we had expected. Christ has indeed descended to the hell in which we all by nature live, in order to ransack it, and liberate the overwhelming majority of its captives. It is surely possible— even probable—that God might deal in irresistible grace in their final moments with millions of people who have not previously responded to the gospel of Christ. Might not Christ be revealed to their souls by the Holy Spirit, and might they not believe for their eternal salvation in the instant before they depart this life and pass into eternity? W. G. T. Shedd, indeed, in advocating the "larger hope," refuses to delay the possibility to the final moments of life. Rejecting the notion of a second opportunity after death, he suggests that the regenerating grace of the Holy Spirit might be made operative in this life in the case of countless "heathen," convicting them of sin and so leading them to the attitude of repentance as they trust in divine mercy, even though they never hear of Christ. Shedd says that "this felt need of mercy and desire for it is potentially and virtually faith in the Redeemer," even though they do not know his name.[64]

While it is true that God's revealed norm is that people cannot believe and be saved without hearing the gospel through a preacher (Rom. 10:14), the Reformation Confessions of Faith show wise pastoral awareness in the way that they word their conviction that faith in Christ and membership in the body of his church are indispensable to salvation.

The Second Helvetic Confession, for example, says that "there is no certain salvation outside Christ." The word "certain" seems to allow for exceptional circumstances. The Confession indicates its refusal to define the word "church" so narrowly as to exclude all who do not outwardly participate in its services, and recognizes that "God had some friends in the world outside the commonwealth of Israel." "Hence," the Confession concludes, "we must be very careful not to judge before the time, nor

63. Michaels, *1 Peter*, on 1 Pet. 4:6.
64. Shedd, *Calvinism*, 128–29.

undertake to exclude, reject or cut off those whom the Lord does not want to have excluded or rejected."[65]

Similarly the Westminster Confession says that outside the visible church "there is no ordinary possibility of salvation."[66] The word "ordinary" stands as an acknowledgement that there may sometimes be extraordinary circumstances.

Clearly such statements are demonstrating an admirable hesitancy about setting limits on the ultimate number of the saved. The word "ordinary" means through the use of the ordinary means of grace. It does not necessarily rule out the possibility that God, whose grace is so immensely lavish that it is uncontainable in the generosity of its mercy, may do the exceptional in achieving the salvation of the vast majority of people. Perhaps the preacher, without hearing whose words sinners cannot believe and be saved, may for most people be the Holy Spirit himself without human agency.

Objection could be raised to this theory on the basis of the New Testament references to the few. Take Matthew 7:14 for example. Jesus says, "Narrow is the gate and difficult is the way which leads to life, and there are few who find it." However, two comments may be made.

The first is to raise the question whether it might be legitimate to read these words not as a statement that few people will finally enter into life, but as a rejection of any human ability to find the way of life unaided by the grace of God: by "few" Jesus actually means "none." Perhaps the Lord's reasoning is the same as in his conversation with his disciples following the departure of the rich young ruler. First he said, "How hard it is for those who have riches to enter the kingdom of God!" This astonished the disciples, but Jesus' next comment baffled them even more: "How hard it is for those who trust in riches to enter the kingdom of God!" You don't have to have riches to trust in them. The disciples rightly understood the implication of Jesus' words, and asked, "Who then can be saved?" Jesus reassured them with the words, "The things which are impossible with men are possible with God" (Mark 10:23–26; Luke 18:27). Few—that is to say, no one at all—will find the way to life from his own resources, but God can do the impossible.

The second comment is to note that, throughout the Sermon on the Mount, Jesus is teaching his disciples. Perhaps in this verse he is

---

65. *Second Helvetic Confession*, ch. 17, paras. 14–15, 18.
66. *Westminster Confession*, 657.

referring not to eternal life in glory, but to the experience of true life in the present available to his followers. It is sadly but a few disciples who enter into everything available to them in the present life. In the previous verses Jesus has spoken about asking, seeking and knocking. He has assured his followers that God will not withhold good things from those who ask (Matt. 7:7-11); Luke 11:13 replaces the words "good things" with "the Holy Spirit." It is in the abundant life of the Spirit that we obtain all the good things which God has in store for us, his children. However, too few of us are so sold out for the Lord that we enjoy the blessings of the Spirit in their fullness.

The similar saying in Luke's Gospel arises from a question addressed to Jesus: "Are there few who are saved?" This was, apparently, a frequent topic of discussion amongst the Jewish rabbis.[67] The questioner is simply curious to know where this new rabbi stands on the issue. The Lord refuses to be drawn into the debate. Instead he presents the challenge to enter through the narrow gate, and not to be numbered amongst the many who will seek to enter but will not be able to do so (Luke 13:23-24). Evidently he has discerned a lack of spiritual seriousness in the questioner, which renders all discussion of such matters superfluous.

The saying "many are called, but few are chosen" (Matt. 22:14) is probably, as Donald Hagner claims, a Semitic idiom in which "many" means "all," emphasizing the universality of the gospel invitation, and "few" is to be understood in a comparative sense, meaning "fewer than the many."[68] This saying therefore rules out absolute universalism, but is not intended to shed light on the relative proportions of saved and lost.

The word "many" is more often used in the New Testament to stress the lavish reach of divine mercy. This is true both on the lips of Christ and in the writings of the apostles. To cite just a couple of examples of each. Jesus revels in the fact that "many will come from east and west, and sit down with Abraham, Isaac, and Jacob in the kingdom of heaven" (Matt. 8:11). His own definition of his purpose is that "the Son of Man did not come to be served, but to serve, and to give his life a ransom for many" (Matt. 20:28). The writer to the Hebrews insists that God is "bringing many sons to glory", and that "Christ was offered once to bear the sins of many" (Heb. 2:10; 9:28).

67. Liefeld, *Luke*, on Luke 13:22-23.
68. Hagner, *Matthew 14-28*, on Matt. 22:14.

It is certainly true that the Scriptural warnings to the unbeliever are stern, and must be taken seriously. However, it is equally true that the whole thrust of the developing revelation of God's grace through Biblical history is towards increasing universalism. "Shall not the Judge of all the earth do right?" (Gen. 18:25). Our confidence is that he most surely shall—and if what is right in his sight is that Christ's descent to hell will finally result in hell being forever virtually unpopulated by sinful human beings, then we shall rejoice with awesome celebration to the praise of the glory of his grace.

Christ's descent to hell as his experience on the cross

However, there is a second way of reading this phrase if *katachthonia* is understood of the experience of lost sinners. This is to take Christ's experience of hell to have occurred during the three hours of darkness as he hung on the cross. Admittedly, this may be, as Grudem caricatures it, "an unconvincing attempt to salvage some theologically acceptable sense" out of the words "he descended to hell," without accurately expounding their original meaning.[69] Nevertheless, this explanation has a worthy pedigree, and, in view of the church's contentment in retaining this clause in the creed, merits consideration.

This is the way in which Calvin takes this clause. In his first catechism he writes:

> It is said that he descended into hell. This means that he had been afflicted by God, and felt the dread and severity of the divine judgment, in order to intercede with God's wrath and make satisfaction to his justice in our name, thus paying our debts and lifting our penalties, not for his own iniquity (which never existed) but for ours.[70]

In his later catechism Calvin defines Jesus' descent to hell as "the fearful agonies with which his soul was tormented."[71] In both contexts he goes on to quote the words of Christ from the cross, "My God, my God, why have you forsaken me?" (Matt. 27:46; Mark 15:34).[72]

---

69. Grudem, *Systematic Theology*, 587.
70. Calvin, *Catechism*, *1538*, 20.iv, 23.
71. Calvin, *Catechism*, *1545*, Q. 65.
72. Calvin, *Catechism*, *1538*, 20.iv, 24; *Catechism*, *1545*, Q. 66.

In his Institutes Calvin expounds this at greater length. He speaks of how the Lord Jesus Christ felt "the weight of divine vengeance," and engaged with "the horrors of eternal death" as "he endured the death which is inflicted on the wicked by an angry God." Again Calvin links this with the cry of dereliction from the cross, and ponders this fact: "

> No abyss can be imagined more dreadful than to feel that you are abandoned and forsaken of God, and not heard when you invoke him, just as if he had conspired your destruction. To such a degree was Christ dejected, that in the depth of his agony he was forced to exclaim, "My God, my God, why have you forsaken me?"

"It is evident," Calvin comments, "that this expression was wrung from the anguish of his inmost soul." From this cry of terror, "we may infer how dire and dreadful were the tortures which he endured when he felt himself standing at the bar of God as a criminal in our stead." His sorrow "was no common sorrow": he engaged with "the power of the devil, the fear of death, and the pains of hell." Smitten and afflicted, "he bore the weight of the divine anger."

Calvin, therefore, understands the descent to hell as a description of Christ's agonies of soul as he hung on the cross. He does face the possible objection that this perverts the order of the creed. It results in the creation of an absurdity, in that "an event which preceded burial [the descent to hell] should be placed after it." However, Calvin sees logic in this:

> After explaining what Christ endured in the sight of man, the creed appropriately adds the invisible and incomprehensible judgment which he endured before God, to teach us that not only was the body of Christ given up as the price of redemption, but that there was a greater and more excellent price—that he bore in his soul the tortures of condemned and ruined man.

The vital importance of this additional phrase in the creed is that "had not his soul shared in the punishment, he would have been a Redeemer of bodies only."

And precisely there we discover the point and purpose of the Savior's agony. It was indeed that he might benefit us, not physically merely, but to the deepest depths of our human nature. He was interposing "between us and God's anger." As "a sponsor and surety for the guilty" he undertook to pay all the penalties which ought to have been exacted from us. Calvin cites the early father, Hilary of Poitiers, in stressing the vicarious object of Christ's spiritual anguish: "Hilary argues, that to this descent we owe our exemption from death. Nor does he dissent from this view in other passages, as when he said, 'The cross, death, hell, are our life.' And again, 'The Son of God is in hell, but man is brought back to heaven.'"[73]

In summary, the death of Christ in its profound spiritual reality "was a proof of true boundless mercy." It would be a mistake, Calvin insists, to find in the Lord's sufferings of soul a detraction from his heavenly glory. On the contrary, in his willingness to bear our infirmities and suffer the consequences of our sin, his goodness becomes more conspicuous.[74]

The Heidelberg Catechism follows Calvin's lead in the interpretation of this clause, and draws out its gracious implications in a warmly personal way: "Why is there added, 'He descended to hell?'—That in my greatest temptations I may be assured, and wholly comfort myself with this, that the Lord Jesus Christ, by his inexpressible anguish, pains, terrors, and hellish agony in which he was plunged during all his sufferings, but especially on the cross, has delivered me from the anguish and torment of hell."[75]

In his Study Guide to the Catechism Williamson makes an interesting observation at this point. He notes that, at first, "it might seem ridiculous to say that Jesus, in a few hours of suffering, could have experienced hell to the fullest." Williamson responds by pointing to the twin facts that Jesus was divine and that as a human being he was sinless. For such a person to be forsaken by God must have meant unimaginably great suffering.[76] Because of who Jesus was, it was possible in his case for an eternity of suffering to be compressed into three hours. Karl Barth says, "Godlessness is existence in hell."[77] Jesus experienced that hell so that we shall never do so.

In his book *The Crucified God*, Jürgen Moltmann has a most suggestive passage in which he contemplates the Godforsakenness of Jesus which is expressed in his cry, "My God, my God, why have you forsaken

---

73. Quoting Hilary, *On the Trinity*, 3.15, 272.
74. Calvin, *Institutes*, 2.16.10–12.
75. *Heidelberg Catechism*, Q. 44.
76. G. I. Williamson, *Heidelberg*, 76.
77. Barth, *Dogmatics*, 118.

me?" Moltmann focusses on the Greek verb *paradidōmi*, used in the passion narratives of Jesus' betrayal,[78] of his handing over to the Roman authorities,[79] of Pilate surrendering him to the will of the Jews,[80] and, in more general terms, of his abandonment to the cross.[81] It is also used of Jesus dismissing his life in the words, "He gave up his spirit."[82] With the possible exception of the last mentioned text, the connotations of the word are clearly negative.

Moltmann draws attention to Paul's threefold use of the same word in the first chapter of Romans. The human race rejected God's revelation, and "therefore God also gave them up" (Rom. 1:24; cf. vv. 26, 28). Moltmann puts it like this: "Men who abandon God are abandoned by God. Godlessness and Godforsakenness are two sides of the same event." This is God's judgment: "God delivers men up to the corruption which they themselves have chosen and abandons them in their forsakenness."

However, "Paul introduces a radical change in the sense of 'deliver up' when he recognizes and proclaims the Godforsakenness of Jesus." Moltmann cites Romans 8:32: God "did not spare his own Son, but delivered him up for us all," and comments: "In the total, inextricable abandonment of Jesus by his God and Father, Paul sees the delivering up of the Son by the Father for godless and godforsaken men." Consequently, "because God 'does not spare' his own Son, all the godless are spared. Though they are godless, they are not godforsaken, precisely because God has abandoned his own Son and delivered him up for them."

Moltmann next takes us to Galatians 2:20, where the Son of God is said to have given himself up. This expresses "a deep conformity between the will of the Father and the will of the Son in the event of the cross." Paradoxically, "this deep community of will between Jesus and his God

---

78. Matt. 10:4; 17:22; 20:18; 26:15-16, 21, 23-25, 45-46, 48; 27:3-4; Mark 3:19; 9:31; 10:33; 14:10-11, 14, 18, 21, 41-42, 44; Luke 9:44; 22:4, 6, 21-22, 48; John 6:64, 71; 12:4; 13:2, 11, 21; 18:2, 5; 21:20.

79. Matt. 20:19; 27:2, 18; Mark 10:33; 15:1, 10; Luke 18:32; 20:20; 24:7, 20; John 18:30, 35; 19:11.

80. Luke 23:35; John 18:36.

81. Matt. 26:2; 27:26; Mark 15:15; John 19:16.

82. John 19:30.

and Father" occurs "precisely at the point of their deepest separation, in the godforsaken and accursed death of Jesus on the cross."[83]

When God sent Hosea to the sinful people of Israel, the prophet came with a devastating word of judgment: "You are not my people, and I will not be your God" (Hos. 1:9). It seems that God had given his people up. However, Hosea was not finished. Towards the end of his prophecy we hear God mulling over in his mind the history of Israel in which he has involved himself. We sense his grief as he says on the one hand, "When Israel was a child, I loved him" (Hos. 11:1), and on the other (using the Revised Standard Version), "The more I called them, the more they went from me" (Hos. 11:2). As God surveys the sin of his nation, he begins to declare horrific judgment. It seems, indeed, that he has given his people up finally.

But then, all of a sudden God seems to check himself. As his anger and grief intermingle, he cries out from the depths of his love, "How can I give you up, Ephraim?" (Hos. 11:8). God feels himself torn apart by contradictory emotions. On the one hand, he gives his people up, on the other he asks, "How can I?" In Hosea 11:9 three times he exclaims, "I will not." How does God resolve the tension in his own recoiling heart?

We find the answer in the twofold truth which Moltmann has highlighted. There is a dichotomy in God. The Father gives up the Son. But in this greatest of divisions Father and Son are also most deeply one, for, in unity of purpose with his Father, the Son gives up himself.[84] The Son stands in for those whom God had given up, and out of that division in God, which is also the center of Trinitarian unity, forgiveness, redemption and restoration flow to us, whom God has given up in our sin.

However, this phrase has been understood, Kelly is right to point out that it does provide the creed with something which would otherwise be missing, namely a mention, albeit in abstruse terms, of the achievement of Christ by his death.[85] While not by any means an exhaustive account of the atonement, the statement that he descended to hell does nevertheless indicate that there was more to his sufferings than the outward event alone. On the basis of this article, believers could find assurance that

---

83. Moltmann, *Crucified God*, 241–44.

84. In addition to Gal. 2:20, this fact is stated also in Gal. 1:4, 1 Tim. 2:6, and Titus 2:14.

85. Kelly, *Creeds*, 383.

their Savior had been to hell "in order that they should not go."[86] In that sense Calvin is right to say that the exposition of this phrase in terms of Christ's sufferings during the hours of his God-forsakenness is "replete with excellent consolation."[87]

I conclude this chapter with a poem based on Psalm 22. Through meditation on its words we will perhaps be led into that "excellent consolation" of which Calvin speaks.

> The God-forsaken God, accursed, hangs on the tree,
> Himself the Lord divine: unfathomed mystery!
> To God he groans with ceaseless cry,
> Yet heaven is silent in reply.
>
> By mocking men despised, insulted: bitter scorn—
> False homage to a hated 'king': a crown of thorn!
> And God, he knows, is on the throne,
> Yet no deliverance can he own.
>
> Anointed from the womb, a miracle his birth;
> God's servant tried and true, of proved and priceless worth.
> Encircling troubles now surround;
> A God far-off will not be found.
>
> Disjointed every bone, like molten wax his heart,
> Pierced through his hands and feet; his strength, his life depart.
> Shall not his precious life at length
> Be rescued by the Lord, his strength?
>
> No respite may he find, forsaken must he be;
> God has abandoned God: perplexing mystery!
> And I recall, with baited breath—
> It was for me he tasted death.
>
> To God unceasing praise and endless power pertain.
> The cry of his afflicted he did not disdain.
> In God by God forsaken see
> God strangely one with God—for me![88]

---

86. Stewart, *Creeds*, 53.

87. Calvin, *Institutes*, 2.16.10.

88. By Jonathan F. Bayes—first written to be sung at a Good Friday Service at Northallerton Evangelical Church, England, in 1992.

11

On the third day he rose from the dead

In his study of John Calvin's first Catechism John Hesselink makes the point that "Calvin does not discuss at great length the significance of Christ's resurrection, for it was not for him a problematic area."[1] Since Calvin's day, however, things have changed, and the resurrection of Jesus Christ from the dead has become a problem in modern times.

Rudolf Bultmann is one who has created a problem out of the resurrection. He claims that there is nothing which can give us any insight into the reality of Christ's resurrection, and then goes on in somewhat baffling terms:

> The resurrection cannot—in spite of 1 Cor. 15:3–8—be demonstrated or made plausible as an objectively ascertainable fact on the basis of which one could believe. But insofar as it or the risen Christ is present in the proclaiming word, it can be believed—and only so can it be believed. Belief in the resurrection and the faith that Christ himself, yes, God himself, speaks in the proclaimed word (2 Cor. 5:20) are identical. . . . The meaning of Jesus' resurrection is not that he is translated to the beyond, but that he is exalted to the status of Lord.[2]

Alasdair Heron interprets Bultmann's understanding of the resurrection, stripped of its "mythical clothing," like this: "The resurrection of Jesus is not his 'rising from the grave' in any literal sense, but his continually confronting us in the *kerygma* of the cross: Christ is risen in the message which expresses the faith of the disciples once they perceived the meaning of the cross itself."[3]

---

1. Hesselink, *Catechism*, 125.
2. Bultmann, *Theology*, 305–6.
3. Heron, *Protestant Theology*, 109.

David Smith describes Process Theology "as one of the most powerful theological movements of the latter twentieth-century."[4] Process theology also makes a problem out of the resurrection. Referring to process theologian Henry Wieman, Smith says:

> When process theologians speak of the resurrection, one must not think that they mean the literal physical resurrection of Jesus. Not at all. Wieman suggests that, with the death of Christ, hope for the future died. But about the third day after his death, that creative power came to life once more in the disciples' band. Because of its past association with Jesus, some of his followers thought that they saw him. "But what rose from the dead was not the man Jesus; it was creative power."[5]

One sometimes gets the impression that those who seek to explain away the resurrection as a myth feel very grown up, sophisticated, and authentically modern (or even postmodern!). The belief in a literal resurrection is dismissed as something natural for primitive believers like the first disciples, living as they did in pre-scientific times, but untenable now. "'Myth' for Bultmann," Harvie Conn has said, "is the undifferentiated discourse of a pre-scientific age."[6]

However, such an attitude betrays appalling ignorance of the thinking processes of ancient men and women. While the technological progress which science has subsequently achieved may have been unknown to ancient people, it is emphatically not the case that their worldview was unscientific. That is to say, they knew as well as we do what things can happen, and what things do not happen in the ordinary course of nature—and the idea of a dead man getting up out of his grave and returning to the realm of life was as foreign to them as it is to us.

The New Testament emphasizes this repeatedly. Although Matthew largely declines to draw attention to the disciples' initial unbelief (he makes just one solitary reference to a measure of doubt on the part of some on the mountain [Matt. 28:17[7]]), the other three gospels give

---

4. Smith, *Contemporary Theology*, 155.
5. Smith, *Contemporary Theology*, 159.
6. Conn, *World Theology*, 34.
7. The suggestion by Carson, *Matthew*, on Matt. 28:17, that "some" here means a wider group around the eleven, and not the eleven themselves, is unnecessary. Even after six weeks of occasional appearances, there could have been some of the eleven who, prior to the coming of the Spirit, were still at something of a loss to explain exactly what was going on (cf. Hagner, *Matthew 1–13*, on Matt. 28:17: "It is natural to believe

prominent emphasis to the fact that no one from the immediate circle of Jesus' friends was anticipating a resurrection.

Mark shows us how, as the women went to the tomb on Sunday morning, the thought that they might not find the body there had not even occurred to them: they bought spices specifically to anoint Jesus' dead body (Mark 16:1). The expectation that the stone might already be rolled away was the furthest notion from their minds (Mark 16:3). When Mary Magdalene brought to the disciples the news that Jesus "was alive and had been seen by her, they did not believe" (Mark 16:11). Even when the same message was later carried by two others, "they did not believe them either" (Mark 16:13). When Jesus appeared to the eleven, he rebuked their skepticism, "because they did not believe those who had seen him after he had risen" (Mark 16:14).

Luke, too, draws attention to the unexpected nature of Jesus' resurrection. He describes the women's preparation of spices, their intention being to anoint Jesus' corpse (Luke 23:56). He introduces the statement that "they found the stone rolled away" with the word "But" (Luke 24:2), indicating the unpredictable nature of this discovery. The fact that "they went in and did not find the body of the Lord Jesus" (Luke 24:3) is recorded as a surprising turn of events—to the extent that it caused the women considerable perplexity (Luke 24:4). Their inability to understand what was going on caused them to be gripped by fear (Luke 24:5). Like Mark, Luke informs us that the disciples greeted the women's announcement of the resurrection with skepticism: "their words seemed to them like idle tales, and they did not believe them" (Luke 24:11). When Peter went to the tomb to check things out for himself, his response was to marvel (Luke 24:12); this probably does not yet mean adoring wonder of what he recognizes as a marvelous divine achievement, but is rather a description of "incredulity."[8] The two on the road to Emmaus had had high hopes of Jesus; now, however, all they can say is a resigned "But" (Luke 24: 21). Even after Cleopas and his companion had told the eleven remaining disciples and their associates of their unmistakable encounter with the risen Lord, the first reaction of the disciples when Jesus finally appeared to them was that "they supposed that they had seen a spirit" (Luke 24:37). Jesus rebuked their troublesome doubts (Luke 24:38), but

---

that the eleven disciples would have been in a state of hesitation and indecision. Too much had happened too fast for them to be able to assimilate it").

8. Liefeld, *Luke*, on Luke 24:12.

On the third day he rose from the dead 111

it was only once he had eaten in their presence (Luke 24:43) that they were convinced.

John tells us that Mary's first thought on finding the tomb empty was that some anonymous person had removed the body and hidden it (John 20:2). She repeated this explanation, which at that stage seemed most probable, to the angels (John 20:13), and even to Jesus himself, until she recognized his voice (John 20:15). In the middle of his account John notes that Jesus' followers had not yet understood the scriptural prophecy "that he must rise again from the dead" (John 20:9). Consequently, and not surprisingly, their naturalistic outlook overrode any miraculous interpretations that there could have been. John puts particular stress on this fact by reporting the absence of Thomas on the occasion of Jesus' first appearance to the disciples. When the others inform him, "We have seen the Lord," he assumes that it is a joke which they have worked out together with the specific intention of springing it on him. Thomas will stubbornly refuse to believe without empirical proof of the resurrection (John 20:25).

Walter Liefeld correctly notes that "this reluctance to believe has an important relation to the evidences for the Resurrection. The disciples were not expecting that event. Thus they cannot be called fit subjects for hallucination, as some would have them be."[9] As John Nolland puts it: "the later testimony of the Apostles is that much more impressive because they have been so hard to convince."[10]

As the apostles began to bear that testimony to the resurrection of Jesus in the ancient Roman world, they met with the same incredulity that had once been their own reaction. At Athens, "when they heard of the resurrection of the dead, some mocked" (Acts 17:32). Richard Longenecker points out that the idea of resurrection was "the height of folly" to the Athenians. He cites some words of the Greek poet, Aeschylus: "When the dust has soaked up a man's blood, once he is dead, there is no resurrection."[11]

To dismiss belief in the resurrection as the fruit of a primitive mindset is, therefore, inept in the extreme. The apostles

---

9. Liefeld, *Luke*, on Luke 24:9–12.
10. Nolland, *Luke 18:35–24:53*, on Luke 24:11–12.
11. Longenecker, *Acts*, on Acts 17:32.

were too discouraged after the death of Jesus to have talked themselves into believing that Jesus was risen from the dead. The only satisfactory explanation for their sudden faith was that Jesus appeared to them. Furthermore, the early Christian community could not have survived if the tomb of Jesus had not been empty. An occupied tomb would have destroyed their faith, and given the Jews a strong argument against the church.[12]

To those for whom the resurrection of Jesus Christ from the dead is a problematical area, Karl Barth offers the following sound advice: "if we should find it difficult to believe, rather than modifying the message, let us pray God that he give us faith, through his Holy Spirit."[13] For Williamson is surely right to say that "there is no such thing as authentic Christian faith without acceptance of the bodily resurrection of Jesus."[14] Does not the apostle say as much in Romans 10:9? "If you confess with your mouth the Lord Jesus and believe in your heart that God has raised him from the dead, you will be saved." To deny the resurrection is to remain in the tragic condition of an unsaved person.

The Apostles' Creed emphasizes the fact that Christ's resurrection took place "on the third day." This phrase occurs thirteen or fourteen times in the New Testament with reference to the Lord's resurrection.[15]

The significance of the inclusion of this phrase in the creed is often seen to lie firstly in that it emphasizes the reality of the resurrection. Like the crucifixion, which took place "under Pontius Pilate," Jesus' resurrection is a datable event, and therefore a historical fact. The dating is precise.[16] The resurrection did not take place just "sometime or other,"[17] and "the idea of a mere spiritual resurrection" is repudiated.[18]

Moreover, the phrase "on the third day" explicitly establishes Jesus' resurrection as a specific fulfillment of prophecy. Paul stated that "he

12. Conn, *World Theology*, 69.
13. Barth, *Faith*, 107.
14. G. I. Williamson, *Heidelberg*, 79.
15. Matt. 16:21; 17:23; 20:19; 27:64; Mark 9:31; 10:34; Luke 9:22; 18:33; 24:7, 21, 46; Acts 10:40; 1 Cor. 15:4, and, possibly, Luke 13:32 (Liefeld, *Luke*, on Luke 13:32, suggests that the phrase here may have been intended to remind Luke's readers of Jesus' resurrection, whereas Nolland, *Luke 9:21–18:34*, on Luke 13:32, apparently sees no connection).
16. Packer, *Christian*, 51.
17. Von Balthasar, *Credo*, 57.
18. McGiffert, *Creed*, 134.

rose again the third day according to the Scriptures" (1 Cor. 15:4). It is often assumed that the Old Testament Scripture in view here is Hosea 6:2, "On the third day he will raise us up, that we may live in his sight."[19] Acknowledging that this prophecy has the church as its direct reference, Witsius continues, "however, it is primarily and literally verified in the Head," and reads it as a definite prediction of the time of Christ's resurrection.[20]

However, it is worth considering an alternative Biblical source for Paul's allusion to the fulfillment of Scripture. The phrase "on the third day" occurs a cluster of times in connection with the Levitical peace offering. The flesh of the sacrifice was not to be eaten "on the third day"; indeed "the remainder of the flesh on the third day must be burned with fire" (Lev. 7:17-18; cf. 19:6-7).

It is no doubt true that there are issues of health and hygiene behind this requirement.[21] However, there may be deeper spiritual significance in addition to this practical provision. Could it also be that the peace offering, typifying the sacrifice of him who "himself is our peace" (Eph. 2:14), the one who "made peace by the blood of his cross" (Col. 1:20), must contain within its provisions a stipulation pointing to the fact that his flesh would no longer be held by the power of death come the third day? Any of the sacrifice remaining by the third day had to be disposed of, since, in the case of the antitype, the third day would mark the end of his sacrifice of himself.

John Gill combines the practical and typological aspects of this provision. He notes that, by the third day, the flesh of the sacrifice would begin to become corrupted, and adds: "perhaps some respect may be had in the type to the resurrection of Christ on the third day, having seen no corruption."[22]

The creed's reference to "the third day" is thought by McGiffert "to emphasize the brevity of the time between Christ's death and resurrection."[23] Massie makes the same point in connection with 1

---

19. Pannenberg, *Creed*, 108, n.

20. Witsius, *Creed*, Vol. 2, 192; cf. Massie, *Corinthians*, 242, against Grosheide, *Corinthians*, 350.

21. So R. K. Harrison, *Leviticus*, 79; Wenham, *Leviticus*, 124; R. L. Harris, *Leviticus*, on Lev. 7:11-18 and Lev. 19:5-8.

22. Gill, *Exposition*, on Lev. 7:17.

23. McGiffert, *Creed*, 133.

Corinthians 15:4, and adds a pertinent cross-reference to Acts 2:24,[24] "it was not possible that he should be held by it [death]." This impossibility made it inevitable that the period in the grave would be short. Witsius, however, finds significance not only in the brevity of the period, viewed from one angle, but also in its length, viewed from another: "It pleased God so to adjust the time of Christ's continuance in the sepulchre, that it might be sufficiently long to evince the reality of his death, and sufficiently short to correspond with the divine purpose respecting the preservation of his body from corruption."[25]

What is the message of Jesus' resurrection from the dead? Calvin puts it like this: "By this he shows himself to be conqueror over sin and death. For by his resurrection he swallowed up death, broke the fetters of the devil, and reduced all his power to nothing."[26]

The moment of the Lord's resurrection is "the point in time at which Jesus' new, deathless life takes its departure from our mortal history."[27] The resurrection ushers in a new era: "Our Lord was pleased to determine that . . . , by his coming forth from the grave, the epoch of a new world, and of a happier age, should commence."[28] As a result, we may legitimately sing,

> No more then as a child of earth
> Must I my lifetime spend—
> His history, his destiny
> Are mine to apprehend.
> O, what a Savior, what a Lord!
> O, Master, Brother, Friend!
> What miracle has joined me to
> This life that never ends![29]

This is not, as Barth rightly insists, the natural sequel to the sinful history which has been running its course since the fall of Adam. What we are talking about here is "an absolute beginning,"[30] a totally fresh

---

24. Massie, *Corinthians*, 242.
25. Witsius, *Creed*, Vol. 2, 175.
26. Calvin, *Catechism, 1545*, Q. 73.
27. Von Balthasar, *Credo*, 57.
28. Witsius, *Creed*, Vol. 2, 176.
29. From the hymn, *O what a mystery I see*, by Graham Kendrick, © 1988, Make Way Music. Used by permission.
30. Barth, *Faith*, 105.

start, something radically new. "Christ's resurrection does not follow his death as morning follows evening, as spring follows winter, and as good days come again after bad days. It is not a consequence independent of the active will of God."[31]

Hence, "every human claim to immortality would be an illusion without this God-given pledge through Christ's resurrection."[32] That is why the superstitious hope of folk-religion is a forlorn and empty disappointment. Immortality is not a natural quality of humanity, nor of any part of our human make-up. Apart from the victory of Christ we are dead, lost forever. If Jesus Christ did not rise from the dead, gospel preaching is vain, biblical faith is futile, we are still in our sins, those who have died in Christ have perished, and our condition is unutterably miserable (1 Cor. 15:14, 17–19). "But now Christ is risen from the dead, and has become the firstfruits of those who have fallen asleep" (1 Cor. 15:20).

The emphasis on Christ as the firstfruits is part of a threefold application which follows from the truth of his resurrection. There is application to our future, our present and our past.

First, then, the fact that Christ is risen from the dead has a glorious application to our own future. He has blazed the trail through death to glory, and we shall follow in the path that he has trod. Calvin puts this vividly: "From his resurrection one may infer a sure confidence that we will obtain victory over the power of death. For as he could not be held back by the pangs of death but overcame all its power, he so blunted all its darts that they cannot now prick us into destruction. Therefore his resurrection is, first, the surest truth and substance of our coming resurrection."[33]

We live in hope because we live in the light of the future which Christ's resurrection has secured for us.

Rufinus also draws out the implications of Christ's resurrection for our future. He notes that Christ descended into death

> not that he might be detained by death according to the law of mortality, but that he might by himself in his resurrection open the gates of death. It is as if a king were to proceed to a prison, and to go in and open the doors, and bring forth, and set at lib-

31. Barth, *Faith*, 100.
32. Barth, *Faith*, 102.
33. Calvin, *Catechism, 1538*, 20.v, 24.

erty the prisoners, and restore those who are sitting in darkness and in the shadow of death to light and life.[34]

The prisoners of death have become the "prisoners of hope" (Zech. 9:12). We, who once faced the darkness of death, because our sin had plunged us into mortality, can now see through the gloom to the light of eternity beyond. As the Lord himself said, "Because I live, you will live also" (John 14:19).

Listen to how G. I. Williamson expresses it: "If Christ really did get up out of his grave, then there is—at last—an answer to man's ultimate problem: the problem of death. If he really arose, then death has been conquered. It can never be looked on as final—as the 'last word'—by the people of Jesus."[35] That is the relevance of Jesus' resurrection for our future, our destiny. Death has lost its sting for us.

Secondly, the fact that Jesus Christ is risen from the dead has a powerful application to our present. There are benefits which flow to us in our present experience. By the virtue of his resurrection "we are raised to newness of life, that we may obey God's will by pure and holy living."[36] With the apostle, we desire to know "the power of his resurrection" (Phil. 3:10). It is by that power that we are enabled to reckon ourselves "dead indeed to sin, but alive to God in Jesus Christ our Lord" (Rom. 6:11).

F. B. Meyer speaks of "Christ's resurrection as primarily affecting spiritual experience." Commenting on Philippians 3:10, he says:

> To the believing soul, the power of the life which resides in Christ pours into the receptive spirit, forthwith it rises from the grave of passion in which it had been imprisoned, escapes from the bondage of corruption by which it was held, and goes forth into the glorious liberty of the sons of God. Just as Christ could not be holden by the bands of death, so the soul which trusts him is emancipated, enthused, raised into an altogether new atmosphere, breathes the ozone of eternity, is thrilled by the powers of the unseen, and meets all appeals from the lower world with an abundance of life.

Meyer sums up the present impact of this truth in these words: "the soul which is infilled with the resurrection power of Christ is more than a

---

34. Rufinus, *Commentary*, para. 17, 1112.
35. G. I. Williamson, *Heidelberg*, 79.
36. Calvin, *Catechism, 1545*, Q. 74.

conqueror in the midst of the most virulent temptation."[37] The challenge is indeed to walk in this reality.

Thirdly, these future and present aspects of the application of the fact of the resurrection of our Lord are only possible because of the gracious application which his resurrection has for our past. The resurrection has been described as the consummation of the cross.[38] Professor Cranfield calls it "God's seal on Jesus' work on the cross," and writes: "The significance of Easter is that it validates what was accomplished on Good Friday as God's own saving deed."[39]

On the cross Jesus suffered the punishment for sin—he died. Was his death effective as a vicarious sacrifice? The resurrection answers the question with a resounding Yes! Jesus was raised from the dead "to prove that the death sentence has been remitted."[40] The resurrection guarantees to every believer that we really are in the clear before God. Jesus our Lord "was delivered up because of our offences, and was raised because of our justification" (Rom. 4:25). Some translations render the second part of this verse, "for our justification." However, I think that the New King James Version is right to translate as it does. For one thing it is a more accurate rendering of the Greek (*dia* followed by an accusative). For another thing, it is theologically more appropriate.

Jesus' death secured our acquittal from guilt. His death was a successful propitiation in turning God's wrath away from us. Jesus' death obtained forgiveness for our sins. His death opened up for us access into God's favor. His death acquired for us a standing before God in righteousness. All that is entailed in justification. And it is just because his death was thus effective, that God raised him from the dead. There was no further need for him to remain under the power of death. The work of salvation was completed. There was no further legitimacy in his remaining under the power of death. The sentence was served. The resurrection is conclusive proof that our salvation is eternally safe, that we are eternally saved.

If ever I find myself entertaining doubts about my ultimate destiny, I have only to remind myself of this fact: Jesus was raised from the dead. God has accepted his work on my behalf. My past is dead and buried.

37. Meyer, *Philippians*, 165.
38. Hesselink, *Catechism*, 125.
39. Cranfield, *Creed*, 36.
40. Praamsma, *Before the Face*, 70.

I may forget the past, and press on, with sin and death behind me, and only glory ahead. The resurrection of Jesus affects my future, my present, and my past.

This is indeed a totally new start, a completely fresh beginning. Christ is alive, so all is new. The world is radically different, because Jesus has broken the power of death. All the miserable consequences of death are nullified. Hope reigns supreme.

And yet it does not. Still I sin. Still I must attend the funerals of those who die. Still despair torments the minds of men and women. Still people live out a miserable existence, held in the prison house of gloom. Still poverty, war, crime, vandalism, hatred, and all the fruits of a discordant humanity rip the world apart. Still homes are wrecked by divorce. Still lives are blighted by abuse and cruelty. Still hearts are plagued by guilt and fear. Has anything really changed, just because Jesus Christ was raised from the dead?

Karl Barth gives a helpful illustration to aid us in making sense of these realities:

> Indeed death and sin continue to exist, but as vanquished things. Their situation is similar to a chess player's who has already lost but has not acknowledged it as yet. He looks on the game and he says: Is it already finished? Does the king still have another move? He tries it. Afterwards he acknowledges there was no more possibility of winning. That precisely is the situation of death and sin and the devil: the king is checkmated, the game is finished and the players do not acknowledge it as yet. They still believe the game will go on. But it is over.

Barth describes the idea that nothing has changed since Easter as "the grand illusion, the sad human illusion."[41] The vision of faith sees through the illusion to the reality above: Jesus has conquered death for us. Things can never be the same again. Death is not the end, and the end is not death. There is no end, for eternal life, endless life, lies beyond the horizon, and the glow of eternity flickers down through the shadows of sin into the present, and beckons us onwards and upwards. "Death is swallowed up in victory" (1 Cor. 15:54). Even God is different now: the resurrection of Christ has become part of the definition of who he is: we believe in "him who raised up Jesus our Lord from the dead" (Rom. 4:24). Hold on in hope, for "he who raised Christ from the dead will also give life to your mortal bodies through his Spirit who dwells in you." (Rom. 8:11).

---

41. Barth, *Faith*, 104.

12

He ascended to the heavens

THE NEW TESTAMENT GIVES us three accounts of the ascension, two of them from the writings of Luke, and one from Mark's gospel. All three emphasize that the ascension was something which happened to Jesus. A passive verb is used in each instance (Mark 16:19; Luke 24:51; Acts 1:9). Jesus ascended to heaven because God the Father reached down and picked up the Son of his love in whom he found great delight.

In his gospel Luke informs us that Jesus was lifted up into heaven as his hands were lifted in blessing (Luke 24:50–51). This no doubt symbolizes the fact that his present position in heaven is one from where he blesses his people incessantly. In Acts 1:12 Luke indicates that the ascension took place from the Mount of Olives. Witsius notes that this was the very place where the final stage of his humiliation had commenced. It was to the Mount of Olives that Jesus had gone from the upper room after the Last Supper (Matt. 26:30; Mark 14:26; Luke 22:39). It was in this vicinity that the agony of Gethsemane took place. Fittingly, it was from the same spot "where he had struggled with infernal hosts" that he ascended in triumph.[1]

Of the many things which might be said about Christ's ascension, I want for present purposes to focus on just three.

THE ASCENSION RESULTED IN JESUS' ABSENCE FROM THE EARTH

Calvin asks whether Christ so ascended "as to be no longer on earth?" He answers in the affirmative, and then explains that, having performed everything necessary for our salvation, "there was no need for him to

---

1. Witsius, *Creed*, Vol. 2, 211.

continue longer on earth."[2] The ascension is "when the time of his absence begins."[3]

Jesus had alerted his followers to the fact that they would not always have him with them (Mark 14:7). He had clearly forewarned them that there would come a time when he would go away (John 7:33; 8:21; 13:33; 16:5). He described his ascension to heaven as his going to the Father (John 14:12, 28; 16:10, 28).

In John 16:16 Jesus says to his disciples, "A little while and you will not see me." These words make it clear that he is talking about his visible presence. We are no longer in a position to see our Lord. The visibility of Jesus points by extension to his humanity. "According to his human nature, he is not now upon earth," is how the Heidelberg Catechism expresses it.[4] This means that Alister McGrath exaggerates to the point of inaccuracy when he says, "In no way does the ascension of Christ mean that Christ is now absent from his world."[5] It is not true to say that Christ is in no way absent. As regards his visible, human presence, we do not have that now. In that way Jesus Christ is most definitely absent from the world.

Wolfhart Pannenberg explains this powerfully, in words that serve as a cautionary warning to us. He notes that during the period of forty days from Easter to the ascension there was a series of appearances of the risen Lord. He points out that the New Testament clearly asserts that Jesus will come again at the dawn of the end-time. However, the inescapable implication of the New Testament doctrine of the ascension is that "in the intervening period there are no direct encounters with the one who is risen."[6]

At times we are tempted to desire visions of Jesus. We long for Damascus Road encounters, which will resolve all our doubts and questions once and for all. However, the post-ascension appearance of the Lord to Saul of Tarsus is unique. It certainly was "a real vision of the ascended Redeemer" in the same body that had been seen by the other apostles prior to the ascension.[7] But it is not such a phenomenon as we

2. Calvin, *Catechism, 1545*, Q. 76.
3. Cranfield, *Creed*, 44.
4. *Heidelberg Catechism*, Q. 47.
5. McGrath, *I Believe*, 74.
6. Pannenberg, *Creed*, 107.
7. Barnes, *New Testament*, Vol. 5, 285.

may ever expect to see repeated. The apostle Paul's own account of it makes this clear. He compares it to an untimely birth, calling himself "the child born out of due time." The presence of the Greek definite article (not easy to reproduce in fluent English) implies "that there were no more of such children afterwards."[8] Paul therefore describes this abnormal appearance as "last of all" (1 Cor. 15:8). There were—and are—to be no more.

This absence of the visible Jesus Christ as a result of his ascension to heaven is not to be taken lightly. It is something which we must take seriously. We are visionary creatures. The catch phrase, "seeing is believing," says much about our dependence on the sense of sight. Like Thomas, before the risen Lord had appeared to him, we feel that we want to say, "Unless I see . . . I will not believe" (John 20:25). In fact, we find it hard to imagine that we *can* believe without seeing.

Arnold Buss, the psychologist, points out that we receive most of our information through vision, and speaks of "the dominance of vision."[9] It is, he suggests, through visionary perception that we seek meaning.[10] We endeavor to extract information from what we see, and as a result we learn, we know.

But we cannot now see Jesus our Lord, except with the non-visionary perception of faith (Heb. 2:9; cf. John 14:19). That is why in the present time we have to "walk by faith, not by sight" (2 Cor. 5:7). And this is why we have to struggle with sufferings, disappointments, perplexity, discouragement, uncertainty, ignorance. This is why the Christian life can seem such a battle, such a frustration. It explains why we sometimes feel so close to giving up. We long for our Lord, and yet he is not here. We cannot see him. "There is only the word of his apostles."[11] We live in "the time of awaiting,"[12] and in this time our aching hearts can sometimes reach desperation point, as we long to see our Jesus.

We can imagine something of the feelings of the first disciples as they stood there on the Mount of Olives that day. Jesus was meeting with them for the last time. They probably did not know that this was the case until, all of a sudden, he was lifted off the earth, and vanished into

8. Grosheide, ,*Corinthians* 352.
9. Buss, *Psychology*, 186.
10 Buss, *Psychology*, 209.
11. Pannenberg, *Creed*, 107.
12. Barth, *Faith*, 113.

the cloud of divine glory which had come down from heaven to receive him. And he was gone. He would never again be seen on earth until the last day. For that first generation of Christians, visions of Jesus were now, permanently, a thing of the past.

Luke tells us that "they looked steadfastly toward heaven" (Acts 1:10), no doubt open-mouthed with astonishment, and perhaps sensing something of a bereavement as it slowly dawned on them that that was it, as far as the sight of the Savior was concerned. Howard Marshall suggests that "they are looking for the reappearance of Jesus or some other happening which will indicate that what they have seen is not the final act in the drama."[13] However, the fact that appearances of the risen Lord are now finished is soon confirmed by the words of the angels (Acts 1:11). Their message was that "the Jesus the disciples had known now had a heavenly existence. This is stressed by the double use of the phrase 'into heaven.'"[14] For the time being, they were not to expect to see him again on earth. Calvin, too, expounds the angels' words as an indication of the bodily absence of Christ from this world, and as a rejection of the desire to have him on the earth.[15] They must walk by faith, not by sight.

Professor Hanson sees the main emphasis of the entire story of the ascension in Acts as being "on the removal of the visible presence of Jesus. The Lord will return some time, but meanwhile mere gaping after wonders is futile."[16] We must walk by faith, not by sight.

Ralph Martin quotes C. K. Barrett's words on 2 Corinthians 5:7: "we live by believing in the absent and invisible Christ, not by looking at visible forms." Martin goes on to suggest that Paul is opposing the attitude which majored on visions and other ecstatic experiences.[17] Such an approach to the Christian life is still around today. It elevates sight, and denies the reality of the believer's struggle. There is a triumphalist mindset. All the emphasis is on victory, and yet it involves living in a world of spiritual make-believe. The fact is that Christ is not here—and therefore our walk is a hard, uphill struggle, which demands faith.

Not long ago I was conversing with a group of pastors, several of them charismatic in ethos. One of them was having to handle a difficult

---

13. Marshall, *Acts*, 61.
14. Longenecker, *Acts*, on Acts 1:11.
15. Calvin, Acts, 52.
16. Hanson, *Acts*, 58.
17. Martin, *2 Corinthians*, on 2 Cor. 5:7.

pastoral situation where a member of his church was struggling with a debilitating terminal illness. Apart from the increasing physical weakness and intense bodily pain which she was feeling, her trust in God was coming under strain too. My colleague commented that Christian ministry into such lives is hard at times like that, because all the normal emphasis in ministry is on victory in Jesus.

I could not help wondering at the time whether such perceived difficulties were the result of a lopsided approach to normal ministry. If our normal emphasis is triumphant victory we shall be ill suited to deal with most human experience, because for most people (including most Christian people), most of the time, life is anything but victory and triumph in Jesus. For most people, most of the time, life is best symbolized by a question mark—and the question is, Where is Jesus when I need him? The absence of the Lord is the troubling reality that dominates the Christian life. He is not now here. He is in heaven, but I am on earth.

In the book of Ecclesiastes Solomon writes, "God is in heaven, and you on earth; therefore let your words be few" (Eccl. 5:2). We have few words which we can speak, because for so much of the time we just do not understand. Life is a burden and a puzzle. Our experience is of sorrow and perplexity. We are unable to articulate any sort of interpretation of things which rings true. In "many words there is also vanity" (Eccl. 5:7). Talk becomes pointless in the face of life's apparent meaninglessness. If Daniel Fredericks is correct to translate the key word in Ecclesiastes (here rendered "vanity") as "temporary,"[18] then this verse might be stressing the provisionality of all our judgments owing to our inability to make sense of things. We are earth-bound and limited, and the absence of Jesus compounds our predicament.

I remember as a young Christian facing an extremely difficult decision. How I wished at that time that the lights of God's guidance could be flashed across the sky, or that I could experience an overwhelming sense inside me of which was the right way to go. Looking back, from the vantage point of maturer years, I can now see that what I was really wishing was that Jesus was still on earth and would tell me what to do. But it does not happen, because for the present time we have to live with the absence of Jesus. Well did our Lord himself say, "you will seek me and not find me" (John 7:34). So we must make our decisions in faith. That will often mean that we have no peace about what we decide. We

---

18. Fredericks, "Ecclesiastes," 553.

will sometimes make our decisions, decisions which will set the direction of our life (or at least a phase or aspect of it) while swamped by intense uncertainty. But that is how it must be, because Jesus is not here, and we walk by faith, not by sight. And very often faith means risk.

In a fascinating book Richard Friedman traces the way in which, through the course of the Old Testament Scriptures, gradually "the deity appears less and less to humans, speaks less and less." He points out that "miracles, angels, and all other signs of divine presence become rarer and finally cease."[19] Turning to the New Testament and referring to Jesus' cry of dereliction from the cross, Friedman sees that "in the climactic moment of the Christian story, the central being of the story speaks of the departure of God."[20] Although Friedman does not mention the ascension, this event would fit well into his reading of the Bible story line in terms of God's disappearance. Certainly, he suggests, in the age of the early Christian mission the "feeling of a divine void, of a hidden face of God" was widespread in both Jewish and pagan contexts,[21] and "Christianity had a sense of the hiddenness of God."[22]

Here is the challenge for our present time. Jesus has ascended. He has gone from the world. He is absent. We walk by faith, not by sight.

THE ASCENSION LED TO THE PRESENCE OF JESUS WITH US BY HIS SPIRIT

Cranfield points out that Luke's comment on the disposition of the disciples which follows the account of the ascension in his gospel is not what might have been expected, given that they had just witnessed their Lord's final departure from this world.[23] Luke says that they "returned to Jerusalem with great joy" (Luke 24:52). This reminds us that to stop short at the fact of the absence of Jesus since his ascension would be to understand the event in far too one-sidedly negative a way.

While the lack of Jesus' visible presence with us on earth now must not be minimized, it would be an excessively pessimistic doctrine of the ascension which said nothing further. For, as a matter of fact, the Lord is

19. Friedman, *Disappearance*, 7.
20. Friedman, *Disappearance*, 135.
21. Friedman, *Disappearance*, 136.
22. Friedman, *Disappearance*, 139.
23. Cranfield, *Creed*, 44.

after all not altogether absent from the world: he is no longer here as far as his humanity is concerned, but, as the Heidelberg Catechism rightly insists, "according to his Godhead, majesty, grace, and Spirit, he is at no time absent from us."[24] Or, as Calvin succinctly puts it, Christ's body is in heaven, but "his virtue . . . is diffused everywhere."[25]

Although, as we have already noticed, Alister McGrath overstates the case in claiming that the ascension "in no way" means that Jesus is absent, he is nevertheless quite right to point to the ubiquity of Christ's spiritual presence.[26] And in view of that spiritual ubiquity, Calvin is right to say, "though he departed from us, it was that his departure might be more useful to us than that presence which was confined in a humble tabernacle of flesh during his abode on the earth."[27]

Jesus himself emphasized to his disciples the advantage which would accrue to them from his departure (John 16:7). He said, "You have heard me say to you, 'I am going away and coming back to you.' If you loved me, you would rejoice because I said, 'I am going to the Father'" (John 14:28). Luke reports that this was exactly their reaction as their Lord left them.

When the Lord spoke of the advantage entailed in his ascension, one of the main aspects which he highlighted was the coming of the Holy Spirit: "it is to your advantage that I go away; for if I do not go away, the helper will not come to you; but if I depart, I will send him to you" (John 16:7). Earlier on in his gospel John explains that Jesus' figurative language concerning living water was an allusion to the Holy Spirit; he then adds this comment: "the Holy Spirit was not yet given, because Jesus was not yet glorified" (John 7:39). The glorification of Jesus in his ascension was the essential first step on the way to the massive outpouring of the Holy Spirit which took place at Pentecost (cf. Acts 2:33). Thus the Heidelberg Catechism lists amongst the benefits which we receive from Christ's ascension into heaven "that he sends us his Spirit."[28]

And it is by the Holy Spirit that the Son of God is everywhere present. The Holy Spirit is "the Spirit of Christ," by whom we are assured that we belong to Christ, for it is by his Spirit that Christ himself is in us (Rom.

24. *Heidelberg Catechism*, Q. 47.
25. Calvin, *Catechism, 1545*, Q. 79.
26. McGrath, *I Believe*, 74
27. Calvin, *Institutes*, 2.16.14.
28. *Heidelberg Catechism*, Q. 49.

8:9–10). The Holy Spirit is "the Spirit of his [God's] Son," by whom we are enabled to enjoy the Father's intimate paternal love, as we are drawn by adoption into Jesus' own relationship with "Abba, Father" (Gal. 4:6). The Holy Spirit is "the Spirit of Jesus Christ," supplied to us to strengthen us in the sufferings and challenges of the Christian life (Phil. 1:19).

So the Pentecostal outpouring was not an end in itself. The significance of the omnipresence of the ascended Lord in his divine nature is that he "*daily* lavishes spiritual riches" upon his people,[29] and so enriches them constantly. Pentecost, though unique as an event, has ongoing implications, because the Holy Spirit, having been sent, remains, for the daily good of Christ's people in every place.

Our ancestors in the faith used to refer to the outpouring of the *gifts* of the Spirit.[30] The Spirit's gifts were the solid tokens of the spiritual presence of Jesus, and the concrete benefits of his ascension. The gifts in view here are not the so-called "charismatic" gifts listed in such passages as 1 Corinthians 12. Our Reformed forefathers had a much broader and fuller understanding of the gifts of the Spirit than has tended to become associated with the term these days. Listen, for example, to Herman Witsius. Witsius notes that the ascended Christ sheds on his people gifts "more precious than gold"; they are "the gifts of his Holy Spirit," who is "the Spirit of wisdom and understanding, the Spirit of counsel and might, the Spirit of knowledge and of the fear of the Lord—the Spirit of adoption."[31]

These echoes of Isaiah 11:2 and Romans 8:15 indicate that, for Witsius, the gifts of the Holy Spirit were all the graces involved in the sanctification of our lives. The ascension of Christ to heaven and the growth of his people in holiness are intrinsically connected, because it was as the direct sequel to the ascension that the outpouring of the Spirit at Pentecost occurred. He is the *Holy* Spirit, and one of his primary tasks in the world today is to replicate within Christ's people Christ's own holiness.

In connection with the ascended Christ's conferment of the gifts of the Spirit, Rufinus quotes Paul's Biblical citation from Psalm 68:18 in Ephesians 4:8: "When he ascended on high, he led captivity captive, and gave gifts to men."[32]

29. Hesselink, *Catechism*, 127.
30. *Heidelberg Catechism*, Q. 51.
31. Witsius, *Creed*, Vol. 2, 232–33.
32. Rufinus, *Commentary*, para. 31, 1122.

The final phrase of the citation, "he gave gifts to men," reads a little differently in the Old Testament original, which says that he "received gifts among men." Dr. Skevington Wood suggests that the explanation of this discrepancy is that "the apostle was drawing on an ancient oral tradition reflected in the Aramaic Targum on the Psalter and the Syriac Peshitta version, both of which read, 'You have given gifts to men,'"[33] although he mentions the fact that "some have claimed that, under the inspiration of the Spirit, Paul felt free to amplify the meaning of the Psalm, since the giving is implicit in the receiving."[34]

Calvin makes another suggestion—that the quotation stops before the words "and gave gifts to men," which are the apostle's additional comment, emphasizing how much more illustrious was Christ's triumph than that depicted in Psalm 68: "it is a more honorable distinction for a conqueror to dispense his bounty largely to all classes, than to gather spoils from the vanquished." In any case, Calvin acknowledges, "the intention of *receiving* was to *give* gifts."[35] He therefore combines both the receiving and the giving, in the course of presenting a concise summary of the entire import of the ascension:

> he has received all the gifts of the Holy Spirit to bestow them, so as by them to enrich those who believe in him. Therefore, although lifted up into heaven, he has removed his bodily presence from our sight; yet he does not refuse to be present with his believers in help and might, and to show the manifest power of his presence. This also he has promised, "Behold I am with you even until the end of the age."[36]

It is sometimes said that the context surrounding Paul's Psalm quotation defines the gifts in view as the ministries of the church designed for the equipping of the saints, of which there is a limited and specific number (Eph. 4:11–12).[37] However, in that verse 8 is linked to the preceding verse by the word "therefore," it seems more likely that verse 7 should guide us in our understanding of the gifts of the ascended Lord. It is probably not, therefore correct to read verses 8–10 as a parenthesis in the flow of the argument from verse 7 to verse 11, as Martyn Lloyd-

---

33. See also Lincoln, *Ephesians*, on Eph. 4:8.
34. Skevington Wood, *Ephesians*, on Eph. 4:8.
35. Calvin, *Galatians and Ephesians*, 273–74.
36. Calvin, *Catechism, 1538*, 20.v, 24.
37. So Hendriksen, *Ephesians*, 191.

Jones claims.[38] Verses 7 and 11 may well be talking about different gifts. The gifts of the ascended Christ are those of verse 7, and at verse 11 a new, though closely associated, section begins.

What the ascended Christ has given to each believer, according to Ephesians 4:7, is "grace." The aorist tense of "was given" needs to be taken seriously. Here is a once-for-all gift, in which each believer participates. This makes it unlikely that the reference is to the ministries enumerated in verse 11, for they are given repeatedly to each generation.

Many commentators see the gift of verse 7 as the function which each of the saints has within the growing body. Thus Francis Foulkes defines the word "grace" here as "the privilege of a special calling in the service of God."[39] This, too, would seem to run into difficulties with the aorist.

The use of the word "grace" as denoting a one-off endowment to the church as a whole seems more probably to relate to the outpouring of the Holy Spirit, and to his gracious working within the life of each believer. In my view, some of the older commentators were right to read verse 7 in this way.

Albert Barnes puts it clearly: "the grace referred to here most probably means the gracious influences of the Holy Spirit."[40] Matthew Poole explains what this grace includes: it comprehends "those graces which are common to all believers as such, faith, love, hope, zeal, etc."[41] Barnes affirms that God has given each believer "the means of living as he ought to do," and that he has made ample provision in the gospel for believers to walk worthy of our calling.[42]

In mentioning the duty of walking worthy of our calling Barnes is echoing the first verse of Ephesians 4, where the apostle exhorts us to commit ourselves to such a walk. Paul then spells out some of the elements which make up a worthy walk: lowliness, gentleness, longsuffering, love, unity, and peace (v. 2–3). This defining context suggests that the grace which the ascended Christ has given is indeed the sanctifying power of his own unfailing presence in the Holy Spirit.

This means that the presence of the ascended Lord with his church is always purposive. It is certainly for our joy, though it is not merely

38. Lloyd-Jones, *Christian Unity*, 147–48.
39. Foulkes, *Ephesians*, 114; see also Stott, *God's New Society*, 155.
40. Barnes, *New Testament*, Vol. 7, 75.
41. Poole, *Commentary*, 672.
42. Barnes, *New Testament*, Vol. 7, 75.

for our joy. It is truly for our encouragement, though never merely for our encouragement. It is indeed for Christian witness, though not for witness alone.

It is perhaps a neglected aspect of the work of the Spirit these days, but one which is vital: the ascended Jesus poured his Spirit upon his church to make us more Christ-like, more holy. Being a Christian is not just reaping the heavenly benefits of the atonement. It is also growing in holiness through the inner working of the Holy Spirit, the gift of the ascended Lord, by whom his presence is channeled incessantly to his people.

In the original text which Paul quotes from Psalm 68:18 there is a line which is not reproduced in Ephesians 4:8. We read, "you have received gifts among men, even among the rebellious." William Plumer makes the ultimate application, with the apostle, to Christ, "who has ascended up far above all heavens, who turned the captivity of his people, who bound their enemies Satan, sin and death, who received great gifts, especially of the Holy Ghost, for men (Acts 2:4, 33); and who bestows his gifts on 'rebellious man.'"[43]

That rebellious man should be the receiver of the gift of the ascended Lord—that is the essence of grace. But the goal of the gift is that we should be rebellious no more. The work of the Holy Spirit is to subdue our rebellion. Spurgeon comments on the grace shown to the rebellious: "Subdued by love, they are indulged with the benefits peculiar to the chosen."[44] The Canons of Dort explain where the work of the ascended Jesus through his Spirit leads in practice:

> he opens the closed and softens the hardened heart, and circumcises that which was uncircumcised; infuses new qualities into the will, which, though heretofore dead, he quickens; from being evil, disobedient, and refractory, he renders it good, obedient, and pliable; actuates and strengthens it, that, like a good tree, it may bring forth the fruits of good actions.[45]

On the cross we view the very heart and center of the work of Christ for us. From his ascension derives his work in us. He is with us, because he has poured out his Spirit. As the Spirit makes us more like Jesus, so

---

43. Plumer, *Psalms*, 665.
44. Spurgeon, *Treasury of David*, Vol. 3, 142.
45. *Canons of Dort*, Third and Fourth Heads of Doctrine, Art. 11.

Jesus becomes more real to us, more close to us. "Strengthened with might through his Spirit in the inner man," we find that Christ dwells in our hearts (Eph. 3:16–17). He is ascended. His human nature is removed from us. But by his Spirit he comes to us constantly, and we live in him increasingly. He fulfils his word, "I will never leave you nor forsake you" (Heb. 13:5).

THE ASCENSION SIGNIFIES THE RECEPTION OF HUMANITY INTO HEAVEN

There is one other aspect of the ascension which we must not fail to mention. Yes, as regards his human nature, Jesus is absent from earth. However, he has not ceased to be human as well as divine. "In assuming our humanity he joined it to his divine nature forever."[46] This means that Christ in his human nature is right now present in heaven. And the glorious truth is that he is there as our representative. There is a human being in heaven—only one as yet, but one who is there emphatically as a human being.

When sin entered human life the Lord's response was to exclude humanity from his presence. Adam was driven out of Eden, and cherubim and a revolving flaming sword were positioned to the east of the garden, confirming and ensuring that there was no way back (Gen. 3:23–24). Gordon Wenham notes the tragic consequences of sin. He points out that in the Garden of Eden "God was uniquely present in all his life-giving power. It was this that man forfeited."[47] Verse 24 stresses that God "actively excludes the sinner."[48]

However, this exclusion owing to sin has been decisively overcome in the human person of Jesus Christ. Since the day of Christ's ascension there has been a man in glory. The ascension of Jesus was the moment of his exaltation, his glorification. It is, of course, true that "he who is now exalted possessed from all eternity, as the eternal Son of God, the glory and authority of his Father." However, something new transpired with his ascension: "it is now as human, as our brother, that he possesses the

---

46. Cranfield, *Creed*, 45.
47. Wenham, *Genesis 1–15*, on Gen. 3:24.
48. Kidner, *Genesis*, 72.

glory, majesty, and power of God."[49] Most appropriately, therefore, Rufinus speaks of "the novelty of flesh ascending to the right hand of God."[50]

There is joy to be found in the doctrine of the ascension because, although our Lord is absent from earth, he is present in heaven. And in his heavenly existence he is glorified and highly exalted. His humanity is resplendent with the elegance, the beauty, the radiance of divine majesty. What the favored three glimpsed just briefly on the Mount of Transfiguration is now the permanent reality for the beloved Son of the Father. His face shines like the sun and his clothes exude celestial whiteness (Matt. 17:2). They retain the perfect whiteness of snow, with a glory unattainable on earth (Mark 9:3). There on the mountain the disciples "were being privileged to . . . anticipate his coming exaltation."[51]

The fact that Jesus Christ has ascended to heaven means that "the person in charge of the universe now is human!"[52] The one "who has passed through the heavens" is our "great High Priest," who is able to "sympathize with our weaknesses" (Heb. 4:14–15). In all our struggles and doubts and questions, all our pains, and anxieties, and griefs, we may look up, assured and comforted "that he who ascended higher than all the heavens . . . is still the same Jesus, filled with the same tender love and sympathetic concern which he showed when, on Calvary's cross, he descended to regions lower than the earth, that is, to the experience of the nethermost depths, the agonies of hell."[53] And knowing that he is indeed in heaven now, we receive a sure and certain guarantee that "our future can never be hopeless,"[54] that the pangs of hell can never take hold of us.

For the deepest source of joy in the fact of Christ's ascension is found in knowing that it is not on his own account only that Jesus is present in heaven. He is there for us. Our humanity is represented in heaven by the representative human being. It is therefore possible to speak of the ascension of Christ as "the unprecedented elevation of human nature to the point of participation in the Father's majesty."[55] It is not merely Jesus

---

49. Cranfield, *Creed*, 45
50. Rufinus, *Commentary*, para. 31, 1122.
51. Carson, *Matthew*, on Matt. 17:2.
52. G. I. Williamson, *Heidelberg*, 84.
53. Hendriksen, *Ephesians*, 193.
54. G. I. Williamson, *Heidelberg*, 84.
55. Von Balthasar, *Credo*, 64.

the human being who is in heaven; it is the very humanity which we share with him which is there.

While it is true, as McGrath says, that the ascension confirms Jesus' unique status,[56] it is equally true that "our flesh, our human nature is exalted in him to God,"[57] and therefore his uniqueness as an exalted man is provisional and temporary. He is unique in his status as a glorified man for now, for the time being, but his achievement of that status contains a promise: it assures us that we shall finally be like him and be with him. Calvin expresses it powerfully: "By his ascent into heaven he opened for us the entry into the kingdom of heaven that had been closed to all in Adam. Indeed, he entered heaven in our flesh as in our name, that already in him we may possess heaven through hope, and hereafter may sit, so to speak, among the heavenly ones."[58] That is why Docetism is such a serious heresy. It renders it impossible for the Savior to make common cause with us, and so destroys our hope of participation at last in what he enjoys already.

For that is the joy of his ascension. His arrival in heaven is the pledge to us that our ultimate future is not to be defined by those trials and sufferings and sorrows and perplexities of this present world. We are destined for glory. It is not merely that our mortality is overcome: Christ's resurrection achieved that for us. His ascension promises us that we shall live forever in a condition that infinitely surpasses the frustrating, painful, tearful reality of life on earth as we know it in this present time.

Let the Collect for the Sunday after Ascension Day sum things up:

> O God, the King of glory, you have exalted your only Son Jesus Christ with great triumph to your kingdom in heaven: Do not leave us comfortless, but send us your Holy Spirit to strengthen us, and exalt us to that place where our Savior Christ has gone before; who lives and reigns with you and the Holy Spirit, one God, in glory everlasting. *Amen.*[59]

---

56. McGrath, *I Believe*, 75.
57. Barth, *Dogmatics*, 125.
58. Calvin, *Catechism, 1538*, 20.v, 24.
59. *Book of Common Prayer*, The Collect for the Seventh Sunday of Easter: The Sunday after Ascension Day, 226.

13

And sat down at the right hand of God the Father almighty

THERE IS SOME DISPUTE about the actual wording of this part of the Apostles' Creed. Are we being informed that Jesus Christ "sat down" at the Father's right hand—a past event, or that he "sits" there—a present state? Karl Barth makes much of the transition from the series of perfect tenses ("He was conceived ... born ... suffered ... crucified ... buried ... descended ... rose ... ascended") to the present tense, "he sits at the right hand of God." For Barth this signals the passage from the time of revelation to a new time, to our time.[1] On the other hand, Christopher Stead insists that the proper wording is "he sat down," and that this phrase terminates the description of the Son's earthly experience, which is central to the creed.[2]

It is true that the received text of the creed reads *sedet*—the present tense.[3] On the other hand, in one of the Greek texts which lie behind the Latin version Hippolytus uses the aorist, *kathisanta*.[4] It is probably neither possible nor necessary to try to resolve the question as to which is "correct." The most that can be said is that examples of both tenses are found in the course of the creed's development. This reflects the New Testament evidence, where present tenses, *kathēmenon*, *kathēmenos*, or *kathou* occur nine times (Matt. 22:44; 26:64; Mark 12:36; 14:62; Luke 20:42; 22:69; Acts 2:34; Col. 3:1; Heb. 1:13) and the aorist, *ekathisen*, six times (Mark 16:19; Eph. 1:20; Heb. 1:3; 8:1; 10:12; 12:2).

---

1. Barth, *Dogmatics*, 124–25.
2. Stead, "Apostles' Creed," 6.
3. Kelly, *Creeds*, 369.
4. Kelly, *Creeds*, 91.

In the end, the matter is not particularly significant, because, even where the past tense draws attention to the event of our Lord's arrival at the Father's right hand, the clear understanding is that, consequent upon the event was a continuing state of seatedness.

These words belong very closely with the creed's previous phrase. The ascension and the heavenly session are intimately related. If the sitting down is regarded as an event, it is the second of a pair of events, the ascension being Jesus' departure from earth, and the sitting down the end of his journey to heaven. Even if the emphasis is placed on the heavenly session as an ongoing activity, it is still the resultant state of which the ascension was the beginning.

CHRIST'S HEAVENLY SESSION DECLARES THE COMPLETION OF HIS EARTHLY TASK

After a hard day's work it is a pleasant experience to sit down and relax. To be free to sit down is to be able to say that the work is done. Although, it would be wrong to press the illustration in terms of relaxation, there are three New Testament texts, all from the book of Hebrews, which seem to link our Lord's session at God's right hand with the completion of his work on earth.

Hebrews 12:2 reads, "Jesus ... for the joy that was set before him endured the cross, despising the shame, and has sat down at the right hand of the throne of God." This simply presents the cross and the session sequentially. The work on earth was finished, and the session in heaven ensues. However, Hebrews 1:3 says, "when he had by himself purged our sins, [he] sat down at the right hand of the Majesty on high," and in Hebrews 10:12 we read, "this man, after he had offered one sacrifice for sins forever, sat down at the right hand of God." In these two verses the connection between the sacrifice of the cross and the heavenly session is portrayed consequentially: it is because his sacrifice for sins was successful as an act of purgation that Christ was entitled to take up his seated position beside the throne of divine majesty. His work on earth is not merely finished; it is accomplished. "The glorious place which our once humiliated Savior has been accorded, supplies conclusive evidence of the value and finality of his redemptive work."[5]

---

5. Pink, *Hebrews*, 566.

Leon Morris describes Christ's posture of sitting at God's right hand as "a way of saying that Christ's saving work is done."[6] He draws the contrast between Jesus' posture and that of the Levitical priests: the latter "stand, for their work is not done but goes on. Christ sits, for his work is done. Sitting is the posture of rest, not of work. That Christ is seated means that his atoning work is complete, there is nothing to be added to it."[7] Or, as Lloyd-Jones puts it: "Sitting down is a sign of finality; it means that nothing further needs to be done concerning our sins. He has done everything."[8]

And that, of course, means that our salvation is eternally secure. As we place our total confidence in the finished work of Christ, we are assured that nothing can ever separate us from God's love in Jesus Christ. Christ "is even at the right hand of God" (Rom. 8:34), and that guarantees that God is for us, such that nothing and no one in hell, earth, or heaven can ever effectively oppose us. John Murray rightly explains Paul's point here: "The apostle's appeal to the exalted glory, authority, and dominion is related directly to the assurance of the security belonging to the elect of God. Since he has all authority in heaven and in earth, no adverse circumstance or hostile power can wrench his people from his hand or separate from his love."[9]

However, the fact that Jesus sat down at God's right hand because his work on earth was completed does not mean that ever since he has been sitting there doing nothing. My earlier reference to relaxation is the point at which the analogy breaks down. The rest in view in Morris's words is specifically rest from the work of obtaining eternal salvation for his people by his death, not rest from all conceivable activity.

CHRIST'S HEAVENLY SESSION INDICATES HIS CONTINUOUS ACTIVITY

One of our hymns opens and closes with words which address our Lord Jesus Christ as "Head of the church, and Lord of all."[10] This phrase neatly

---

6. Morris, *Hebrews*, on Heb. 1:3.
7. Morris, *Hebrews*, on Heb. 10:12; see also Hewitt, *Hebrews*, 158; Kistemaker, *Hebrews*, 281.
8. Lloyd-Jones, *Romans*, 430.
9. J. Murray, *Romans*, Vol. 1, 329.
10. *Head of the Church and Lord of all*, by Joseph Tritton (1819–87).

expresses the two aspects into which Christ's continuing ministry in heaven may be analyzed.

Christ's work as Head of the Church

The Heidelberg Catechism declares: "Christ ascended into heaven for this end, that he might appear there as head of his church."[11] Hebrews 8:1 connects Christ's position "at the right hand of the throne of the majesty in the heavens" with his work as High Priest on our behalf. We may distinguish two elements in Christ's work in heaven as head of his church.

HE IS PREPARING A PLACE FOR US

Jesus himself stated that the purpose of his departure from this world included the task of preparing a place for his disciples (John 14:2). These words may convey a homely illustration of Jesus decorating and furnishing the apartments in his Father's eternal home, and stocking up the larder, so that when his wider family eventually join him there they find that ample provision has been made for their needs and their comfort.

Both Witsius and Cranfield link this with the description of Jesus as "the forerunner" (Heb. 6:20).[12] Jesus is portrayed as the representative human being taking up residence in heaven in order to book an area where all his people can be together around him for all eternity.

However, it is pertinent to note the use of the same word "go" (*poreuomai*) in Luke 22:22, where it alludes to Christ's death. Jesus' route to the Father's right hand went by way of the cross. In his dying he prepared our place. Until the accomplishment of redemption at Calvary, heaven's doors were securely locked, barred and chained against the whole of sinful humanity.

> He only could unlock the gate
> Of heaven, and let us in.[13]

Jesus' death turned the key in the lock. The work of the cross severed the bars and broke the chain. Then Jesus sat down in heaven and so claimed the right of admission for all his people.

---

11. *Heidelberg Catechism*, Q. 50.
12. Witsius, *Creed*, Vol. 2, 232; Cranfield, *Creed*, 48.
13. From the hymn, *There is a green hill far away*, by Cecil Frances Alexander (1818–95).

This aspect of Jesus' work on our behalf is summed up beautifully by the seventeenth-century Scottish preacher George Hutcheson:

> As Christ by his death did purchase a right and title to heaven for saints, so by his ascension into heaven he prosecutes and applies that right; for in his ascension he is declared righteous and acquitted in our name. . . . As harbingers go before to prepare rooms for those who are to follow after, so he ascended as a common person to take possession in our name.[14]

He is protecting us

As our exalted head, the Lord Jesus Christ "defends and preserves us against all enemies."[15] By his protection he preserves his church "safe from all harm."[16] Two aspects of this work may be distinguished, for there are two categories of harmful enemy from which we need his protection: we need to be defended against our own corruption and the wrath of God which it attracts; we also need to be defended against the devil's attempts to undermine us spiritually. Correspondingly, Jesus serves in heaven as our advocate and our intercessor.

As our Advocate

The Heidelberg Catechism calls Jesus Christ "our Advocate in the presence of his Father in heaven."[17] The description comes from 1 John 2:1: "if anyone sins, we have an advocate with the Father, Jesus Christ the righteous." "We have nothing that we can plead before God to gain us forgiveness for our sins, but Jesus Christ acts as our advocate and enters his plea for us."[18]

The setting of this imagery is the law court.[19] Jesus is the counsel for the defence. When we sin, he counteracts the accusations and insinuations of the devil by reminding his Father that the sentence due to us has already been served (in his death on the cross), and that we may therefore legitimately be acquitted and released. To put it like that must not be construed as meaning that the Father would forget that he

---

14. Hutcheson, *John*, 293.
15. *Heidelberg Catechism*, Q. 51.
16. Calvin, *Institutes*, 2.16.16.
17. *Heidelberg Catechism*, Q. 49.
18. Marshall, *Epistles of John*, 116.
19. Smalley, *1, 2, 3 John*, on 1 John 2:1.

could forgive us if Jesus was not there to jog his memory. We are dealing here with picture language. It is, of course, the case that the Father has appointed Jesus as our advocate. The picture is a vivid way of repeating what the apostle has said a couple of verses earlier, that God "is faithful and just to forgive us our sins" (1 John 1:9)—faithful in the first instance to his Son, who has carried our guilt and paid the penalty in our name. Hesselink refers to Calvin's powerful account of how Christ "fills with grace and kindness the throne that for miserable sinners would otherwise have been filled with dread."[20]

There is perhaps another reference to Jesus' heavenly work as our advocate, although that particular word is not used, in Hebrews 2:17, which describes his work as "a merciful and faithful High Priest" as being "to make propitiation for the sins of the people."

Most commentators appear to assume, even if they do not explicitly say so, that the locus of Christ's propitiation in Hebrews 2:17 is the cross. Connected with this assumption is the view, represented by F. F. Bruce that the reason why Jesus is called "high priest" in Hebrews, and not merely "priest" is because the author "views his redemptive work as the antitypical fulfilment of the sacrificial ritual of the day of atonement, where the high priest in person was required to officiate."[21] Similarly, Barnes notes that "the Jewish high-priest was the successor of Aaron," and refers to the privilege that was his alone of entering the most holy place on the annual Day of Atonement. "The Lord Jesus," Barnes continues, "became in the Christian dispensation what the Jewish high-priest was in the old."[22]

However, I am not convinced that Bruce and Barnes are right. There are two reasons why I am doubtful.

First, throughout its account of the ritual requirements of the Day of Atonement, the Septuagint uses, not the verb *hilaskomai*, used here, but its compound form *exilaskomai*. It seems likely that the writer of Hebrews, had he wished at this point to call to mind that ceremony, would have chosen to use the compound verb.

Second, the word used by our author to describe the Lord (*archiereus*) does not occur in the Septuagint, although we know from the Gospels and Acts that it was the title given to the High Priest (though

---

20. Hesselink, *Catechism*, 126–27.
21. F. F. Bruce, *Hebrews*, 52, n. 85.
22. Barnes, *New Testament*, Vol. 9, 74–75.

not uniquely to him[23]) in the days of our Lord's earthly life and of the primitive Church. In the Septuagint the High Priest is generally called *ho hiereus ho megas*,[24] and occasionally *ho hiereus ho prōtos*.[25] Even Aaron was not actually denominated "High Priest." He was known simply as "Aaron the priest."[26] Even though the term *archiereus* was current at the time when Hebrews was written, it seems more likely, given the author's care in building up his argument from the Old Testament, as familiar to him in the Greek version, that, had he intended to portray Jesus as the true successor of Aaron, he would have used a Biblical term.

Two verses later the writer describes Jesus as "the Apostle and High Priest of our confession" (Heb. 3:1). The following verses go on to make a comparison between Jesus and Moses; Aaron does not figure in the argument at all at this stage. Perhaps, then, Peake is right to propose that the writer saw Moses as both apostle and high-priest under the Old Covenant, the high-priestly function having been delegated by him to Aaron.[27] It has been pointed out that Philo saw Moses as fulfilling the dual role of prophet and priest,[28] which means that this need not have been a totally novel idea amongst the addressees of Hebrews. Moreover, the whole point of the argument later in the Epistle is that Jesus is precisely not a priest after the order of Aaron (7:11); the one point of comparison between the two is only the general one that every high priest is called by God, a truth which applies equally to Aaron and Jesus (5:4). However, no sooner is that fairly obvious point made, than the writer distances Jesus from Aaron by introducing the concept of a priesthood after a different order—that of Melchizedek—as the true type of that of Christ. Perhaps he also saw Moses as having stood in that order, and therefore the fact that Moses was not in the Aaronic priesthood in no way affects his argument. Furthermore, that Christ's High Priesthood has present relevance and is part of his post-ascension heavenly work, may be deduced also from Hebrews 6:20 and 9:24–25.

---

23. See (e.g.) Matt. 26:3; Mark 14:53.

24. Lev. 21:10; 2 Kgs. 12:10; 22:4, 8; 23:4; 2 Chr. 24:11; 34:9; Neh. 3:1, 20; 13:28; Hag. 1:1, 12, 14; 2:2, 4. Zech. 3:1, 8; 6:11.

25. 2 Kgs. 25:18; Ezra 7:5; Jer. 52:24.

26. E.g. Exod. 39:41.

27. Peake, *Hebrews*, 114.

28. F. F. Bruce, *Hebrews*, 55, n. 7.

If these observations are pertinent, then I would suggest that the key to understanding the concept of propitiation in Hebrews 2:17 is Moses' pleading with the Lord in Exodus 32. Apparently, what turned away the anger of God with its concomitant death-threat was Moses' advocatory prayer. The Lord was propitiated by the prayer.

Similarly, for the author of Hebrews, propitiation is what the Lord Jesus is doing now in heaven on behalf of his people: he turns away the anger of God from them through his ministry of advocatory prayer as the antitype of Moses, the Old Testament advocate-priest.

These considerations suggest that we are not necessarily right to assume that Hebrews 2:17 is asserting the truth that Christ achieved propitiation on the cross, although that truth is not in dispute. According to our verse, Christ's propitiation is also his continuing ministry as his people's advocate.

Additional support for this view can be found in the fact, noted by some commentators, that the form of the verb in this context, *ilaskesthai*, is the present infinitive. Westcott interprets this to signify that "the one (eternal) act of Christ . . . is here regarded in its continuous present application to men."[29] Now undoubtedly Christ's work as advocate is rooted in his sacrifice, and his sacrifice was propitiatory. However, the author of Hebrews seems to be saying rather more than only that the advocacy is the application of the sacrifice of the cross. The word *ilaskomai* seems to have been selected in order to denote the advocacy as being in itself propitiatory. That is to say, perpetually as Christ sits at God's right hand as advocate for his people, the anger of God which threatens with destruction even Christ's own people is being daily turned away. This is indeed because of what Christ did on the cross, but more: it is an act of propitiation in its very exercise. Peake is, I think, correct to say: "The tense suggests a continual process, not an act performed once for all."[30]

Neither is this to overlook the fact that in Hebrews much is made of the once-for-all nature of Christ's sacrifice; it is simply to assert that that is not the point which is being made in this particular verse. The overwhelming balance of the evidence lends support to the theory that it is the present heavenly ministry of Christ as advocate for his people by which he is exercising a propitiatory ministry towards God because of their sins. Perhaps it may be expressed like this: undoubtedly, the form

29. Westcott, *Hebrews*, 57.
30. Peake, *Hebrews*, 111.

which Christ's advocacy takes is that he applies the work of the cross, he pleads the merits of his blood by which his people's sins are purged; as he does so he continues to protect them from the wrath of God and to render God favorable to them. It is not merely that the advocacy is the application of propitiation, but that the advocatory application of the blood is the work of propitiation.

Louis Praamsma finds an illustration of Jesus' advocacy in Zechariah 3:1–5.[31] Joshua, "clothed with filthy garments," is being opposed and accused by Satan. However, the LORD rebukes Satan, proclaims to Joshua, "I have removed your iniquity from you," and reclothes him in rich robes. It is interesting to note that Satan is seen standing at Joshua's right hand—"the place of accusation under the law,"[32] just as the place of defence, the position of our defender, is found at the right hand of God.

Although Jesus' work as our advocate takes place in heaven and before God his Father, it does nevertheless hold immense consolation and assurance for us. F. B. Meyer brings this out when he describes the LORD's advocacy on Joshua's behalf as "spontaneous and unsought." Meyer continues: "Before Joshua had time to say, 'Shelter me,' his faithful Friend and Advocate had cast around him the assurance of his protection, and had silenced the adversary."[33]

As our Intercessor

While Christ's work as advocate and his role as intercessor are often effectively equated, it is probably better to keep them distinct. John Brown acknowledges that "some would understand the words "make intercession" as just equivalent to "interpose favorably in their behalf." He, however, believes that a larger meaning is in view: Jesus is praying to God on our behalf.[34] We may express the distinction between advocacy and intercession like this: as our advocate Jesus pleads our case before God in the face of our own sin and the devil's consequent accusations; as intercessor he pleads for the Father's protection for us in the face of the devil's attempts to defeat us, whether by using external adverse circumstances, or by tempting us internally.

---

31. Praamsma, *Before the Face*, 74.
32. K. L. Barker, *Zechariah*, on Zech. 3:1.
33. Meyer, *Prophet of Hope*, 41.
34. Brown, *Hebrews*, 352.

There are just two references in the New Testament to our Lord's intercessory ministry as he sits at the Father's right hand. Hebrews 7:25 says that Jesus "ever lives to make intercession" for his people, and Romans 8:34 tells us that Christ "makes intercession for us."

Those who distinguish Christ's intercessory ministry from his work as advocate see the intercession as his permanent prayer for the Father's blessing, so that in all the struggles and battles of the Christian life we are preserved from falling: "he intercedes for us at the throne of grace, whatever our need may be."[35] It is "for his struggling people on earth"[36] that Christ intercedes.

Bruce points to the way in which Jesus used to pray for his followers during his incarnate life. He refers to the Lord's words to Peter, "I have prayed for you, that your faith should not fail" (Luke 22:32), and concludes: "if it be asked what form his heavenly intercession takes, what better answer can be given than that he still does for his people at the right hand of God what he did for Peter on earth?"[37]

Andrew Murray makes the same link with the Savior's prayer for Peter: "he prayed for Peter that his faith might not fail. Because his work of intercession never pauses or ceases, our faith and our experience of the power of that intercession need never fail."[38]

Commenting on the Hebrews text, Pink notes that believers "are still left here in the Enemy's country." Consequently, there is constant opposition to the work of completing our salvation. That is why we need Christ's intercession, in response to which the Father sends us the Spirit, renews to us daily grace, delivers us from our foes, and so keeps us to the end.[39] As Kistemaker notes, in answer to Jesus' prayers for our preservation and protection, "God grants us everything we need for the furtherance of his name, his kingdom, and his will."[40]

In Romans the words regarding Jesus' intercession lead into a catalog of experiences which are potentially spiritually destructive. The apostle mentions tribulation, distress, persecution, famine, nakedness, peril, and sword (Rom. 8:35). These are things which might threaten

---

35. E. F. Harrison, *Romans*, on Rom. 8:31–36.
36. Sanday and Headlam, *Romans*, 221.
37. F. F. Bruce, *Hebrews*, 154–55.
38. A. Murray, *Holiest*, 253.
39. Pink, *Hebrews*, 418.
40. Kistemaker, *Hebrews*, 204.

the believer's security. However, Paul is able to write: "I am persuaded that neither death nor life, nor angels nor principalities nor powers, nor things present nor things to come, nor height nor depth, nor any other created thing, shall be able to separate us from the love of God which is in Christ Jesus our Lord" (Rom 8:38–39). The reason for this confidence is that our Savior is interceding for us.

In the course of our Christian lives we all face different challenges. Some of us are vulnerable to certain temptations which have no attraction to others. They, however, feel their acute weakness when other temptations come which pass us by. How good, then, to believe that John Murray is right to speak of "the particularity of concern and provision" in the Savior's intercession: "intercession must have regard to the distinctive situation of each individual."[41]

In John 17 we have an account of what is often termed Christ's "High Priestly Prayer," implying that its content is the pattern for his ongoing intercessory ministry as he is now seated in heaven.[42] Beasley-Murray traces the title "High Priestly Prayer" to a Lutheran theologian of the sixteenth century, David Chytraeus,[43] though Lindars claims that it goes back as far as Cyril of Alexandria,[44] a fifth-century writer. Leon Morris notes C. K. Barrett's objection to the imposition of this title on the grounds that it "does not do justice to the full range of material contained in it." Morris replies sagely: "everything I suppose depends on what range one would expect to find in a 'high priestly prayer.'"[45] While it would be foolish to overemphasise the title, as the Scriptures do not themselves use it, if our understanding of the distinction between advocacy and intercession is valid, then the range of content in this prayer is indeed just what one would expect to find in Jesus' ministry at the Father's right hand. "As he then interceded, so now he intercedes 'ever living.'"[46]

Jesus prays that his people may be kept from the evil one while they remain in the world (John 17:11, 15), that they may be sanctified by the truth (John 17:17), that his church may be characterized by evangelistically powerful unity (John 17:21 [cf. v. 11]), and that ultimately they may be with him to behold his glory (John 17:24).

41. J. Murray, *Romans*, Vol. 1, 330.
42. See Hutcheson, *John*, 351.
43. Beasley-Murray, *John*, on John 17, Form/Structure/Setting, para. 2.
44. Lindars, *John*, 516.
45. Morris, *John*, 716.
46. Moule, *High Priestly Prayer*, 220.

These themes may well indicate the concerns of our Lord's ministry at the Father's right hand. For the present, we remain on earth with a gospel mandate and a moral challenge. The evil one will try incessantly to frustrate our evangelistic efforts, either by dulling our own gospel ambition or by stirring up persecution against the message. Alternatively, the evil one may sow the seeds of error within the church so that the evangelistic message gets lost, or he will spread division so that the message loses credibility in the eyes of the world. He will also target the individual Christian, seeking to inculcate a lax attitude which militates against growth in holiness. However, in the face of this fierce opposition the Lord prays for his people, and the result is that, whatever our weaknesses, individually or corporately, along the way, we shall be preserved to see him in glory at the last.

In addition to this great exemplar of Christ's intercession, we have in his earthly ministry also a beautiful illustration of his prayer on our behalf in an incident reported by both Matthew and Mark.

The disciples are in a boat on the sea when a strong head wind gets up, and they find themselves tossed by the waves. It is the small hours of the morning, and in the darkness they are straining hard to row. All of a sudden they see a misty figure appearing through the murky darkness walking on top of the water. Their first reaction is to assume that it is a ghost. However, Jesus quickly identifies himself, quietens their fear, and calms the wind. Significantly, immediately prior to this incident we read that Jesus is alone on a mountain praying (Matt. 14:23–27, 32; Mark 6:46–51).

Here is a telling picture of our situation in the world today. Sometimes we feel that we have to labor for the Lord in an atmosphere of intense moral darkness. It is a strain to be a believer in this world. We seem to be tossed about, and it is so hard to make any headway. But from the mountainous vantage point of his heavenly seat, our Lord sees absolutely everything that is happening to absolutely every one of his dear people. He is praying for you. In answer to his prayers, he comes to us by his Spirit. Our fears can be quieted. The storm is stilled.

Christ's work as Lord of all

The parallelism in Psalm 110:1–2 makes it clear that to sit at the Lord's right hand is to rule. When the Apostles' Creed states that Jesus Christ "sat down at the right hand of God the Father almighty" there is clearly an intentional echo of the opening clause of the creed, where we affirmed our belief in just such a God as "the Father almighty." We saw there that God's almightiness means his rule over everything. To say that the man Christ Jesus sat down at the right hand of the God who rules over everything is to declare that the sovereign, universal rule of God the Father has been delegated to his Son. It is to make the stupendous claim that the one who exercises universal sovereignty in the world today is a man like us, but more specifically, the man who is our loving Savior, our committed friend.

Karl Barth brings out the force of this with characteristic insight:

> There is no divine almightiness without Jesus Christ. To declare that God governs the world amounts to saying: Jesus Christ governs the world. The power revealed in the reconciliation of the cross, in the forgiveness of sins, in the act of divine justice and mercy, is identical with the power of the *God Almighty* over the whole world, mentioned significantly at this point of the creed. Here we see concretely how the first article (on God the Father and on creation) must be understood. Here we are shown God's power in its exact and concrete manifestation: Christ's power.[47]

What this means is that the goal and direction of the exercise of divine rule in this world in the present age, as in every age, is the glorification of Christ, the Savior, along with the people whom he has redeemed. God's right hand man is the Savior of the world: the salvation of the world is therefore God's ultimate priority. In exercising universal sovereignty, the overriding ambition of the triune God is to save lost and sinful humanity. It means also that universal sovereignty is personal and merciful. It is indeed embodied in this particular person, Jesus Christ.

In this connection it is instructive to note the frequency of references in the Old Testament to the Lord's right hand. The first occurs in Exodus 15:6. The deliverance of Israel through the Red Sea represents the glorious power of the Lord's right hand which has destroyed his and Israel's enemy. It was the Lord's right hand which was stretched out to cause the waters to overflow the pursuing Egyptian army (Exod. 15:12). The association between the Lord's right hand and the deliverance or salvation of his people is common in the Psalms.[48] And the close connection between the saving strength of the Lord's right hand and his

---

47. Barth, *Faith*, 109.

48. Pss. 18:35; 20:6; 44:3; 60:5; 74:11–12; 77:10; 78:54; 98:1; 108:6; 118:14–16; 138:7 (cf. Ps. 63:8).

tender mercy, his marvellous lovingkindness, is clear.[49] Consequently, his right hand is the place of eternal pleasure (Ps. 16:11).

And now that right hand of saving power and astonishing mercy is identified with Jesus Christ. In all the saving works of the Lord towards Israel, executed in mercy, we see our Lord and Savior prefigured, and indeed, already at work, in the interests of his chosen people. We see Jesus ruling in mercy, bringing salvation to his world.

This fulfilment of the Lord's right hand power in Jesus Christ is prophesied most directly in Psalm 80:17. This Psalm laments the parlous condition to which the Lord's people are reduced. They are the vineyard which God's right hand had planted, and yet the vineyard is burned down, the people perish (v. 15–16). In response to this tragic situation the Psalmist utters the plea, "Let your hand be upon the man of your right hand, upon the son of man whom you made strong for yourself."

Anderson admits that there was a Messianic understanding of these words in ancient Israel, though he himself thinks it an improbable interpretation.[50] Derek Kidner rightly notes that "the context points to Israel in the first place," but suggests that it is not here, but in other Old Testament passages, that we find Israel's calling focussed in a single individual "son of man."[51]

However, given that, ultimately, all Scripture is messianic, and that Jesus could expound "in all the Scriptures the things concerning himself" (Luke 24:27), I think that Matthew Henry shows deeper insight. He too acknowledges the initial reference to the king of Israel contemporary with the Psalmist, but then adds, with approval, "But many interpreters, both Jewish and Christian, apply this to the Messiah."[52] Spurgeon agrees: "There is no doubt here," he says, "an outlook to the Messiah;" he goes on:

> It is by the man Christ Jesus that fallen Israel is yet to rise, and indeed through him, who deigns to call himself the *Son of Man*, the world is to be delivered from the dominion of Satan and the curse of sin. O Lord, fulfil thy promise to the man of thy right hand, who participates in thy glory, and give him to see the pleasure of the Lord prospering in his hand.[53]

---

49. Pss. 17:7; 48:9–10; 89:13–14.
50. Anderson, *Psalms*, 586.
51. Kidner, *Psalms*, 292.
52. Henry, *Commentary*, 665; see also Plumer, *Psalms*, 771; van Gemeren, *Psalms*, on Ps. 80:14b–19.
53. Spurgeon, *Treasury of David*, Vol. 3, 391.

And it is when God's pleasure prospers in Christ seated at his right hand that those eternal pleasures come to sinners who are saved by the Lord's infinite mercy. His infinite mercy is that it is his pleasure to give eternal pleasure to sinful humanity.

The extent of this divine rule of love embodied in Jesus is truly universal. It embraces the whole of creation. This is nicely brought out in words of the second-century martyr, Polycarp. He says that God gave our Lord Jesus Christ a throne at his right hand, and that to him "all things in heaven and on earth are subject, [and] every breeze serves him."[54] The word which I have translated "breeze" (*pnoē*) may mean either a breath of wind, or human and animal breathing. It can denote the gentlest movement of air,[55] and can also speak of a fragrance wafted on the breeze.[56] Jesus Christ is Lord, not only of the big things, not only of the large, sturdy, magnificent elements of creation. His Lordship reaches down to the tiniest and gentlest of created realities.

On the other hand *pnoē* is used in the New Testament of the "rushing mighty wind" of Pentecost (Acts 2:2). In the Septuagint, although, it generally represents the unobtrusive gentleness of breath, in Ezekiel 13:13 it describes the bursting forth of a sweeping blast. Viewed from this side, we may say that Jesus Christ as Lord is in control even of those elements of creation which are too big for our mastery here on earth. Exalted to the Father's right hand, this man has acquired the power to rule invincibly.

In Jesus' ascension to God's right hand we see, in principle already, the restoration of human dominion over the works of the Creator's hands, so sadly distorted by the fall. Psalm 8:6 praises the Lord for the creation of humankind in these words: "You have made him to have dominion over the works of your hands; you have put all things under his feet."

The writer to the Hebrews sees Christological significance in these words. He quotes Psalm 8:4–6, and then comments: "in that he put all in subjection under him, he left nothing that is not put under him. But now we do not yet see all things put under him. But we see Jesus" (Heb. 2:8b–9a). The implication is that the real fulfilment of this celebration of human dominion can be found only in Jesus Christ, and now awaits its final eschatological consummation in "the world to come" (Heb. 2:5).

---

54. Polycarp, *Philippians*, 2.1.
55. So *Online Bible Greek Lexicon*, 5923.
56. Liddell and Scott, *Lexicon*, 567.

Calvin admits that, at first, the Psalm "seems to be unfitly applied to Christ," since it speaks of the dominion bestowed upon mankind. However, as soon as Adam alienated himself from God through sin, he was deprived of this rule, and thus must "the right lost in Adam be restored in Christ." Calvin concludes: "There is, then, no doubt but that we are to look to him whenever the dominion of man over all creatures is spoken of."[57] Similarly, F. F. Bruce argues that "it is as the true representative of humanity that Christ is viewed as fulfilling the language of the Psalm, and as fulfilling therewith the declared purpose of the Creator when he brought man into being."[58]

In Christ the universal sovereignty of the God of mercy is a reality, but it is in him as the representative of the whole human race that this is so. Our destiny, therefore, is to participate in God's universal sovereignty in partnership with him in his Son.

And this rule over all things includes very specifically dominion over the spiritual forces of wickedness. The heavenly session is the proclamation of "Christ's victory over the powers of hell."[59] Rufinus compares Jesus' entry into heaven to a conqueror returning from battle to the acclaim of trumpets.[60] Thus, Jesus "assumed the government at the Father's right hand, so that the devil and all powers might be subject to him and lie at his feet."[61] Paul explains it in these words: the Father seated Christ "at his right hand in the heavenly places, far above all principality and power and might and dominion, and every name that is named, not only in this age but also in that which is to come" (Eph. 1:20–21). No doubt these words may include within their scope benign powers,[62] but they certainly do not exclude evil forces, and hostile beings.[63] The same is true of 1 Peter 3:22, where the "angels and authorities and powers" which have been made subject to Christ must include "every power, whether

---

57. Calvin, *Hebrews*, 56–58.
58. F. F. Bruce, *Hebrews*, 36.
59. Hesselink, *Catechism*, 127.
60. Rufinus, *Commentary*, para. 31, 1122.
61. Luther, *Larger Catechism*, 61.
62. *Pace* Stott, *God's New Society*, 60.
63. See Lincoln, *Ephesians*, on Eph. 1:20, 21.

good or evil, in the universe."⁶⁴ Truly, our Savior has been "invested with universal dominion."⁶⁵

The Savior's Lordship over the powers of evil means that we have nothing to fear from the powers of evil even as they continue to manifest themselves in this world, and, apparently to dominate. Whether it be the demonic forces of Islam, or of political correctness, we have nothing to fear. Whether it be the way that the name "Christian" or even "Evangelical" is hijacked by the American government in order to try to neutralize the witness of the church, or whether it be the way that Christianity in general and Evangelicalism in particular is marginalized, castigated, and ridiculed by the British government in an attempt to destroy its credibility and negate its influence, we have nothing to fear. Let the powers that be do as they will, Jesus Christ is Lord of all, and that's that, and nothing can ever change that.

Indeed, the universal rule of Christ embraces all humankind also. This follows from his representative position as the true human being. Karl Barth rightly says that "every man is under the dominion of Christ, whether he knows it or does not know it." He defines the difference between the church and the world like this: "in the church the Lord of the world is acknowledged and confessed, whereas in the world he is still ignored. But," Barth continues, "the same Lord rules over both."⁶⁶ In this sense, the Lordship of Jesus is, as Packer puts it, "a cosmic fact."⁶⁷

It is this truth which validates the church's gospel mission. Just prior to his ascension the Lord entrusted his disciples with this evangelistic mandate: "All authority has been given to me in heaven and on earth. Go therefore and make disciples of all the nations" (Matt. 28:18–19). As their Lord departs, the apostles remember this, spurred on by the angelic challenge quoted in Acts 1:11, "why do you stand gazing up into heaven?" "They don't remain standing, rooted to the spot, completely overwhelmed by the fact that Jesus has returned to heaven. Their thoughts return immediately to earth—for there is work to be done."⁶⁸ As Mark puts it, the Lord "sat down at the right hand of God, and they went out and preached everywhere" (Mark 16:19–20).

64. Michaels, *1 Peter*, on 1 Pet. 3:22.
65. Hodge, *Romans*, 290.
66. Barth, *Faith*, 111.
67. Packer, *Christian*, 55.
68. McGrath, *I Believe*, 74.

Moreover, we can pursue our evangelistic mandate with great confidence in view of Jesus' universal rule over all people, and all peoples. "The Christ is not a novelty for the pagan. Of his own Lord the pagan hears as he listens to the missionary."[69] The preaching of the gospel must succeed, because it points men and women to the reality which their very own consciences bear witness to them is the truth.

That said, we do have to face the fact that the church's gospel proclamation in this world does not always run smoothly. Hebrews 2:8 is very obviously true: "we do not yet see all things put under him." His Lordship "is still a hidden lordship in this present world."[70] It is "veiled," and there is much "that at present denies and mocks his kingship."[71] For this reason the hidden character of the rule of Christ will "show itself in the rejection which the Christian message comes up against."[72] The universal rule of God in Christ as love and mercy is not recognised by all people. Moreover, it is certainly not the case that the state of the world provides immediate and incontestable evidence of the Lordship of Jesus Christ over everything, everyone, and every place. As a result "only Christians already acknowledge it,"[73] and sometimes (perhaps we should say "quite often") Christians, too, doubt it emotionally even as they profess it theologically.

Repeatedly we ask, or at least we wonder, Why? And, as long as we live between the time of the inauguration of Christ's rule in his heavenly session and the time of its consummation when the kingdom comes in its fullness, we have to live in hope of that complete unveiling of the rule of God the Father almighty in Jesus Christ his Son, our Lord, at the end.

Meanwhile, the fact that he is seated at the right hand of the Father "gives us a new perspective on the chores of everyday life. It sets before us a vision that keeps us going."[74] So we heed the apostolic injunction, "seek those things which are above, where Christ is, sitting at the right hand of God" (Col. 3:1).

---

69. Barth, *Faith*, 111.
70. Pannenberg, *Creed*, 126.
71. Cranfield, *Creed*, 47.
72. Pannenberg, *Creed*, 127.
73. Pannenberg, *Creed*, 126.
74. McGrath, *I Believe*, 83–84.

14

From there he will come to judge the living and the dead

In the text on which the doctrine of Christ's heavenly session is based, Psalm 110:1, the Lord says to his appointed king, "Sit at my right hand till I make your enemies your footstool." The word "till" sets a time limit for Jesus' seated position at the Father's right hand. "One day Jesus will rise from his place at God's right hand, and will return."[1] This *terminus ad quem* is indicated repeatedly in the New Testament. Citations of, or allusions to, the final phrase of Psalm 110:1, "till I make your enemies your footstool," occur six times,[2] and Acts 3:21 states that "heaven must receive [him] until the times of restoration of all things." This creates a close link between the Lord's present position in heaven and his future coming, a link which Jesus himself makes in Matthew 26:64 and the parallel passage, Mark 14:62. He is seated there pending the moment for his return to earth.

In the course of Christian history, not least in recent times, there has been much quite unhelpful speculation about the return of Christ. The sensationalism of a writer like Hal Lindsey[3] threatens to bring the doctrine of the second coming of Christ into disrepute.

In contrast to all tendencies towards speculative sensation, the Apostles' Creed, in restrained language, focusses not so much on the second coming itself as on its purpose.[4] "He will come"—but to what end? That is the concern of the creed, and the answer is clear: "to judge the living and the dead."

1. Praamsma, *Before the Face*, 78.
2. Matt. 22:44; Mark 12:36; Acts 2:35; 1 Cor. 15:25; Heb. 1:13; 10:13.
3. Lindsey, *Late Great Planet*.
4. Cf. McGiffert, *Creed*, 43.

We must take our lead from the creed. We should be less concerned with attempts to work out God's prophetic programme, to discern the eschatological timetable, than with heeding the challenge and comfort of God's ultimate purpose in our present history. Debate around the millennium and related issues is perhaps of some interest. Discussion of conflicting theories may have its time and place. However, the creed sets such arguments firmly in their place—in second place. The exact conclusions which we reach on eschatological matters, views on which we differ, do not feature in a summary of the basics and essentials of the Christian faith. There is to be a last day, and it will be the day of judgment. Judgment is "the last act of the reign of Christ, the brightest manifestation of the divine glory."[5] That is what is important.

Our first reaction on hearing of judgment may well be to feel threatened. The English word "judgment" carries a legal connotation. It conveys the idea of a sentence, of retribution. We need, then, to pay attention to Calvin's "graceful representation of the judgment."[6]

In his earlier catechism Calvin speaks of the "remarkable comfort" which comes to us from this reference to the last judgment, "because we hear that judgment has been transferred to him whose coming could be only for our salvation."[7] Even as he speaks of judgment, Calvin rejoices that the only possibility, given that the Judge is the Savior, is that salvation has to be the outcome.

Later, Calvin emphasized this point if anything even more strongly. Here are his questions and answers in his later catechism:

> Does it give any happiness to our conscience to know that Christ will one day judge the whole world?
>
> Indeed, a quite peculiar happiness. For we know that he will come for our salvation only.
>
> Then is it not proper that we should dread this judgment as though it struck terror in us?
>
> No, indeed, since we shall stand only at the tribunal of a judge who is also our advocate, and who has taken us into his faithful protection.[8]

---

5. Witsius, *Creed*, Vol. 2, 267.
6. Barth, *Faith*, 118.
7. Calvin, *Catechism, 1538*, 20.v, 24.
8. Calvin, *Catechism, 1545*, Qs. 86–87.

Calvin finds in the doctrine of the last judgment a source of intense joy, because he is confident that the outcome of the judgment can be nothing other than salvation. Further, Calvin rules out fear in the face of the final judgment as a totally inappropriate emotion. To contemplate the judgment with foreboding would be an insult to our Jesus. It would imply that we do not really believe that we are to be judged by the very one who right now sits at the Father's right hand as our advocate. To fear the judgment entails the denial that the one who will judge us is the very one who has committed himself to be our protector. He protects us now as we journey on through the years of time. He will protect us as our earthly pilgrimage reaches its end at our dying day. How can he possibly fail to remain our protector still when we stand before him as judge?

This is a marvellously encouraging vision of judgment. It is quite at odds with some popular caricatures of judgment day. It has been pointed out that in Michelangelo's painting entitled "Last Judgment" the returning Christ is portrayed with a clenched fist[9]—ready to strike the hearts of people with terror. Such a view of judgment is a far cry from the Biblical understanding of the judge as the God of stupendous, astounding, radical grace, "scandalous grace," as it has most aptly been labelled.[10]

Calvin's is truly a view of judgment driven by the conviction that the God who is judge is the God of amazing grace, the lover of our souls, the Father of mercies. Given the portrayal of God, Father and Son, in the creed up to this point, how could it be otherwise?

The God in whom I profess to believe is indeed my loving Father, the one whose whole aim and objective as the almighty, sovereign ruler in the course of the current history of his own creation is to save sinners through the conception, birth, sufferings, crucifixion, death, burial, and descent to hell of his Son, our Lord Jesus Christ. He is the God who raised Jesus from the dead, received him up in glory, and seated him at his right hand. He is the God whose mighty acts proclaim in unison that he is for us. He is the God who has committed himself passionately to us and to the cause of our salvation. How he could it be possible that Christ should suddenly turn against us at the last? The section of the creed dealing with Jesus Christ cannot but end on a note of triumphant

---

9. Barth, *Faith*, 118; *Dogmatics*, 134.

10. In the titles of two books: Bragan, *Scandalous Grace*; Barnhill, *Scandalous Grace*.

certainty, of glorious, victorious comfort, of hope and assurance, of unbounded joy!

Following Calvin, the Heidelberg Catechism asks, "What comfort is it to you that Christ shall come to judge the living and the dead?" The answer begins: "That in all my sorrows and persecutions, with uplifted head, I look for the self-same one who has before offered himself for me to the judgment of God, and removed from me all curse, to come again as Judge from heaven."[11]

The judge has already borne the judgment of this world. Therefore the judgment carries no terror, it poses no threat.

The reference in the Heidelberg Catechism to "sorrows and persecutions" points to one aspect of the joy of judgment. Our pathway through life is often hard. Difficulties and setbacks, griefs, pains and heartaches—these are the common features of human existence. What a happy thought that it shall not always be like this. There is a day coming when the wrongs of time shall be righted. Pannenberg points out that "the course of this world is marked by the prosperity of the godless, by the rule of conditions and modes of behavior which are a mockery of man's humanity, and by the suffering of the innocent."[12] Living in such a world, our hearts cry out for a judgment day when all wrongs will be righted, when all that is evil will be overthrown, when human life will be conclusively marked by justice and joy.

In this connection it is important to catch the proper Biblical flavor of the word "judgment." Karl Barth explains that "in the Biblical world of thought the judge is not primarily the one who rewards some and punishes others; he is the man who creates order and restores what has been destroyed."[13] Thus Barth can define the first consequence of judgment as "the establishment of order in the world, the public and irrefutable and victorious proclamation of the truth."[14]

A glance at the Biblical language of judgment suggests that Barth's point is well made. The New Testament verb meaning "to judge" is *krinō*. Walter Schneider finds the basic meaning of this word and its cognates in the idea of sifting.[15] The notion of punishment and condemnation is

11. *Heidelberg Catechism*, Q. 52.
12. Pannenberg, *Creed*, 121.
13. Barth, *Dogmatics*, 135.
14. Barth, *Faith*, 117.
15. Schneider, "*krima*," 362.

entirely secondary. The primary sense is a separation of what is bad from what is good so that what is good may be established securely.

In the Septuagint *krinō* vocabulary most frequently translates the Hebrew verb *šāpaṭ* and its cognate noun *mišpāṭ*. The *Theological Wordbook of the Old Testament* points out that "to judge" is a misleading translation of verb *šāpaṭ*, and that "judgment" is a defective rendering of noun *mišpāṭ*. Rather, the terms denote all the functions of governmental rule.[16] Schneider, too, notes that these Hebrew terms can be validly translated in terms of ruling, so that "he who judges brings salvation, peace and deliverance, especially to the persecuted and oppressed."[17]

This leads to a far more positive view of the judgment than our English terminology initially suggests. The primary purpose of judgment is not the legal decision against those deserving punishment, but the loving decision in favor of those to whom the Judge of all the earth has made an unbreakable covenant commitment. God's judgments "are in harmony with his faithfulness, whereby he espouses the cause of his chosen people, guides them and ensures their safety. Thus God's judgment is motivated by love, grace and mercy, and its outcome is salvation."[18]

Richard Schultz would concur with Schneider's reading of the Old Testament vocabulary. He acknowledges that verb *šāpaṭ* can sometimes refer to judgment in a narrower sense,[19] and that this may include the idea of punishment.[20] However, these are merely specific applications of a more general meaning, by which the verb "describes a range of actions that restore or preserve order in society, so that justice . . . is guaranteed."[21] Essentially, to speak of God as Judge is to affirm that he will rule the earth in righteousness, establishing justice unequivocally.[22]

These claims may be validated by reference to a few representative texts. The Psalms are rich with the positive celebration of the Lord's judgment.

---

16. *Theological Wordbook of the Old Testament*, 2443.
17. Schneider, "krima," 363.
18. Schneider, "krima," 363–64.
19. Schultz, "špṭ," 216.
20. Schultz, "špṭ," 217.
21. Schultz, "špṭ," 214.
22. Schultz, "špṭ," 216, 217.

In some of the Psalms this celebration takes on an intensely personal tone. When David prays, "Judge me, O Lord, according to my righteousness, and according to my integrity within me" (Ps. 7:8), he is appealing to the Lord to show favor. Similarly in Psalm 9:4, a Psalm replete with expressions of joy and praise, the Lord's righteous judgment is equated with his maintenance of David's right and cause. The first line of Psalm 7:9, immediately after the prayer for judgment, reads: "Oh, let the wickedness of the wicked come to an end": that is the ultimate outcome of divine judgment—the absolute, final, total end of wickedness.

In addition to these personal expressions of God's judgment, the Psalms also declare the cosmic role of the Lord as Judge.

Psalm 58:11 places side-by-side as two things of equal certainty the fact that there is a reward for the righteous and the truth that God judges in the earth: the judgment holds no terrors for the righteous—it will be the occasion when they shall reap the benefits of their love for the Lord. Psalm 67:4 sets as parallel ideas God judging the people righteously and ruling the nations on earth: to judge is to rule. Moreover, divine judgment is a cause for joyful song! According to Psalm 76:9, for God to arise to judgment involves delivering all the oppressed of the earth. Psalm 82:8 links God's judgment of the earth with his inheritance of all nations. Calvin interprets this to mean that God will "restore to order what is embroiled in confusion."[23] That will be the result of the return of Christ.

These Old Testament perspectives on divine judgment may be summed up in the words of van Gemeren: "God, the righteous Judge, will order everything on earth in accordance with his will. He does not tolerate anything that does not satisfactorily meet his requirements."[24]

When we turn to the New Testament, we find a number of texts which presuppose this larger, more positive view of judgment. Jesus once said, "Now is the judgment of this world; now the ruler of this world will be cast out" (John 12:31). Here the ejection from the world of the devil is portrayed as the judgment of the world: world government is now to be restored to its rightful Lord.

Writing to the Thessalonians Paul sees "manifest evidence of the righteous judgment of God" in their being "counted worthy of the kingdom of God" (2 Thess. 1:5). Here God's judgment is a positive decision in favor of his people. Consequently, we may face the final judgment

---

23. Calvin, *Psalms*, Vol. 3, 336.
24. Van Gemeren, *Psalms*, on Ps. 50:5–6.

with boldness and without fear, because God's perfect love has united us to Christ (1 John 4:17-18)—the very one who is to come as Judge.

The creed's statement that Christ will come to judge, therefore, means that once and for all our Lord and Savior will set the world to rights. And, as Calvin recognizes, that is definitely something to which we may look forward with joyful anticipation.

It is true that, often in our present situation, "God seems to be far from his people."[25] This final clause on the person and work of Jesus Christ assures us that, in the end, "he will come." His coming to judgment will truly be "the public vindication of God's prior decision."[26] God in Christ has made his decision in our favor. His grace has chosen us in the Savior from all eternity. He has pledged himself to be our God for ever. For now, there is a hiddenness about our privilege and standing. Even we ourselves sometimes fear and doubt and question. But in the end, "he will come." Consequently, we can live with confidence, even amid the uncertainties and sadnesses of life, even at those times when we feel abandoned and alone in the world.

The creed takes up the words of Scripture as it tells us that his coming for judgment will relate to "the living and the dead." This is a phrase which occurs three times in the New Testament. Peter told the household of Cornelius that Jesus of Nazareth "was ordained by God to be Judge of the living and the dead" (Acts 10:42). Peter again, writing his first letter, explains that Christ "is ready to judge the living and the dead" (1 Pet. 4:5), while Paul issues his charge to Timothy "before God and the Lord Jesus Christ, who will judge the living and the dead at his appearing and his kingdom" (2 Tim. 4:1).

Rufinus, rather unconvincingly, took "living and dead" to mean souls and bodies.[27] Augustine suggested, equally implausibly, that the phrase could mean just and unjust.[28] Calvin observes that "some ancient writers appear to have hesitated as to the exposition" of these words. He comments soberly that the clear and plain meaning is that "both those whom that day shall find alive, and those whom death shall previously

---

25. Hesselink, *Catechism*, 128.
26. G. I. Williamson, *Heidelberg*, 87.
27. Rufinus, *Commentary*, para. 33, 1123.
28. Augustine, *Creed*, para. 12, 699.

have removed from the society of the living" will stand before Christ when he comes as Judge.[29]

The phrase "the living and the dead" has been described as a "stereotyped expression,"[30] or a "fixed formula,"[31] which is equivalent to saying "everyone." Michaels writes: "The universality of the phrase is a universality of time: God is Lord and Judge not only over the present, but over the past as well. If 'the living and the dead' means 'each person,' it is each person who has ever lived, from the creation of the world until the day of judgment."[32]

However, it may be fair to take "the living and the dead" in a broader way than a reference to human individuals alone. Jesus will come as the Judge of every generation, including, for sure, the individual human beings from every generation, but embracing also the generational totality of culture and commerce, of art and science, of war and peace, of religion and politics. Certainly, commenting on Romans 14:9, where the terms "dead" and "living" occur in reverse order, and Jesus is declared to be Lord of both, Dunn writes: "It is the completeness of the lordship which is in view here: no condition known or imaginable to humankind escapes his rule."[33]

That day will bring to light every condition and situation which has ever arisen, stretching backwards through time to time's very commencement. No wrong which has ever taken place will remain unresolved. All the damage which has been done to God's world and to human existence within it, however far back its roots extend, will be rectified, as the government of the world reverts, obviously, to its rightful sovereign. Jesus will make an utter, full, complete, total, wonderful reconstruction of creation in its entirety. Therein lies the joy which rightly characterizes us as we anticipate the day of judgment.

When the judgment is viewed in this positive way, the prospect of Jesus' coming becomes a powerful antidote to our contemporary tendency to despair. Packer is quite correct in his observation that "in today's world, pessimism prevails because people lack hope. They foresee only the bomb, or bankruptcy, or a weary old age—nothing worth

---

29. Calvin, *Institutes*, 2.16.17.
30. Michaels, *1 Peter*, on 1 Pet. 4:5; cf. Kelly, *Peter*, 171–72.
31. Guthrie, *Pastoral Epistles*, 165; Hendriksen, *1 and 2 Timothy and Titus*, 308.
32. Michaels, *1 Peter*, on 1 Pet. 4:5.
33. Dunn, *Romans 9–16*, 808.

while."[34] However, we have a sure and certain hope, from which we derive a steadfast assurance: Jesus Christ will come again to judge—to reorder and put right—the whole of time, the entirety of creation. And then, as the hymn writer states it in eloquent poetry:

> All men shall dwell in his marvellous light,
> Races long severed his love shall unite,
> Justice and truth from his scepter shall spring,
> Wrong shall be ended when Jesus is King.
>
> All shall be well in his kingdom of peace,
> Freedom shall flourish and wisdom increase,
> Foe shall be friend when his triumph we sing,
> Sword shall be sickle when Jesus is King.
>
> *Come let us sing: Praise to our King.*[35]

---

34. Packer, *Christian*, 57.

35. From the hymn, *Sing we the King who is coming to reign*, by Charles Silvester Horne (1865–1914).

15

I believe in the Holy Spirit

"What do you believe concerning the Holy Spirit?" With that question the Heidelberg Catechism turns its attention to this clause of the Apostles' Creed.[1] Williamson points out that this is the only question in the Catechism which is completely devoted to the Holy Spirit. By contrast, the subject of the person and work of Christ occupies a whole succession of questions. This observation leads Williamson to begin his comment on this question and answer by noting that "the Heidelberg Catechism is out of step with the times."[2] What he means is that in many Christian circles today much of the emphasis seems to be on the person and work of the Holy Spirit.

A friend of mine once visited a Christian bookshop. She noticed that shelf after shelf was full of books about the Holy Spirit. She went up to the person behind the counter, and, perhaps a bit mischievously, asked, "where are your books about God the Father and God the Son?" A fascination with "the experience of the Holy Spirit"[3] has grown up, which has threatened to displace the saving purpose of God in Christ into a subordinate position, even though that is the very heart of what God is all about. When that happens, a proper concern to understand the truth about the Holy Spirit has descended into an unhealthy subjectivism.

Jim Packer indicates the imbalance in an excessive preoccupation with the Holy Spirit when he quotes Jesus' words about the Spirit from John 16:14, "he will glorify me." Packer likens the Holy Spirit to "a floodlight trained on Christ, so that it is Christ, not the Spirit, whom we see." He pictures the Holy Spirit "standing behind us as it were to throw light

---

1. *Heidelberg Catechism*, Q. 53.
2. G. I. Williamson, *Heidelberg*, 90.
3. Gumbel, *Questions*, 124.

over our shoulder on to Jesus."[4] Williamson is therefore right to say that "the Biblical way to see the full glory of the Holy Spirit is to see it—so to speak—indirectly."[5] It is impossible rightly to envisage the Spirit independently of Jesus Christ. "The Holy Spirit is the Spirit of Jesus Christ," as Barth rightly stresses.[6] He comments: "the Holy Spirit distinguishes himself from any other spirit by his absolute identity with the person and work of Christ."[7]

If the Heidelberg Catechism is out of step with our times, the same is true of the Apostles' Creed. This short phrase together with the reference to the conception of Jesus constitute the sum total of what the creed has to say about the Holy Spirit. By contrast the section devoted to Christ runs to seventy-five words.

Furthermore, Wolfhart Pannenberg has pointed out "how far our contemporary theology is from a doctrine of the Holy Spirit which corresponds to the breadth of Biblical statements about that Spirit."[8] Much contemporary concern focusses on "receiving the Spirit," being "baptized with the Spirit," and manifesting the gifts of the Spirit, with speaking in tongues often given pride of place.

Take the Alpha Course as an example. It devotes three sessions to the topic of the Holy Spirit. The first asks "Who is the Holy Spirit?" The second deals with the work of the Spirit, while the third addresses the practical question, "How can I be filled with the Spirit?" These chapters cover forty-five pages, with fifteen of them devoted to the third section.[9] By contrast, only two sessions, covering thirty-three pages,[10] address the person and work of Christ. To be sure, there is much good material in the chapters on the Holy Spirit. However, nine pages (one fifth of all the teaching on the Holy Spirit, and three fifths of the practical section) are devoted to the matter of speaking in tongues.[11] This suggests something of an imbalance. Surely glossolalia does not comprise one fifth of the

---

4. Packer, *Christian*, 62.
5. G. I. Williamson, *Heidelberg*, 91–92.
6. Barth, *Faith*, 125.
7. Barth, *Faith*, 129.
8. Pannenberg, *Creed*, 134.
9. Gumbel, *Questions*, 123–67.
10. Gumbel, *Questions*, 23–55.
11. Gumbel, *Questions*, 159–67.

totality of a Biblical doctrine of the Spirit, nor does sixty percent of a Christian's spiritual experience involve speaking in tongues.

The Old Testament account of the construction of the tabernacle brings out something of the breadth of Biblical teaching about the Holy Spirit to which Pannenberg refers. In Exodus 31:3-5 and 35:31-33 Bezaleel's artistic skill, his prowess as a craftsman, his wise knowledge by which he understood his appointed task, are attributed to the filling of the Spirit of God. An earlier text, similarly, had spoken of those who were "gifted artisans," responsible for making Aaron's garments, because the Lord had filled them with "the Spirit of wisdom" (Exod. 28:3).

It is a pertinent question whether this Spirit-filled artistic creativity was a special gift just because these particular artisans were responsible for the construction of the tabernacle, the home of Israel's worship, or whether their experience is a paradigm for the involvement of the Holy Spirit in all human art and creativity.

Commentators on Exodus and theologians of the Spirit divide over this question. On the one hand there are those who limit the involvement of the Spirit in the case of Bezaleel to the fact that his creative artistry was directed to "the manufacture of the various media of worship"[12]

C. H. Mackintosh links the necessity of the endowment of the divine Spirit with the fact that it was specifically with the work of "a sanctuary which was to be hallowed and blessed by the presence and glory of the God of Israel" that Bezaleel was involved; he contrasts this with the work of Tubal-Cain and others of Cain's descendants in Genesis 4, who "were endowed with unhallowed skill."[13] Hywel Jones likewise thinks that men were required who were not only skilled, but also spiritual, because of the nature of the work.[14] John Durham sees Bezaleel's special endowment by the filling of the Spirit as an addition to his natural ability,[15] and Matthew Poole believes that the filling of the Spirit was needed to make up for the lack of education available to the Israelites in Egypt: they "therefore needed inspiration."[16]

On the other hand Alan Cole acknowledges that the Old Testament credits "every form of skill and strength and excellence" to the Spirit of

12. Durham, *Exodus*, on Exod. 31:1-5.
13. Mackintosh, *Exodus*, 323.
14. Jones, "Exodus," 136; see also Meyer, *Bible Commentary*, 49.
15. Durham, *Exodus*, on Exod. 31:1-5.
16. Poole, *Annotations*, 236.

God because "God is rightly seen as the source of all wisdom."[17] Similarly, in the *Treasury of Scripture Knowledge* we read:

> No man, by course of reading or study, ever acquired a genius of any kind: we call it natural, and say it was born with the man: Moses teaches us to consider it divine. The prophet Isaiah, (Isa. 28:24–29) pointedly refers to this sort of teaching as coming from God, even in the most common and less difficult arts of life. Dark as the heathens were, yet they acknowledged that all talents and the seeds of all arts came from God.[18]

Matthew Henry expresses this in beautifully expansive terms:

> Skill in common arts and employments is the gift of God; from him are derived both the faculty and the improvement of the faculty. It is he that puts even this *wisdom into the inward parts* (Job 38:36). He teaches the husbandman discretion (Isa. 28:26), and the tradesman too; and he must have the praise of it. God dispenses his gifts variously, one gift to one, another to another, and all for the good of the whole body, both of mankind and of the church. . . . The common benefit is very much supported by the variety of men's faculties and inclinations; the genius of some leads them to be serviceable one way, of others another way, and *all these worketh that one and the self-same Spirit* (1 Cor. 12:11).[19]

Calvin, too, reads the case of Bezaleel as illustrative of the Holy Spirit's involvement in all instances of human art and craft:

> Although the call of Bezaleel was special, because . . . God entrusted to him an unusual and by no means ordinary work, we gather that no one excels even in the most despised and humble handicraft, except in so far as God's Spirit works in him. For, although *there are diversities of gifts*, still it is the same Spirit from whom they all flow (1 Cor. 12:4), and also as God has seen fit to distribute and measure them out to every man. Nor is this only the case with respect to the spiritual gifts which follow regeneration, but in all the branches of knowledge which come into use in common life. It is, therefore, a false division, when ungodly men ascribe all the means of our support partly to nature and God's blessing, and partly to the industry of man, since man's industry

---

17. Cole, *Exodus*, 210.
18. *Treasury of Scripture Knowledge*, on Exod. 31:3.
19. Henry, *Revised*, on Exod. 31:1–11.

itself is a blessing from God. The poets are more correct who acknowledge that all which is suggested by nature comes from God; that all the arts emanate from him, and therefore ought to be accounted divine inventions . . . Moses applies many epithets to the Spirit, because he is speaking of so remarkable a work; yet we must conclude, that whatever ability is possessed by any emanates from one only source, and is conferred by God.[20]

Another writer who takes this line is Abraham Kuyper, a remarkable man—a minister in the Dutch Reformed Church from 1864–80, a university lecturer and administrator from 1880–1901, and Prime Minister of the Netherlands from 1901–5.[21] In his huge book entitled *The Work of the Holy Spirit* Kuyper has one chapter devoted to the subject of "Gifts and Talents,"[22] in which he considers "the Holy Spirit's work in bestowing gifts, talents, and abilities upon artisans and professional men." He notes the role of the Holy Spirit in equipping Bezaleel for the task of tabernacle construction, and infers from that instance that the Spirit is evident in ordinary skilled labor too. He then extrapolates this principle to other spheres of human activity, including "military genius, legal acumen, statesmanship, and power to inspire the masses with enthusiasm," and concludes that "the Holy Spirit has a work in connection with mechanical arts and official functions—in every special talent whereby some men excel in such art or office." Recognizing that different people have different abilities, Kuyper notes that "one is adapted for the sea, another for the plough. One is a bungler in the foundry, but a master at wood-carving, while another is the reverse. This depends upon the personality, nature, and inclination. And since the Holy Spirit lights the personality, he also determines every man's calling to trade or profession."[23]

Contrary to the opinion of C. H. Mackintosh referred to above, Kuyper is quite clear that this operation of the Spirit is seen amongst Cain's descendants just as much as amongst the people of God.

Such a view of the operation of the Spirit is lofty indeed. Clearly many of our Reformed forebears had a far grander doctrine of the Holy Spirit than is familiar in these days of charismatic emphasis. We raised

20. Calvin, *Last Four Books of Moses*, 291–92.
21. De Vries, "Biographical Note," i–ii.
22. Kuyper, *Holy Spirit*, 38–42.
23. Kuyper, *Holy Spirit*, 41.

the question whether the case of Bezaleel was unique—that he was Spirit-filled for the work of artistic creativity solely because it was with the construction of the tabernacle that he was concerned, or whether his experience of Spirit-enabled craftsmanship is paradigmatic for all human creativity. My personal inclination is to side with the giants of Reformed theology, Calvin, Matthew Henry, Kuyper, and to find the Holy Spirit at work in all human art, craft, music, literature, learning, agriculture, horticulture, industry, commerce, politics—to recognize that human achievement is always ultimately the work of the gracious Spirit of God, who has not given up on this sinful world, and still operates within even the vilest of sinners to enhance something of the glory of the image of God in creation. In another work, Kuyper notes that art must derive from God, the Supreme Artist, because "art cannot originate from the Evil One; for Satan is destitute of every creative power. All he can do is to abuse the good gifts of God."[24] When Calvin declares that "Christ accomplishes whatever good there is through the power of his Spirit," and that "through that power he empowers and sustains all things,"[25] we are probably to set no restriction whatsoever on his meaning.

Such an elevated view of the meaning of the declaration "I believe in the Holy Spirit" prompts two practical reflections. First, we should welcome, love, and admire every achievement of human beings, because in all of them we see the Spirit of God. Our admiration of human achievement is the worship of the Creator. Second, whatever gifts and talents we may personally possess, we should nurture them, develop them to the full, and seek in whatever field of life we have God-given aptitude, to excel to the maximum of our capacity. The experience of Spirit-filled service is not just for the Christian minister, nor merely for the functions which we all exercise within the gathered life of the church, but for absolutely everything that we are and do. Jesus said, "Without me you can do nothing" (John 15:5). We must take him literally. We must refuse to reduce the relevance of his words to some religious sphere. We must also remember that Jesus made that statement in the course of teaching on the Holy Spirit, the abiding helper (John 14:16), who "will teach you all things" (John 14:26), not excluding the abilities and insights which we need to fulfil our role in the secular world.

---

24. Kuyper, *Calvinism*, 155.
25. Calvin, *Catechism, 1538*, 20.vi, 25.

This clause of the creed contains three indications that the Holy Spirit is a divine person, the third member of the holy Trinity. The first is the repetition of the words "I believe." Although Barth reads this as signalling a new departure, a change of direction, as indicating a shift of concern from God to man,[26] I prefer to see it as a way of deliberately tying this part of the creed to the first part. "I believe in God," the creed begins. Part of what that means is that "I believe in the Holy Spirit": he is unquestionably God. Secondly, the word "in" signifies that the Holy Spirit is God, for it speaks of giving myself over to him in a way that would not be possible to some merely impersonal power.[27] Thirdly, the word "Holy" emphasizes that the Holy Spirit belongs to the holy Trinity: this word "should impress on us that we are concerned here with God's own Spirit, the Spirit who is himself God."[28]

To acknowledge the Holy Spirit, to commit myself to him, as God, is, as Leanne Van Dyk points out, not only to make a positive statement of faith, but also to declare that there are alternatives which I reject. Van Dyk puts it like this: "I believe in the Holy Spirit (not in my spirit as the final measure of reality)."[29] Because the Spirit is God, I bow to him as Lord, as the executor of the Lordship of Jesus Christ. I submit my preferences, my opinions, my outlook, my ambitions, to the direction of the Spirit of God as articulated in the Word of God.

However, the main intention of the statement "I believe in the Holy Spirit," as the following clauses indicate, is not so much to affirm his essential deity, and certainly not his mere existence. It is rather to rejoice in the part played by the Holy Spirit on my behalf in the work of grace. Thus, having given an ontological definition of the Spirit's absolute divinity, the Heidelberg Catechism continues, "he is also given to me, to make me by a true faith partaker of Christ and all his benefits, to comfort me, and to abide with me forever."[30]

Cranfield is surely correct to say that whereas "in thinking about the creed's second article (about Jesus Christ) we have been concerned with what God has done, is doing, and will do *for* us," in this third article our

---

26. Barth, *Dogmatics*, 137.
27. See von Balthasar, *Credo*, 76.
28. Cranfield, *Creed*, 54.
29. Van Dyk, "Conversation," 23
30. *Heidelberg Catechism*, Q. 53.

concern moves to "what the eternal God does *in* us."[31] The Heidelberg Catechism brings out this subjective aspect of the united work of the holy Trinity for our salvation, the aspect which is particularly the responsibility of the Holy Spirit. As Calvin puts it, "God, as he has redeemed and saved us by his Son, makes us by his Spirit heirs of this redemption and salvation."[32]

It is at this point that we find something disappointing in the current so-called "charismatic" emphasis which has captured so much of the wider evangelical church. Where a proper concern with subjective spiritual experience degenerates into subjectivism, much of the depth and breadth of the Spirit's work is lost sight of. Karl Barth is right to insist that it is an error to consider the work of the Holy Spirit "as something new and peculiar beside the sole truth of faith and the life of faith."[33] However, in refusing to see the Spirit's work as an extra, additional to the work of Christ, we do not minimize it; rather, the vastness of what the Spirit does, as the "means by which the historical Christ becomes 'contemporaneous' with us,"[34] is displayed in all its wonder.

It is when we become preoccupied with the Spirit's manifestations in phenomena such as speaking in tongues that we insult him and reduce his work, even perhaps to trivial proportions, whereas a full-orbed understanding of the Spirit's part in God's total purpose of grace gives us a rich and glorious perspective on his role. Calvin expresses it dramatically when he says that "until our minds are intent on the Spirit, Christ is in a manner unemployed."[35]

The role of the Spirit in our personal salvation begins, as the above quotation from the Heidelberg Catechism indicates, when he grants us faith, and so makes us true believers. He is, as Calvin puts it, "the seed and root of heavenly life in us."[36] It is not possible to become a Christian at all unless the Holy Spirit does the work within us, a point stressed by Luther in both his catechisms: "I believe that I cannot, by my own reason or strength, believe in Jesus Christ my Lord, or come to him; but

---

31. Cranfield, *Creed*, 54.
32. Calvin, *Catechism, 1545*, Q. 89.
33. Barth, *Faith*, 128.
34. Hesselink, *Catechism*, 183.
35. Calvin, *Institutes*, 3.1.3.
36. Calvin, *Institutes*, 3.1.2.

the Holy Spirit has called me through the gospel."[37] Calvin calls faith the Spirit's principal work: our regeneration as new creatures is his achievement.[38] Barth wisely draws attention to Jesus' words in John 3:8: "The wind blows where it wishes, and you hear the sound of it, but cannot tell where it comes from and where it goes. So is everyone who is born of the Spirit." The sovereign freedom and uncontrollability of the Spirit means that we cannot always discern where he is at work; consequently, as Barth insists, "I can now no longer do otherwise than hope the best for all."[39]

From the Spirit's role in initiating our Christian identity, it follows that all the benefits of Christ are communicated to us by the Holy Spirit.[40] These include justification and cleansing, sanctification, and our preservation to the end and for eternity. The entire Christian life, in its commencement, its continuation, and its consummation is the outworking of the indwelling Holy Spirit. Calvin puts it like this: "the Holy Spirit . . . kindles our hearts with the fire of love both toward God and toward our neighbor, and day by day he boils away and burns up the vices of our inordinate desire so that if there are in us any good works, they are the fruits of his grace and his excellencies."[41]

This is what Jeremiah means by the writing of God's law on the heart of the believer (Jer. 31:33), an experience which the Lord describes through Ezekiel in these terms: "I will give you a new heart and put a new spirit within you; I will take the heart of stone out of your flesh and give you a heart of flesh. I will put my Spirit within you and cause you to walk in my statutes, and you will keep my judgments and do them" (Ezek. 36:26–27).

I shall finish this chapter by quoting a passage from Calvin's *Institutes*, where he points out the Scriptural titles for the Holy Spirit, and so emphasises the largeness of the Spirit's activities:

> First, he is called the *Spirit of adoption*, because he is witness to us of the free favor with which God the Father embraced us in his well-beloved and only-begotten Son, so as to become our Father and give us boldness of access to him; nay he dictates the very

---

37. Luther, *Enchiridion*, 80; cf. *Large Catechism*, 62.
38. Calvin, *Institutes*, 3.1.4.
39. Barth, *Dogmatics*, 138–39.
40. Calvin, *Institutes*, 3.1.1.
41. Calvin, *Catechism, 1538*, 20.vi, 25.

words, so that we can boldly cry, *Abba, Father*. For the same reason, he is said to have *sealed us, and given the earnest of the Spirit in our hearts*, because, as pilgrims in the world, and persons in a manner dead, he so quickens us from above as to assure us that our salvation is safe in the keeping of a faithful God. Hence, also, the Spirit is said to be *life because of righteousness*. But since it is his secret irrigation that makes us bud forth and produce the fruits of righteousness, he is repeatedly described as *water*. Thus in Isaiah, *Ho, every one that thirsts, come to the waters*. Again, *I will pour water upon him that is thirsty, and floods upon the dry ground*. Corresponding to this are the words of our Savior, to which I lately referred, *If any man thirst, let him come to me and drink*." Sometimes, indeed, he receives this name from his energy in cleansing and purifying, as in Ezekiel, where the Lord promises, *Then will I sprinkle you with clean water, and you shall be clean*. As those sprinkled with the Spirit are restored to the full vigor of life, he hence obtains the names of *Oil* and *Unction*. On the other hand, as he is constantly employed in subduing and destroying the vices of our concupiscence, and inflaming our hearts with the love of God and piety, he hence receives the name of *Fire*. In fine, he is described to us as a *Fountain*, whence all heavenly riches flow to us; or as the *Hand* by which God exerts his power, because by his divine inspiration he so breathes divine life into us, that we are no longer acted upon by ourselves, but ruled by his motion and agency, so that everything good in us is the fruit of his grace.[42]

---

42. Calvin, *Institutes*, 3.1.3.

16

The holy catholic church

IF, AS WE SAID in the previous chapter, the words "I believe in" signal the divine personality of the Spirit, are we not driven to teach the divine personality of the church and the other things listed in the final section of the Apostles' Creed (since they are all dependent clauses following those words)? Kelly admits that one or two of the very earliest post-apostolic Christian writers did at least come close to regarding the church as "an incarnation of eternal Spirit."[1] Generally, however, it has been recognized as obvious that a distinction must be maintained between the Holy Spirit and the other realities mentioned at this point in the creed.

Kelly, as has already been noted,[2] describes "the holy catholic church," and the other four blessings which follow, as "the fruits of the Spirit in action." Perhaps it is better to see them, as Kelly puts it, as being "appended to the mention of the Holy Spirit," rather than as being dependent on the words "I believe in," and there is then clear logic in "attaching these items in immediate association with the Holy Spirit."[3] Although grammatically, we have here one main clause and five dependent clauses, theologically, we have the one main clause, "I believe in the Holy Spirit," followed by five aspects of what the Holy Spirit does in the lives of believers and in the life of the believing community. Perhaps this could be clarified to some extent by punctuating with a colon after the main clause, provided that we do not thereby reduce the doctrine of the Holy Spirit to these five elements in Christian experience, so denying his essential reality.

1. Kelly, *Creeds*, 155.
2. See above, chapter 3.
3. Kelly, *Creeds*, 155–56.

Rufinus helpfully explains this distinction between the Spirit and his works:

> It is not said "in the holy church," nor "in the forgiveness of sins," nor "in the resurrection of the flesh." For if the preposition *in* had been added, it would have had the same force as in the preceding articles. But now in those clauses in which the faith concerning the Godhead is declared, we say *in God the Father*, and *in Jesus Christ his Son*, and *in the Holy Spirit*, but in the rest, where we speak not of the Godhead but of creatures and mysteries, the preposition *in* is not added. We do not say, "We believe in the holy church," but "we believe the holy church," not as God, but as the church gathered to God: and we believe that there is forgiveness of sins; we do not say, "we believe in the forgiveness of sins"; and we believe that there will be a resurrection of the flesh; we do not say, "we believe in the resurrection of the flesh." By this monosyllabic preposition, therefore, the Creator is distinguished from the creatures, and things divine are separated from things human.[4]

Calvin also notes that the particle *in* ought not to be inserted when we speak of the church, because to do so "would make the expression improper:" He continues: "We declare that we believe in God, both because our mind reclines upon him as true, and our confidence is fully satisfied in him. This cannot be said of the church, just as it cannot be said of the forgiveness of sins, or the resurrection of the body."[5]

This reference to the church is intrinsically tied in to the rest of the creed. We have affirmed our faith in, our passion for, our allegiance to, the triune God. Now we acknowledge that there is a church, and it consists of all those who, as sons and daughters of the Lord almighty (cf. 2 Cor. 6:18), believe in him as Father. It is because we believe in Jesus Christ that we "belong to a dynamic community that spans the centuries,"[6] for the church is "the one effect" of Christ's death.[7] It is the work of the Holy Spirit, in whom we believe, to create the church, because he it is who induces the faith[8] through which men and women, boys and girls, are incorporated into the church.

4. Rufinus, *Commentary*, para. 36, 1126.
5. Calvin, *Institutes*, 4.1.2.
6. McGrath, *I Believe*, 91.
7. Calvin, *Catechism, 1545*, Q. 94.
8. Packer, *Christian*, 64.

In this clause of the creed we have three key words, the noun "church" itself, which translates the Latin term *ecclesia*, a transliteration of the Greek original, and the two attached adjectives, "holy" (*sancta*) and "catholic" (*catholica*). Our study of this phrase will examine each of these three words in turn.

CHURCH

Etymologically the Greek noun *ekklēsia* means an assembly resulting from a summons.[9] The call has gone forth, and the people have come out and come together.

The two words, *call* and *people*, are equally vital in the definition of the church. The word *call* stresses the fact that "the church is not formed by a human gathering of people who would have the same opinions." Rather, it is God's summons which brings together "individuals until then scattered at the mercy of their opinions."[10] In the immediate aftermath of Pentecost it was the Lord "who added to the church daily those who were being saved" (Acts 2:47). Addressing "the church of God which is at Corinth," Paul affirms that they were "called to be saints" (1 Cor. 1:2).

The word *people* contrasts emphatically with the popular idea of a church as the building where people meet for worship. Such a use is remote from the Biblical meaning of the term. It is true that the church can be described as "God's building" (1 Cor. 3:9; cf. Eph. 2:21), and that the growth of the church can be pictured as a building project (Matt. 16:18). Nevertheless, this is metaphorical language, and refers not to a literal building, but to the people who are the church.

The Reformers and their early successors were insistent on the church being understood as people. Calvin called the church "the body and society of believers."[11] According to Witsius the church is "a society of believing and holy men"[12] (which includes women, of course!). In speaking of the building of believers into a spiritual house in Jesus Christ, Peter describes us as "his own special people" (1 Pet. 2:9).

---

9. See Coenen, "*Church*," 291.
10. Barth, *Faith*, 136.
11. Calvin, *Catechism, 1545*, Q. 93.
12. Witsius, *Creed*, Vol. 2, 350.

In the Reformers' definitions of the church, the contrast which is assumed is less with the idea of a building than with that of an institution. The break with the elaborate organization which the Roman Church had become meant that for the Reformers the institutional aspects of the church were secondary. The matter of primary importance was that it was the company of elect, redeemed, believing people who constituted the church.

This does not mean that the church is already there as an abstract entity to which people join themselves. The church is not the elect considered as an ideal, even prior to their personal experience of salvation. It is as those who are God's elect are led by the Spirit to justifying faith in Christ that the church comes into being. Until there are people who are believers in Christ, there is no church, for the church simply is those people. The society of believers is a body (to take up Calvin's terminology) because the people who are believers have come together in response to that divine summons of grace in the gospel. Calvin's starting point is the fact that there are people who are chosen and who believe, and from there he extrapolates to the existence of the church. As he puts it in another place: "The whole number of the elect are joined by the bond of faith into one church and society and one people of God, of which Christ is Leader and Prince, and, so to speak, Head of the one body, just as in him before the foundation of the world they were all chosen to be gathered into God's kingdom."[13]

It is true that there have been those who have taught the pre-existence of the church. The writer known as 2 Clement is the best example. He speaks of the church as "barren before children were given to her,"[14] and conceives of the church as an eternal existent, which can be construed independently of those who would become its members. He refers to "the first church, the spiritual one which was created before the sun and moon," the church which "belongs not to the present, but has existed from the beginning." 2 Clement pictures the church as an eternal spiritual reality, existing with the pre-incarnate, spiritual Christ; when Christ became manifest in the flesh he brought to earth with him that first, eternal, spiritual church, which began to become filled up with its children after his return to heaven.[15]

13. Calvin, *Catechism, 1538*, 20.vii, 25.
14. 2 Clement, *Corinthians*, 2.1.
15. 2 Clement, *Corinthians*, 14.1–3.

For the Reformers, this idea of a church existing before it had any members was inconceivable. It is the members who are the church. As far as they were concerned, a memberless church would be nothing at all. If my reading of Calvin is correct, then Karl Barth misreads his emphasis. Barth claims that, for Calvin, "the body of Christ exists prior to its members."[16] However, this does not appear to be Calvin's view. While it is clear that, for Calvin, the elect were chosen to be gathered together, it is not until the gathering together takes place that the church emerges.

This means that, despite the Reformers' insistence on the primacy of the church as a gathering of people, it is still the case, nevertheless, that the church is a visible institution on earth. It is true that the Reformation Confessions maintained an important distinction between the visible and the invisible church. The invisible church is the full number of the elect, while the visible church consists of all who profess to be Christians at any given time. The distinction arises from the recognition that, in the present world, where sin still affects Christians and churches, there are people in the church who are not actually true believers, and people who, for exceptional reasons, are outside the church, who are, nevertheless, true believers.

The distinction between the visible and the invisible church should not be pressed to the point of an absolute separation: it is, as Williamson rightly stresses, precisely the invisible church which becomes visible as the church in the world,[17] even though its visibility may be somewhat obscured by the presence of unbelievers. However, Pannenberg is quite right to see it as belonging to the essence of the Christian church, "as the community of the incarnate God, to take on physical shape in institutional form."[18] Consequently, as Barth insists, "if the church has not this visibility, then it is not the church."[19]

This is clear from the fact that in the New Testament, the word *ekklēsia* most often refers to a local, identifiable, visible body of believers. Of 109 uses of *ekklēsia* with reference to the Christian church, only seventeen (or perhaps eighteen—1 Corinthians 10:32 is ambiguous) refer to the church universal. A few examples must suffice to demonstrate the

---

16. Barth, *Faith*, 136.
17. G. I. Williamson, *Westminster Confession*, 187.
18. Pannenberg, *Creed*, 146.
19. Barth, *Dogmatics*, 142.

local sense of *ekklēsia* on the overwhelming majority of occasions when it is used.

On three occasions the phrase "the whole church" appears, but in each case it refers to the whole of a particular church—the whole church in Jerusalem in Acts 15:22, the whole church in Corinth in Romans 16:23, and again in 1 Corinthians 14:23, though in that case, the warning that "if the whole church comes together in one place, and all speak with tongues," and some unbelievers happen to come in, they will conclude that they have visited a lunatic asylum, is, in principle, applicable to any congregation. On sixteen occasions a qualifying phrase links the reference to the church with a particular place. For example, Romans 16:1 speaks of "the church in Cenchrea," Colossians 4:16 of "the church of the Laodiceans," and Revelation 2:1 of "the church of Ephesus."

Furthermore, some statements about the church only make sense with a local understanding. We shall cite just three examples. When Jesus said of an unresolved disciplinary issue, "tell it to the church" (Matt. 18:17), this is obviously restricted to the local company. When the apostles came to Antioch and "gathered the church together" (Acts 14:27), it was only that one local church to which they reported. An elder's role—to "take care of the church of God" (1 Tim. 3:5)—is limited to one particular church family.

It is often pointed out that the presence of the clause, "I believe . . . the holy catholic church," in a Christian credal summary indicates that the fact of the church is a matter of faith rather than sight. Thus Karl Barth can say that it is a question of "seeing the visible church—believing in the invisible church through her earthly and present expression."[20] This is a matter of faith, and often a profound challenge to faith, because, as Calvin says, "oftentimes no difference can be observed between the children of God and the profane, between his proper flock and his untamed herd."[21]

There is nothing unusual about this. Even in New Testament times, the apostles had frequently to rectify inappropriate behavior in the churches. In 1 Corinthians 11:18–22 Paul has to rebuke a church where there are divisions, and where some members are showing shameful contempt towards the church, and the letters to the seven churches in Revelation 2–3, with two exceptions (Smyrna and Philadelphia) include

20. Barth, *Faith*, 148.
21. Calvin, *Institutes*, 4.1.2.

words of reproof and correction. Paul said to Timothy, "I write so that you may know how you ought to conduct yourself in the house of God, which is the church of the living God" (1 Tim. 3:15): this implies that right conduct could not simply be taken for granted.

This is an important observation, because it is so easy to become disillusioned with the church as we know it.[22] The church "bears every stamp of human imperfection."[23] The public scandal of the Anglican communion battling it out over homosexuality, or the petty squabbles which beset a local congregation—both demand that it is by faith that we see that even there the church of God is found. The Christian "acknowledges the church in spite of its faults and deficiencies: he acknowledges the church as the field of activity of the Spirit of Christ."[24]

This does have practical ramifications for our relationship to our own local congregation, which is the place where we encounter the church in its most down-to-earth form. Karl Barth insists that to say that we believe the existence of the church means first of all that we believe our own particular congregation to be a congregation of Christ in which the work of the Holy Spirit takes place: "*Credo ecclesiam* means that I believe that the congregation to which I belong, in which I have been called to faith and am responsible for my faith, in which I have my service, is the one, holy, universal church. If I do not believe this here, I do not believe it at all. No lack of beauty, no 'wrinkles and spots' in this congregation may lead me astray."[25]

Barth is not saying that, as far as I am concerned, I may limit my interest in "the holy catholic church" to my own congregation, that, for me, "the holy catholic church" finishes at the boundaries of my local assembly. What he means is identical with how Kelly interprets Ignatius of Antioch's teaching on the church: "his point was that the local community only had reality, life and power in proportion as it formed part of the universal church."[26] My local congregation is "the holy catholic church" in so far as we retain our sense of belonging to the whole people of God. This is why the word *ekklēsia* occurs thirty-five times in the plu-

---

22. Cf. G. I. Williamson, *Heidelberg*, 99.
23. Barth, *Faith*, 140.
24. Pannenberg, *Creed*, 145.
25. Barth, *Dogmatics*, 143–44.
26. Kelly, *Creeds*, 385.

ral: there is more than one church on earth, but each assembly is truly *ekklēsia*—a limb of the one body.

However, Barth's words would also lead us astray if we use them to justify the assumption that every gathering of people which goes by the name of "church" is a church in the valid sense of the word. How may we distinguish between a congregation which, however poorly, with however so many weaknesses, is nonetheless a true Christian church, and one which has forfeited its right to such a title?

The Reformation Confessions typically answered that question by identifying three marks of the church. Let the Scottish Confession serve as representative. It confesses the marks of the true church to be:

> first, the true preaching of the Word of God, in which God has revealed himself to us, as the writings of the prophets and apostles declare; secondly, the right administration of the sacraments of Christ Jesus, with which must be associated the Word and promise of God to seal and confirm them in our hearts; and lastly, ecclesiastical discipline uprightly ministered, as God's Word prescribes, whereby vice is repressed and virtue nourished.[27]

Where these three things were present, the Reformers believed, a local church could be accepted as genuine, whatever imperfections may remain.

Several comments are worth making on the subject of the marks of the church. First, the Westminster Confession appears to add a fourth mark, namely purity of worship.[28] Second there are those who suggest that another mark ought to be added too—mission, as a defining feature of the church.[29] Third, I rather prefer the way that Heinrich Heppe words the third traditional mark. He speaks not of church discipline, but of "the serious and zealous practice of disciplined Christian life."[30] This removes the third mark from the sphere of occasional emergencies to a description of the practical lifestyle commitment which should mark the members of the church at all times. Fourth, the exact interpretation of how the marks of the church take concrete form may vary from time to time and from place to place. We should not, therefore be over dogmatic about what the marks imply in practice, while remaining insistent on the

---

27. *Scottish Confession*, 18, 176–77.
28. *Westminster Confession*, 658.
29. So Stotts, "After Barmen," xx.
30. Heppe, *Reformed Dogmatics*, 669.

undergirding principles. Fifth, all these marks come down in the end to one thing, which the Belgic Confession summarizes like this: "all things are managed according to the pure Word of God, all things contrary thereto rejected, and Jesus Christ acknowledged as the only Head of the church."[31] According to J. N. D. Kelly, Irenaeus would have been happy with such a summary. In his understanding the church meant "a worldwide society which was clearly demarcated from its rivals by a common acceptance of the doctrine long ago proclaimed by the prophets of the old dispensation, preached by the Son of God himself, and transmitted to later ages by his apostles and others charged to safeguard the precious deposit."[32]

HOLY

It is rightly noted that "holy" does not, at least in the first instance, bear a moral meaning in this context. "It does not mean that these people are particularly suited to come near to God, to deserve his revelation."[33] Rather, it denotes that the church "belongs to God and to his activity in the world."[34] Kelly puts it like this: "The church is described as *holy* in the creed because it has been chosen by God, because he has predestined it to a glorious inheritance, and because he dwells in it in the Person of the Holy Spirit."[35] The holiness of the church distinguishes it from "a mere voluntary association:" it is "an institution founded by and belonging to God, not man."[36]

Alexander Stewart finds in the word "holy" the "bond of connection" with the previous clause. He cites Kattenbusch, who discerned in early Christianity's mention of "the holy . . . church" an understanding of the church "as a branch or colony upon earth of the City of God which is heaven."[37] Such imagery is based on Philippians 3:20, which depicts believers as a truly privileged people. Philippi had been awarded the status of a Roman colony. This meant that the citizens of Philippi "were

---

31. *Belgic Confession*, 419–20.
32. Kelly, *Creeds*, 158.
33. Barth, *Faith*, 138.
34. Pannenberg, *Creed*, 145; see also Kelly, *Creeds*, 158.
35. Kelly, *Creeds*, 159.
36. McGiffert, *Creed*, 153.
37. Stewart, *Creeds*, 55.

also citizens of Rome with all of the rights and privileges awarded to any Roman born in the imperial city."[38] Still more wonderfully, the church and its members, even while located on earth, are the beneficiaries of all the holy privileges of heaven.

The fact that the church is holy, that it belongs to God, contains a far-reaching challenge. It means, as Clifton Kirkpatrick points out, that the church is not ours.[39] We must therefore handle the church with care. We must live and serve within the church with humility. We must remember that our personal opinions and preferences are far less important than God's pleasure.

God once complained that the worship of his people did not bring him satisfaction (Isa. 43:24). Our whole aim through all our involvement in the life of the church must always be to satisfy God. If our criteria for assessing a church or a service of worship center around what we enjoy, if we make our judgments on the basis of our personal tastes, our likes and dislikes, we have forgotten that what God wants is paramount, that his satisfaction is what matters. Commenting on Isaiah 43:24, Alec Motyer reminds us that the point of all religion is not that it should please people, or help people, "but that it should please and satisfy God."[40]

Cranfield connects the word "holy" with the church's origin—in God's sovereign decision, its allegiance—to the God who is its owner, its function—to bear witness in the world to God and his grace, and its character—as the object of God's undeserved grace.[41]

Cranfield's final comment draws attention to the fact that the church's holiness is not all extrinsic to the church's being. The church is that company of people who stand in the holiness of Christ. Though by nature unholy, a holy standing has been conferred on them "as a matter of the fact that God has chosen them."[42] That is why Paul refers to "the churches of the saints" (1 Cor. 14:33). The juxtaposition of "church" and "saints" equates the church with the holy people, but as Paul acknowledges in the same letter, our sanctification is "in Christ Jesus" (1 Cor. 1:2): we are holy in him, in his holiness.

---

38. Hawthorne, *Philippians*, on Phil. 3:20.
39. Kirkpatrick, "Preface," xi.
40. Motyer, *Isaiah*, 339.
41. Cranfield, *Creed*, 61–62.
42. Barth, *Faith*, 138.

However, this holiness is more than only a holy standing in Christ (though such a gracious conferment is certainly not to be minimized). Calvin says that the church is holy "because as many as have been chosen by God's eternal providence to be adopted into the number of the church—all these are made holy by the Lord through spiritual regeneration."[43]

That Calvin is referring here to the moral impact of that definitive sanctification which we are freely given in Christ is suggested by his comment in his later Catechism: he asks, "In what sense do you call the church holy?" His answer runs: "In this sense, that all whom God chooses he justifies, and remakes in holiness and innocence of life (Rom. 8:29), so that in them his glory may be displayed. This is what Paul intends, when he affirms that Christ sanctifies the church which he redeemed, that it might be glorious and free from all stain (Eph. 5:27)."[44]

Here Calvin seems to make a distinction between justification—the imputation of Christ's righteousness—and holiness, which his reference to Romans 8:29 appears to equate with being "conformed to the image of his Son." The reference to Ephesians 5:27, likewise, implies moral renovation. Skevington Wood sees Paul's concern here as Christ's ultimate aim in giving himself for the church, namely "that that at the end of the age he might be able to present her to himself in unsullied splendor."[45] Developing holiness along the way is a movement towards that glorious goal. In similar vein, Lincoln writes on Ephesians 5:27:

> it then becomes crystal clear from the final *hina* clause that this bride's beauty is moral. She is to be holy and blameless, the two terms found so frequently in Old Testament contexts of cultic and ethical purity, used with the language of presentation in Colossians 1:22, and already taken up earlier in this letter in 1:4, where the display of such holiness and blamelessness is seen as the purpose of God's election of believers from before the foundation of the world.[46]

---

43. Calvin, *Catechism, 1538*, 20.vii, 25.
44. Calvin, *Catechism, 1545*, Q. 96.
45. Skevington Wood, *Ephesians*, on Eph. 5:27.
46. Lincoln, *Ephesians*, on Eph. 5:27.

CATHOLIC

This epithet has nothing to do with Roman Catholicism. Catholicity is a mark of the true church, and the catholic spirit should be a quality of every Christian. The word "catholic" means "universal," and there are two ways in which the church is seen to be catholic.

Catholic in composition

The members of the church are drawn from the whole of humankind. The church is universal in composition: "it embraces all Christians everywhere."[47] "All those belonging to the universal church, including the Reformed, belong to a catholic body."[48] There are four aspects to this, neatly summarized by Witsius as "diversities of places, times, persons, and states."[49]

Geographical universality.

Cyril of Jerusalem, preaching to young Christians in the middle of the fourth century, said that the church is called *catholic* "because it extends over all the world, from one end of the earth to the other."[50] In our generation the marvelous reality of this can be felt as never before, as the Christian church now is truly global. This is the fulfillment of the great Old Testament vision, which anticipated the spread of Messiah's dominion "from sea to sea, and from the river to the ends of the earth" (Ps. 72:8), when "all the ends of the earth [should] see the salvation of our God" (Isa. 52:10).

Historical universality.

The church does not only extend across the world at any given time, it also stretches backwards and forwards through time. All true believers who have ever lived are part of the church, and all who are yet to be will become its members in their turn. The Heidelberg Catechism emphasizes this aspect of the church's catholicity when it says "that out of the whole human race, from the beginning to the end of the world, the Son of God, by his Spirit and word, gathers, defends, and preserves

---

47. Packer, *Christian*, 65.
48. Praamsma, *Before the Face*, 87.
49. Witsius, *Creed*, Vol. 2, 359.
50. Cyril, *Catechetical Lectures*, 18.23, 328.

for himself unto everlasting life, a chosen communion in the unity of the true faith."[51]

In this connection, Professor Cranfield sounds a note of warning. He stresses the importance for the church (and, we might add, for any particular local church) of striving "to maintain and to value its continuity with the church of past ages and to guard against the pride that makes us try to be independent of our fathers and mothers in the faith and to indulge in individualism and desire for the latest novelty."[52]

This does not mean that nothing should ever change. However, it does mean that change should be natural, gradual, and appropriate, and should never be so revolutionary as to divorce us from the church life of earlier generations. It may also mean that it is necessary sometimes to reverse more recent innovations in order to restore our unity with the historic church of God.

CULTURAL UNIVERSALITY.

Witsius points out that this originally meant the breaking down of the divide between Jew and Gentile, as both were incorporated together into the one church of Christ.[53] This was what caused Paul so much joy as he said that Christ "is our peace, who has made us both one, and has broken down the middle wall of partition between us" (Eph. 2:14).

However, the extension of the removal of that dividing wall is that the church "is limited by no barrier, either of state, or of race, or of culture."[54] The church's cultural universality anticipates the day when the redeemed shall finally be gathered around the throne in heaven "out of every tribe and tongue and people and nation" (Rev. 5:9). Kirkpatrick's paraphrase of the word "catholic" is that "the Christian community welcomes the broad diversity of the human family."[55] Williamson urges the practical implication of this truth: since the church "always transcends the culture of any nation," it must "resist conformity to the spirit of any culture or era."[56]

---

51. *Heidelberg Catechism*, Q. 54.
52. Cranfield, *Creed*, 63.
53. Witsius, *Creed*, Vol. 2, 359.
54. Barth, *Faith*, 139.
55. Kirkpatrick, "Preface," xi.
56. G. I. Williamson, *Heidelberg*, 95.

GENERATIONAL UNIVERSALITY.

The generation gap, so frequently remarked on in contemporary western culture is not (or at least, idealistically, should not be) replicated in the church. The believing teenager and the believing eighty-year old have far more in common with each other than the believing teenager has with an unbelieving teenager or the believing eighty-year old has with an unbelieving eighty-year old. "The church is equally for young and old and middle-aged: for a congregation to value the young above the old or the old above the young is an abandonment of its catholicity."[57]

The practical challenge of the church's catholicity in composition is stressed by Calvin, when he says, "every one of us must maintain brotherly concord with all the children of God."[58] It is sadly true that we see the church "divided by the barriers which circumstances or ignorance or prejudice have erected;" nevertheless, all true believers are "one in heart, one in love and service of the one Lord, one in the glorious hope of their calling."[59] It is, therefore, our duty to work at practical catholicity with all our brothers and sisters in Christ, wherever they may be found.

Catholic in mission

Stewart sees in the insertion in the creed of the word "catholic" the church's "consciousness of her mission, as extending to all men the benefits of salvation, and designedly excluding none."[60] Loius Praamsma expresses this graphically: God's "call of salvation goes out to all people without exception. No one is left out, no place is forgotten, whether it is an inner city slum or an African tribe. Jesus calls prostitutes and tax collectors into his kingdom. That is why we speak of a universal or catholic church."[61]

The combination of the terms "holy" and "catholic" means, as von Balthasar reminds us, that the church is not "a *holy* enclave within a profane, godless world," but rather the movement which communicates salvation to all nations.[62] As the *catholic* church, the church is open to all

---

57. Cranfield, *Creed*, 63.
58. Calvin, *Institutes*, 4.1.3.
59. Stewart, *Creeds*, 60.
60. Stewart, *Creeds*, 56.
61. Praamsma, *Before the Face*, 87.
62. Von Balthasar, *Credo*, 84.

people, all peoples; it must ever retain its outward-looking orientation, and never become confined within the bounds of its own self-interest, or its own self-serving activities. Pannenberg sees this outward orientation as the standard for the church's self-understanding:[63] without the universal outward perspective, the church has lost its authenticity as the recipient of the divine commission to "Go into all the world and preach the gospel to every creature" (Mark 16:15).

Calvin's distinction between God's "proper flock" and "the untamed herd"[64] is suggestive. It implies the possibility of taming and inclusion in the flock. Our catholic mission has as its goal the taming of the herd, until the flock attains its co-extensiveness with the elect of God.

Packer describes the local congregation as "a spearhead of divine counter-attack for the recapture of a rebel world."[65] In our locality, and through our sending and support of missionaries, the local church must take responsibility for the universal mission of the whole church. It is not a task to be left to specialist societies, nor (necessarily) something which can only be done by congregations acting in concert, though that may increase missional efficiency in some instances. However, even in joint endeavors, each participating local congregation must preserve its missionary priority.

A concomitant of this missional catholicity is the confidence that the church's message is universally relevant, valid for every time, every place, every situation.[66] Western culture tries to intimidate us these days into doubting the truth of this. However, we must place our confidence in God and his word, heeding Paul's exhortation to "hold fast the pattern of sound words which you have heard" (2 Tim. 1:13), and holding forth that word of life to the whole human race. We have to accept that "the Acts of the Apostles and Paul's life alone are a singular testimony to the fact that the church's catholic mission always proves itself victorious only in persecution, failure, and martyrdom."[67] Are we ready for the cost of being the church in the world with a universal mission?

---

63. Pannenberg, *Creed*, 147.
64. Calvin, *Institutes*, 4.1.2.
65. Packer, *Christian*, 67.
66. See McGrath, *I Believe*, 93.
67. Von Balthasar, *Credo*, 85.

17

The communion of saints

INTRODUCTION

THERE ARE THOSE WHO have taken this phrase as a definition of the previous phrase: "the communion of saints" equals "the holy catholic church," since the church is the community of men and women accounted holy by God's grace in Christ. Kelly mentions several medieval writers who took this line.[1] It was also Luther's view.[2] However, given the structure of this section of the creed, where five balanced phrases follow the reference to the Holy Spirit, it seems unlikely that the first two phrases should be synonyms. "It can scarcely be doubted that 'communion of saints' means much more than 'church' in the creeds."[3] It expresses what Calvin calls "the quality of the church,"[4] rather than the mere fact of the church.

There are, however, two possible interpretations of the original Latin phrase, *sanctorum communionem*, deriving from the fact that *sanctorum* may be either neuter (communion of holy things) or masculine (communion of holy persons). It has sometimes been maintained that the phrase was used by the early church "with a full consciousness of its ambiguity."[5] If this is so, then it becomes unnecessary to try to make a judgment as to which gender is correct: both meanings may be embraced in parallel.[6] This will be our approach. I am in no doubt that

---

1. Kelly, *Creeds*, 394.
2. Luther, *Larger Catechism*, 63–64; see also G. I. Williamson, *Heidelberg*, 98.
3. Kelly, *Creeds*, 390.
4. Calvin, *Institutes*, 4.1.3.
5. Stewart, *Creeds*, 57, citing Kattenbusch.
6. So Cranfield, *Creed*, 64; Pannenberg, *Creed*, 149–50.

Barth is right to say that "only when both interpretations are retained side by side, does the matter receive its full, good meaning." Barth goes on to bring out the connection between the two interpretations: Christians are holy people because God has set them apart for holy things—for holy gifts and holy works.[7]

OUR COMMUNION IN HOLY THINGS—SANCTORUM AS NEUTER

If the neuter is read, then communion in holy things may be read in either of two ways.

A general way

This understanding of the clause is clearly spelt out by Cranfield, though it figures in various forms in different writers. Cranfield writes: "the members of Christ's church share the holy things, that is, all that God has done, is doing, and will do for us in Jesus Christ, all the benefits and obligations that come from God's actions."[8]

This general reading of the neuter phrase is given as part of the answer of the Heidelberg Catechism to the question, "What do you understand by *the communion of saints*?" All believers are said to be partakers of Christ and all his treasures and gifts.[9] Packer draws attention to the glorious reality emphasized by this clause: "that in the church there is a real sharing in the life of God."[10] God has, indeed, called us "into the fellowship of his Son, Jesus Christ our Lord" (1 Cor. 1:9). We have come into fellowship with the divine nature, as 2 Peter 1:4 would perhaps be better translated, "and truly our fellowship is with the Father and with his Son Jesus Christ" (1 John 1:3).

It must be said that this aspect of the communion truly is basic to all the rest. As Pannenberg rightly says, it is through their communion with Christ himself that believers are in turn joined together in communion with one another.[11] Moreover, it is only because of our communion with God himself, Father, Son, and Holy Spirit that we share communion in the holy things which God has done for us in Christ.

---

7. Barth, *Dogmatics*, 144.
8. Cranfield, *Creed*, 64.
9. *Heidelberg Catechism*, Q. 55.
10. Packer, *Christian*, 65.
11. Pannenberg, *Creed*, 151–52.

A specific way

More often, however, communion in holy things is understood more specifically, of the participation of all the church members together in the bread and wine at the Lord's Table. By virtue of their sacramental use, the elements are set apart as holy. Kelly notes that this has been an increasingly popular reading of the clause since the nineteenth-century.[12]

On this reading, the words become a reminder to all of us of the importance of our participation in the Lord's Supper if we are members of the church. That is why it is so vitally important for each local congregation carefully to consider the timing of communion so that every member can be present at the same time. If we celebrate the Lord's Supper, when some members are absent, we are failing to put into practice this communion in these holy things, for it is around them that the church assembles.[13]

The Lord's Supper is the family meal. To absent oneself when the family gathers around the table is one way to "despise the church of God" (1 Cor. 11:22). It amounts to the declaration that I do not regard myself as belonging to this company of people; I do not count my fellow believers as worthy of my friendship. The Lord's Supper has been described as "a feast of the fellowship of the covenant of grace."[14] That being so, to neglect it entails the rejection of an interest in the covenant of grace, and a refusal to acknowledge one's fellow beneficiaries of God's grace in Christ.

The main teaching passage in Scripture on these holy things is 1 Corinthians 11:20–34, along with the accounts of the Last Supper in the Synoptic Gospels. Paul teaches that it is impossible to celebrate the Lord's Supper if the church is riddled with self-interest (v. 20): the sacramental significance of the occasion is undermined where loving concern is lost. The family meal is symbolic of the care which the members of the congregation have for the needy amongst them (v. 21–22).

We highlight twelve things in the apostle's outline of the procedure for the meal.

---

12. Kelly, *Creeds*, 390.
13. Von Balthasar, *Credo*, 85.
14. Heppe, *Reformed Dogmatics*, 635.

The Lord's Institution of the Supper (v. 23)

Paul received these instructions from the Lord; that is to say, he received them from those who had been apostles before him, and passes on the words of the Lord at the Last Supper as recorded in the Synoptic Gospels.[15] There are many echoes of the gospels in Paul's words, as we shall see. The Lord's Supper is not a matter of human tradition, nor of individual preference. The Lord has commanded us to break bread together. To fail to attend the communion service is to be in a position of rebellion against Christ.

The Occasion Which Is Commemorated (v. 23)

It was "on the same night in which he was betrayed" that Jesus instituted this meal. The Supper and the main event to which the betrayal led—the cross and the Lord's sacrificial death—are inextricably bound together. Calvin explains this clearly:

> This circumstance as to time instructs us as to the design of the sacrament—that the benefit of Christ's death may be ratified in us. For the Lord might have some time previously committed to the apostles this covenant-seal, but he waited until the time of his oblation, that the apostles might see soon after accomplished in reality in his body, what he had represented to them in the bread and the wine.[16]

For the church to hold a communion service without the Lord's crucifixion as the uppermost consideration would be to miss the point entirely. "Jesus bids us commemorate, not his birth, nor his life, nor his miracles, but his death."[17] Moreover, it is specifically his death as a sacrifice which is commemorated, "so that if this idea be kept out of view the sacrament loses all its significance and power."[18]

Moreover, the occasion of the Last Supper was the Passover meal (Luke 22:14). The apostle elsewhere describes Christ as "our Passover" (1 Cor. 5:7). To summarize it in a nutshell, the significance of the Passover was that a lamb died instead of the firstborn amongst God's people: the blood on the lintel and doorposts was a sign that a death had already

---

15. So Mare, *1 Corinthians*, on 1 Cor. 1:23–24, and Grosheide, *Corinthians*, 269; against Hodge, *Corinthians*, 221–3, and Morris, *Corinthians*, 159–60.
16. Calvin, *Corinthians*, 373.
17. Carson, *Matthew*, on Matt. 26:26.
18. Hodge, *Corinthians*, 226.

occurred in that house (Exod. 12:13, 23). In that God's people were his firstborn (Exod. 4:22), the lamb died instead of the entire people. In celebrating the sacrament we acknowledge the Savior's death as the death which liberates us from death. He died instead, and we live eternally.

THE GIVING OF THANKS (V. 24)

The provision of bread and wine for the Supper remind us of God's daily provision for all our physical needs. The sacramental use of the bread and wine points us to his provision of the bread of life, who is Jesus Christ (John 6:35), the one and only answer to our every spiritual need. On both counts, thanksgiving has to be a central feature whenever the church assembles around the Lord's Table. Calvin again puts the point well:

> Paul observes elsewhere, that every gift that we receive from the hand of God "is sanctified to us by the word and prayer" (1Tim. 4:5). Accordingly, we nowhere read that the Lord tasted bread along with his disciples, but there is mention made of his giving thanks (John 6:23), by which example he has assuredly instructed us to do the like. This *giving of thanks*, however, has a reference to something higher, for Christ *gives thanks* to the Father for his mercy towards the human race, and the inestimable benefit of redemption; and he invites us, by his example, to raise up our minds as often as we approach the sacred table, to an acknowledgment of the boundless love of God towards us, and to have our minds kindled up to true gratitude.[19]

Paul's reference to giving thanks takes up Luke's words (Luke 22:19), which are echoed in the other gospels by the statement that Jesus "blessed" the bread (Matt. 26:26; Mark 14:22), a word taken up by Paul in 1 Corinthians 10:16 with reference to the cup. It is the articulated expression of gratitude which sets these particular elements apart as vehicles of blessing. Matthew and Mark do mention that Jesus gave thanks before distributing the cup (Matt. 26: 27; Mark 14:23). The phrase "when he had given thanks" translates the Greek participle *eucharistēsas*, from which the name Eucharist as a title for the Lord's Supper is derived.

THE IMPORTANCE OF THE BREAKING OF THE BREAD (V. 24)

The Synoptic evangelists all tell us that Jesus broke the bread (Matt. 26:26; Mark 14:22; Luke 22:19). His example sets the pattern for our

---

19. Calvin, *Corinthians*, 374.

practice. But this is not a mere ritual for the sake of it. The breaking of the bread is vital as a picture of the brokenness of Jesus' body as he was battered on the cross. It serves as a reminder that our broken lives are repaired by the shattering of his holy person. Such is the import of the words "for you," which indicate the vicarious nature of Jesus' suffering: "there was purpose in his suffering, and that purpose was directed towards his people."[20]

In Luke's account of the Last Supper, Jesus is quoted as saying, "This is my body which is given for you" (Luke 22:19). It is the word "given" which Paul replaces with "broken," so emphasizing that the brokenness of Jesus was his gift to us, not a tragic atrocity, and that it was precisely to this experience of brokenness that he gave himself. The apostle omits the mention in the gospels that Jesus gave his disciples the bread (Matt. 26:26; Mark 14:22; Luke 22:19), but the fact is still implicit. Jesus' act of giving the bread serves as a signpost to the significance of the cross as the greatest of all acts of self-giving. Heinrich Heppe says, "The breaking of the bread is not to be regarded as an indifferent use, but is necessarily to be used in solemnizing the Supper, as a symbol ordained by Christ of his broken body and of the communion which the many believers have in the one Christ."[21]

Donald Senior draws an insightful comparison between the breaking of the bread at the Last Supper and Jesus' two earlier feeding miracles, both of which involved breaking bread (Matt. 14:19 [Mark 6:41]; Matt. 15:36 [Mark 8:6]). Senior says that the first of these miracles (the feeding of the five thousand) took place in Jewish territory, the other (the feeding of the four thousand) among Gentiles. Taken together, therefore, they "express the very intent of Jesus' messianic mission," moving from the Jews to the world. Both feeding miracles took place in desert regions (Matt. 14:13 [Mark 6:35]; Matt. 15:33 [Mark 8:4]), and both were "driven by compassion" (Matt. 14:14 [Mark 6:34]; Matt. 15:32 [Mark 8:2]).[22] Similarly, Jesus' impending death provides spiritual, eternal sustenance for those whose lives without him are barren, and it was the same motivation – compassion – which lay behind the cross, and compassion is the ultimate divine attribute.

---

20. Morris, *Corinthians*, 161.
21. Heppe, *Reformed Dogmatics*, 634.
22. Senior, *Matthew*, 65–66; Senior, *Mark*, 54–58.

THE ACTIVE RECEPTION ON THE PART OF THE CONGREGATION (V. 24)

Paul cites Jesus' command to his disciples to "take" the bread in order to eat it (cf. Matt. 26:26; Mark 14:22): "the disciples' active participation in the action (the command to share in the bread and the cup and the actual carrying out of the command) is clearly stressed."[23] In each account the command is *labete*. A lexicon would explain this verb with phrases such as these: "to lay hold of something in order to use it, to take something to oneself and so make it one's own, to take something so as not to let it go, to take possession of a thing, to receive something that is offered as a gift."[24] These definitions suggest active participation, personal commitment, determination. To take the bread is to give expression to your passionate love for Jesus, your resolve that he shall be yours and you shall be his forever, but also to acknowledge that everything which you receive as you take him comes freely from God as pure gift.[25]

THE SYMBOLIC IDENTIFICATION OF THE ELEMENTS (VV. 24, 25)

All four accounts reveal that Jesus said, very definitely, "this is my body" (see also Matt. 26:26; Mark 14:22; Luke 22:19), and also used the personal pronoun with reference to the new covenant blood (see also Matt. 26:28; Mark 14:24; Luke 22:20). In Biblical thought the body was far more than something merely exterior, detachable, in principle at least, from the real person. The body was one way of referring to the real person, to the self in its entirety.[26] Jesus' identification of the sacramental bread with his body, was a way of explaining that he was to give "his very self,"[27] that his entire being was to be consumed for the sake of those for whose life he was dying. "The food is Jesus himself," and there is a "personal bonding of Jesus with his disciples."[28] Our affection in the sacrament is not for the elements, not even for the cross as such, but for the very person who gave himself to that death. He gave himself, and we love him.

---

23. Senior, *Mark*, 54, n. 15.
24. Thayer, *Lexicon*, 370–71.
25. See Siede, "*lambanō*," 748.
26. See Wibbing, "Body," 233, 235.
27. Senior, *Mark*, 58.
28. Senior, *Luke*, 61.

The Supper as an act of remembrance (vv. 24, 25)

In the breaking of bread and the drinking of the cup we remember the Lord Jesus. Here Paul quotes Luke 22:19. The word translated "remembrance" is *anamnēsis*. The prefix, *ana*, means "upwards," and signifies a goal, or it can suggest repetition or renewal.[29] To remember the Lord around his table is not a bare act of historical recollection. It is more than a mere memory exercise. To remember the Lord is to be led upwards into deepened fellowship with him, the goal being that the church's sense of union with its head in heaven should be constantly renewed as a part of our felt experience while we remain on earth. "The communion leads to Christ."[30] As F. F. Bruce says, "In the Biblical sense *remembrance* is more than a mental exercise; it involves a realization of what is remembered.... At the Eucharist Christians experience the real presence of their Lord."[31]

Senior speaks of "dynamic memory" as the way in which the link between Jesus and the church is maintained: remembering entails "the continuing presence of the risen Christ."[32] This is why the Lord's Supper is "a sacrament, an effective means of God's grace to all who receive it in faith."[33]

The cup as the new covenant in the Savior's blood (v. 25)

In Exodus 24:8 we read of "the blood of the covenant." The covenant is something which the Lord makes with people, and the blood is taken from burnt offerings and peace offerings sacrificed on the altar (Exod. 24:5–6). The purpose of this combination of offerings was primarily to provide "a sweet aroma to the Lord" (Lev. 1:9, 13, 17; 3:5; cf. 3:16). The function of a sweet aroma is defined in Genesis 8:21: it tranquilizes the Lord's anger against sin, so that he is able to say "never again" at the thought of implementing judgment.

Exodus 24:8 is quoted in Hebrews 9:20, in a passage which sees Christ as the true fulfillment of all the Old Testament provisions: "with his own blood he obtained eternal redemption" (Heb. 9:12); he has "put away sin by the sacrifice of himself" (Heb. 9:26). He is the Mediator of the new covenant" (Heb. 9:15; cf. Heb. 12:24).

---

29. Thayer, *Lexicon*, 35.
30. Grosheide, *Corinthians*, 270.
31. F. F. Bruce, *Corinthians*, 111–12.
32. Senior, *Luke*, 63–64.
33. Burrows, *Mark's Passion Narrative*, 8.

The newness of the new covenant is that the coming of Christ and his self-sacrifice "once for all" (Heb. 7:27; 9:12, 26, 28; 10:10) renders it complete, as distinct from the merely provisional nature of the old covenant.[34] Because the new covenant is complete, our sins are remembered "no more" (Heb. 8:12; 10:17). This is the equivalent of the words "never again" in Genesis 8:21. They draw attention to the fact that Jesus offered himself as "an offering and a sacrifice to God for a sweet-smelling aroma" (Eph. 5:2). It is the sacrifice of Christ on the cross—he who "himself is our peace" (Eph. 2:14)—which forever tranquilizes God's anger against a sinful world, such that judgment is now in the past, completed at the cross, so that never again shall redeemed sinners face that judgment. Like the old covenant, the new covenant too is one which the Lord makes on his own gracious initiative.

The three Synoptic writers each put a slightly different slant on these words of Jesus. Mark 14:24 simply announces that Jesus' blood of the new covenant "is shed for many," "the many" being a common description of the whole company for whose life and salvation Jesus gave up his life to the death of the cross. The same term is used in Hebrews 9:28. The words echo Isaiah 53:12, where it is the "many" whose sin the Savior bore. "*The many* underlines the immeasurable effects of Jesus' solitary death: the one dies, the many find their lives 'ransomed, healed, restored, forgiven,' a great host no man can number."[35] The choice of the word "many" to delineate God's elect helps to emphasize the lavish vastness of God's grace in his secret, sovereign choice of the vast majority of human beings for salvation.

Matthew 26:28 indicates the benefit which the many derive from Jesus' sacrifice: "the remission of sins." That is "the full significance of Jesus' redemptive mission,"[36] the heart of his achievement as viewed from our side. It is the effect of the tranquilizing of God's anger: he renounces his claim against us for retribution, accepting his Son's offering as the requisite satisfaction in our name. Our debt towards him is cancelled.

Luke 22:20 makes this all very personal. Jesus says, "This cup is the new covenant in my blood, which is shed for you." And you and I may, by faith in Jesus, include ourselves within the scope of Jesus' personal address.

34. See Grosheide, *Corinthians*, 271.
35. Carson, *Matthew*, on Matt. 20:28.
36. Senior, *Matthew*, 69.

The Particular Cup in View (v. 25)

The words "this cup" distinguish the cup in view from other cups on the Passover table, and, indeed, from all other cups. The word "this" draws emphatic attention to the particular cup which Jesus is holding. We learn from 1 Corinthians 10:16 that it was "the cup of blessing" which served this sacramental purpose. "This cup was the third of the Passover cups."[37] Traditionally, four cups were used during the Passover meal,[38] the other three being the cup of sanctification, the story cup, and the cup of praise.[39] Jesus took this cup, the cup of blessing, so declaring the incalculable blessings which would flow to his followers from his death on the cross. In drinking this cup we "unfold all the treasure of God's goodness, and call to mind those mighty gifts."[40]

Perhaps there is an intentional contrast too with the cup which the Lord was so soon to face, and from which he shrank away during his agony in Gethsemane (Matt. 26:39, 42; Luke 22:42). The reference to "the cup" here must be understood in the light of Isaiah 51:17 and Jeremiah 25:15, which speak of the cup of the Lord's fury. The Lord Jesus shrank from facing the fury of his Father against the world's sin, and yet at the same time committed himself to submit to the Father's will. He therefore went on to drink to its dregs the cup of divine wrath. There is then an exchange of cups: we deserve the wrath, but he took it for us. His was the blessing, but he shares it forever with us.

The Duty of Frequent Participation in the Lord's Supper (vv. 24–26)

The words "as often as you drink it" and "as often as you eat this bread and drink this cup" are a Pauline addition, not recorded in any of the gospels. They certainly imply that it was the expectation that the Lord's Supper would be celebrated often. Further, the repeated command, "do this" "is present continuous: 'Keep on doing this.'"[41]

We need this feast of remembrance at frequent intervals because of the constant battle we face with our sinful flesh, which would turn our eyes away from Jesus to foolish confidence in our own works and efforts.

---

37. Mare, *1 Corinthians*, on 1 Cor. 11:25–26.
38. Liefeld, *Luke*, on Luke 22:14–18.
39. Klappert, "Lord's Supper," 522.
40. Chrysostom, *Corinthians*, Hom. 24.3, 320.
41. Morris, *Corinthians*, 161.

We need to participate in the Supper often, also, because, as the family meal, this is what keeps the family together in unity and love. To neglect the Supper, or to attend merely occasionally betrays a half-hearted commitment to Christ, and a lukewarm love towards our brothers and sisters in him.

The proclamatory power of the Lord's Supper (v. 26)

God achieves his saving work in his people's hearts through the preaching of his Word. The Word spoken audibly appeals through the hearing to the mind. Just as the Jews at Passover recounted the story of the exodus, so the Lord's Supper has to include "a public narration of the death of Christ."[42]

However, beyond that, the sacraments are God's Word presented to the other senses. In the Lord's Supper, God appeals to our sense of sight, as we observe the elements positioned on the table, to our sense of taste as we place the bread and wine in our mouths, to our sense of smell as the fragrance of baked bread and fermented grape wafts into our nostrils, to our sense of touch as we handle the bread and the cup. The Lord's Supper is an event in which Calvary is vividly proclaimed as the saving moment to which we commit our trust. "The solemn observance of Holy Communion is a vivid proclamation of the Lord's death. In word and symbol Christ's death for men is set before them. 'The Eucharist is an *acted* sermon, an *acted* proclamation of the death which it commemorates.'"[43]

As such, it serves to deepen the assurance of believers, as their entire bodily functions are caught up into the reception of God's Word.

The Lord's Supper is also a dramatic evangelistic presentation of the gospel. For that reason, we should beware of fencing the table too strictly. An excess of anxiety about who is present may result in some who might encounter the gospel in the sacrament being robbed of the opportunity. It would be quite wrong, too, for the children of believers to be excluded from coming to the table. To witness the church in its celebration of God's grace in Christ will help to lead the children of the covenant into the faith which dwells first in their parents (see 2 Tim. 1:5).

---

42. F. F. Bruce, *Corinthians*, 113–4.
43. Morris, *Corinthians*, 162, quoting Robertson and Plummer.

The Eschatological Perspective of the Lord's Supper (v. 26)

The time frame for the Lord's Supper is terminated by the words "until he come." No doubt this is the apostle's summary of Jesus' eschatological vision as he shared the Passover meal with his disciples. He said to them, "I will not drink of this fruit of the vine from now on until that day when I drink it new with you in my Father's kingdom" (Matt. 26:29; cf. Mark 14:25). Senior describes the "until" as "defiant": this phrase "is a stunning prediction of hope and victory planted in a story that rushes toward death."[44]

The "until" is intimately connected with the words "with you": that is what Jesus looked forward to—to eating and drinking in heaven with his people. This is what his people look forward to—to seeing our Savior face to face, and feasting with him at the heavenly banquet, tasting the joys of eternity. The earthly sacrament is a foretaste of that glorious, endless festivity which will be our portion when the kingdom of God comes in its everlasting fullness. Therefore, "what is from one point a view a memorial act is from another point of view an act of anticipation."[45]

Having set out the procedure and indicated the symbolic meaning of the Lord's Supper, the apostle then stresses the duty of self-examination prior to participation. Personally, I rarely read these words when the congregation is assembled around the table. It is a bit late then to start the process of self-examination. This is not the task of a couple of minutes while we are already at the table, but the work of the week that leads up to the gathering of the church.

"Worthiness" in this context means "discerning the Lord's body" (v. 29). Most probably, this is a reference to the church as the body of the Lord.[46] The next chapter speaks of the church as "the body of Christ" (1 Cor. 12:27). To discern the body is to treat fellow believers with a special care, above and beyond what would be normal in human relationships. It is to recognise that the new humanity in Christ is unique and distinct in the world, that to belong to it is an inestimable privilege, and that membership demands the loving commitment, which cares for every member, and rejoices to serve.

---

44. Senior, *Mark*, 61.
45. F. F. Bruce, *Corinthians*, 114.
46. So F. F. Bruce, *Corinthians*, 115.

To fail in this duty is to "be guilty of the body and blood of the Lord" (v. 27), because it is to fail to value the people whom he valued so much that for them he gave his body to brokenness and shed his precious blood. It is to despise the sacrifice of Calvary by failing to cherish the fruits of Calvary in lives transformed by the grace of the Lord Jesus Christ. As the second-century work known as The Didache puts it, "Anyone who has a difference with his fellow is not to take part with you until they have been reconciled."[47]

OUR COMMUNION WITH HOLY PERSONS—SANCTORUM AS MASCULINE

If "saints" is taken as masculine, and therefore as referring to people, "the communion of saints" may be understood in more than one way. There is one interpretation which may be discounted immediately. Kelly notes that "saints" may be taken "in a narrow sense of the saints proper and martyrs,"[48] distinguishing those who have been "canonized" from the generality of Christian people.

According to *The Catechism of the Catholic Church*, the canonization of some of the faithful involves the solemn proclamation "that they practised heroic virtue and lived in fidelity to God's grace," by which, as saints, they are proposed "as models and intercessors."[49] However, such a use of the word "saints" is quite foreign to Scriptural usage: in the Bible "saint" is the normal term for a believer.[50] Moreover, the procedure of canonization is an entirely human invention. The idea that the church or its leadership can create a saint is without any Biblical warrant whatsoever. We cannot, therefore, read the clause in this restrictive way.

However, there are two other possible meanings of the phrase understood in a masculine sense. They are not mutually exclusive. Witsius speaks of both,[51] although McGiffert, wrongly in my view, rules out the second.[52]

---

47. *Didache*, 14.
48. Kelly, *Creeds*, 390.
49. *Catechism of the Catholic Church*, para. 828.
50. See, e.g., Deut. 33:3; 1 Sam. 2:9; Pss. 31:23; 34:9; 50:5; 148:14; Dan. 7:27; Rom. 1:7; 1 Cor. 1:2; Eph. 2:19; Col. 1:2; Rev. 14:12.
51. Witsius, *Creed*, Vol. 2, 378–79.
52. McGiffert, *Creed*, 33.

All the saints of every age and generation

On this understanding the clause will be a description of the fullness of the church across time, "that ultimate fellowship with the holy persons of all ages,"[53] reminding every generation of its togetherness with believers from every period of history. Stewart expresses this lyrically:

> The *communion of saints* is a reality to those who have thus realized their oneness in Christ. We have communion with all the saints of all the ages; there is nothing good of which we cannot claim to be the inheritors; before our faith even the veil falls away, and the Church militant and the Church triumphant are seen to be one—the great cloud of witnesses, whose voices join in one great hymn of praise.[54]

Packer finds Biblical support for this idea of the communion "of the church 'militant here in earth' with the church triumphant" in Hebrews 12:22–24,[55] where believers now are said to "have come . . . to the spirits of just men made perfect".

Although this communion stretches forward as well as backwards in time, it is perhaps "with the saints departed"[56] that it is most evident. It is not obvious that talk of communion with people who do not yet exist is even meaningful, except in the somewhat abstract sense that "from the beginning of the world patriarchs, prophets, martyrs, and all other righteous men who have lived, or are now alive, or shall live in time to come, comprise the church."[57] However, "the *saints* or faithful Christians in this life and the saints who rejoice in heaven"[58] are contemporaneous today: the latter, as the Christmas Eve Service so beautifully puts it, "rejoice with us, but upon another shore and in a greater light."[59]

Jim Packer points out that the modern mind-set comes to the Bible with a "pervasive sense of difference between cultures and epochs." However, he applauds the wisdom of the Puritans, who saw things differently: "instead of feeling distant from biblical characters and their expe-

---

53. Kelly, *Creeds*, 391.
54. Stewart, *Creeds*, 60.
55. Packer, *Christian*, 65.
56. Stewart, *Creeds*, 57; see also Kelly, *Creeds*, 392.
57. Words of Nicetas of Remesianus, quoted by Kelly, *Creeds*, 391.
58. Stead, "Apostles' Creed," 10.
59. From The Bidding Prayer, Festival of Nine Lessons and Carols (King's College, Cambridge).

riences because of the number of centuries between them, the Puritans felt kinship with them because they belonged to the same human race, faced, feared, and fellowshipped with, the same unchanging God, and struggled with essentially the same spiritual problems."[60] It is that felt kinship which is "the communion of saints" on this larger scale.

All the saints on earth at any given time

If we take this as the reference of this phrase, it will then be a reminder of the joy and the duty of unity and fellowship with all God's people everywhere alive today. This goes beyond a mere definition of the church to a celebration of the real experience of global belonging which grips the hearts of Christian people, and to a challenge to practise this fellowship in whatever ways are possible.

Stewart understands the Westminster Confession to interpret the phrase like this.[61] Although the Confession does not explicitly state that this is its understanding, and does not rule out other possible readings, it is certainly true that what it says about "the communion of saints" points in the direction of this understanding. It speaks of communion in gifts and graces and of the obligation to perform such duties as serve the common good.[62] This appears to be Thomas Aquinas' reading of this phrase too.[63]

Witsius analyzes this communion under three headings: intimate union, common enjoyment of the most invaluable blessings, and reciprocal kindnesses. The third of these he further subdivides into three, as entailing sympathy in times of evil, whether afflictions or sins, mutual sharing of all good things, and prayer for one another. He then explains, in lovely terms, the place of this clause in a creed:

> we recognize and celebrate the admirable power of our God, which unites believers of every nation, age, condition and sex, often separated from one another by such vast intervening spaces of land and sea, of such dissimilar capacities and tempers, and engaged in such diversified pursuits; and so closely conjoins them by one Spirit, that they most harmoniously concur in the same sentiments and feelings respecting God and Christ, and in the

60. Packer, *Among God's Giants*, 129.
61. Stewart, *Creeds*, 57.
62. *Westminster Confession*, 659.
63. Kelly, *Creeds*, 394.

same devout prayers and praises, and discern in each other, with mutual congratulation and applause, the same effects of the same divine grace; so that, even at their first meeting, a most delightful interchange of love often arises.[64]

Witsius' words remind me of my own experience as a teenager in 1975. I had left my home and my home church in London for university in Bradford. Attending the evening service at Sunbridge Road Mission on my very first Sunday as a student, I found myself sitting behind a couple called Mr. and Mrs. Stocks. I had never met them before, but they turned to me, and warmly welcomed me at the end of the service. On discovering that I was new to the city, Mrs. Stocks generously invited me to their house for supper. In their home I met their daughter and her husband. Supper consisted of poached eggs. The memory of that egg will live with me all my days! It was a thoroughly practical, and lovingly spiritual, expression of the communion of saints. I never attended a Sunday service at another church throughout my time in Bradford, unless I was preaching. When we know the Lord, we have instant friends wherever we go. We are strangers for no more than a few minutes.

Commenting on this communion, in which believers mutually communicate to one another all the blessings which God bestows on them, Calvin quotes Acts 4:32,[65] "the multitude of those who believed were of one heart and one soul; neither did anyone say that any of the things he possessed was his own, but they had all things in common."

The wording of this text is interesting. The word translated "multitude" (*plēthos*) refers to a huge number of people, but in the case of the primitive Christian church, though their numbers were growing rapidly, they did not remain a thoroughly disparate group, but found themselves bonded together as "one heart and one soul." "The common life of *the body of believers* continued, being based on their spiritual unity; even the word *own* was discarded."[66] This placing of possessions at the disposal of one's fellow Christians was "the practical expression of the deep sense of fellowship"[67] between believers in Christ. "There could scarcely be a stronger expression of the unity prevailing in the infant church, and not

---

64. Witsius, *Creed*, Vol. 2, 381–82.
65. Calvin, *Institutes*, 4.1.3.
66. Rackham, *Acts*, 62.
67. Neil, *Acts*, 92.

confined to sentiment or language merely, but extending to the interchange of social advantages and legal rights."[68]

This mutuality of pooled and shared resources was spontaneous and voluntary. It was truly a fruit of the regenerating work of the Spirit of Christ within each member. This is emphasized by the words "neither did anyone say": it was a matter of individual and personal choice and joy. About the same time as the gospel was taking root and making its early headway in the world, the Jewish Essene sect of Qumran was also active. At Qumran sharing of goods was imposed as a matter of community legislation. In the Christian community, by contrast, the sharing "was the expression of the love of the Spirit."[69]

Acts 4:34–35 continues this theme of the practical communion of saints with its statement that there was no one amongst the believers who was constricted by poverty, because the body distributed to those in need. Howard Marshall sees here the fulfilment of the promise in Deuteronomy 15:4, that "there may be no poor among you; for the Lord will greatly bless you."[70] And it was the Lord's blessing, the sanctifying grace of the Spirit, which so bonded the believers together. Rackham rightly says, "It was only divine grace which enabled the wealthier individuals to overcome selfishness and make community of goods a reality."[71]

No doubt it is significant that, sandwiched between these two allusions to practical Christian fellowship, verse 33 reads: "with great power the apostles gave witness to the resurrection of the Lord Jesus." It is out of vibrant Christian fellowship that powerful evangelism flows. The depth of mutual belonging and the extent of practical caring are what give credibility to Christian testimony.

Calvin describes genuine Christian belonging within "the communion of saints" like this: "if they are truly persuaded that God is the common Father of them all, and Christ their common head, they cannot but be united together in brotherly love, and mutually impart their blessings to each other."[72]

One perhaps lesser known aspect of Paul's apostolic ministry was the collection which he made from Gentile churches for the support of the

68. J. A. Alexander, *Acts*, Vol. 1, 175.
69. E. F. Harrison, *Acts*, 90.
70. Marshall, *Acts*, 109.
71. Rackham, *Acts*, 62.
72. Calvin, *Institutes*, 4.1.3.

Jewish believers who were facing a time of financial hardship. Two texts in which words from the *koinōnia* group (signifying *communion* or *fellowship*) and the word "saints" occur in close proximity relate to this. They are Romans 15:26 and 2 Corinthians 8:4. Before the Corinthians Paul holds the example of the Macedonians, who had been so eager to hand over to Paul "the gift and the fellowship [or 'communion' (the *koinōnia*)] of the ministering to the saints." Writing to the Romans, Paul commends the Macedonian and Achaian Christians, who had made "a certain contribution for the poor among the saints who are in Jerusalem." More precisely, these believers are said to have been pleased "to do some fellowship [or 'communion' (the *koinōnia*)] towards the poor among the saints."

The verse from 2 Corinthians seems to distinguish between the gift and the fellowship, whereas the Romans text effectively equates the two. To be sure, the two may be distinguished, but they are so closely tied together, the gift being a way of making fellowship an experienced reality, that the distinction must ultimately break down: fellowship has to mean giving.

This emphasizes the active nature of the communion of saints. It is not merely a feeling of belonging, but putting that mutual belonging into practice in very tangible ways, not just within a local congregation, but between congregations too. James Dunn suggests that the use of the word the *koinōnia* implies that "Paul wanted his converts to regard their resources as held in common with and for other Christians," such that financial sharing becomes "the expression of their common life in Christ."[73]

The apostle regarded this contribution on the part of the Gentile believers for the poor Jewish Christians as vitally important: it demonstrated "the sort of close fellowship which Gentile and Jewish Christians ought to have with one another—helping one another in every way they could."[74] It gave "material expression to their participation in Christian *fellowship*."[75] Without that material expression Christian fellowship remains ethereal and suspect. When our communion with other holy people becomes as tangible as this, then even our material possessions and financial resources become holy things.

Although this clause of the creed has to be taken in a large sense, it is, of course, in the local church, or at least, in the fellowship of particular

---

73. Dunn, *Romans 9–16*, 875.
74. Bowen, *Romans*, 194.
75. Hendriksen, *Romans*, 494.

congregations in a specific locality, that "the communion of saints" finds its most concrete expression in the love of believers for one another. The practice of Christian love is only possible with those fellow believers whom we actually meet, and for most believers the option of travel for global fellowship is extremely limited.

There is one other text (Romans 12:13) in which *koinōnia* vocabulary and the word "saints" are juxtaposed. It emphasizes the duty and joy of mutual sharing as the opportunity arises in the first instance within the local church.

The apostle here urges on us the duty of "distributing to the needs of the saints." More literally, this could be rendered "entering into fellowship [or 'communion' (*koinōnia*)] with the needs of the saints." In its most practical expression, "the communion of saints" means doing what one can to help fellow believers who are in need, and so experiencing real fellowship. This practical help may be couched in terms of fellowship, since it is a reflection of the love of Christ, whose motivation was to help us in our direst need. Charles Hodge points out the significance of the use of this verb:

> "Taking part in the necessities of the saints; regard them as your own." Believers are *koinōnoi* in everything, because they are all members of the body of Christ. The members of the same body have the same interests, feelings, and destiny. The joy or sorrow of one member, is the joy or sorrow of all the members. The necessities of one are, or should be, a common burden.[76]

Alister McGrath highlights the practical application of this doctrine:

> Draw comfort and support from others! That is one of the practical consequences of the doctrine of "the communion of saints." Read Hebrews 11:1–12:3 and realize that you share in the faith of these great figures of old. You all belong to the same great family. They have all been through the trials, struggles and temptations of faith before you. They are now "a great cloud of witnesses" (Heb. 12:1) cheering you on as you run the same race. Try to visualize the scene: you are in a great Roman amphitheatre, with the racecourse ahead of you and crowds shouting their support and encouragement as you aim to complete the race and gain your crown of laurel.[77]

---

76. Hodge, *Romans*, 397; see also J. Murray, *Romans*, Vol. 2, 133.
77. McGrath, *I Believe*, 108.

18

The remission of sins

KARL BARTH DRAWS ATTENTION to the fact "that the Apostles' Creed, speaking of the Christian life in the present time, mentions only the forgiveness of sins." Barth notes that the Reformers followed suit, and deems them to be right "in thus narrowing down all Christianity, all the Christian life and faith to one single point." He explains: "the forgiveness of sins is the basis, the sum, the criterion, of all that may be called Christian life or faith."[1] McGrath calls "the remission of sins" the creed's compressed summary of "the full richness of the New Testament understanding of the work of Jesus Christ."[2] As Ephesians 1:7 and Colossians 1:14 imply, "the forgiveness of sins" is the whole, or at least the heart, of our "redemption through his blood." "Redemption and forgiveness are not exactly parallel or identical concepts, but by putting the two terms in apposition to each other, the apostle teaches that the central feature of redemption is the forgiveness of sins."[3]

Part of what is involved in affirming belief in "the remission of sins" is the recognition of our duty to forgive those who wrong us. Jesus teaches us to pray, "forgive us our sins, for we also forgive everyone who is indebted to us" (Luke 11:4). He stressed to Peter the challenge of lavish, endless, unrecorded forgiveness, backing it up with the parable of the servant whose master forgave him an immense debt, but who then unacceptably refused to forgive a fellow servant a much smaller amount (Matt. 18:21–35). However, for now I want to focus on our faith in God's forgiveness extended towards us.

---

1. Barth, *Faith*, 157–58.
2. McGrath, *I Believe*, 98.
3. C. Vaughan, *Colossians*, on Col. 1:14; see also O'Brien, *Colossians*, 28; Lincoln, *Ephesians*, on Eph. 1:7, 8.

It is a sad fact that in the early centuries of the Christian era the church somehow lost the fullness of the gospel. Dr. Kelly is certainly right to say of that ancient period that "one of the grand convictions of Christians was that in baptism all their past sins were washed away once and for all." However, our first ancestors in the Christian faith had a blind spot when it came to forgiveness for sins committed after baptism.[4]

Both Augustine and Rufinus bring out the wonder of God's lavish forgiveness bestowed in baptism (or in the experience of conversion which baptism signified). Augustine spoke of the perfection of forgiveness upon reception of baptism. To believers who feared that they had committed sins so heinous that they were beyond the reach of God's forgiveness, he pointed out that the worst possible sin was the killing of Christ. Of this the Jews were guilty, and yet many of them subsequently came to believe on him, and this worst of sins was forgiven. How much more then will our sins, even those which we shudder to think about, be forgiven us![5]

Rufinus, likewise, celebrated the largesse of God's indulgence towards sinners. He acknowledged the ridicule which Christians often faced from pagans: "they say, 'can he who has committed murder be no murderer, and he who has committed adultery be accounted no adulterer? How then shall one guilty of crimes of this sort all of a sudden be made holy?'" Rufinus replies like this:

> He is King of all who has promised it; he is Lord of heaven and earth who assures us of it. Would you have me refuse to believe that he who made me a man of the dust of the earth can of a guilty person make me innocent? And that he who when I was blind made me see, or when I was deaf made me hear, or lame walk, can recover for me my lost innocence?[6]

However, those early believers failed to embrace the fullness of the gospel, and were therefore deficient in their understanding of the future impact of the forgiveness first received at conversion. McGiffert interprets the extant Christian literature of the second-century as picturing God more as lawgiver and judge than as loving Father. He acknowledges that "there was general agreement among Christians that

---

4. Kelly, *Creeds*, 160–61.
5. Augustine, *Creed*, para. 15, 700.
6. Rufinus, *Commentary*, para. 40, 1129–30.

repentance and baptism effected the remission of a man's pre-baptismal sins, and enabled him to start upon the Christian life with a clean record." Thereafter, however, the chief emphasis was on ethical rigor, on judgment rather than forgiveness, so that for the believer in those early days, "it was the thought of the divine severity, not the divine mercy, which was to control his life."[7]

This may be illustrated by reference to *The Shepherd of Hermas*, a second-century work composed at Rome. It was written out of concern that something of the radical nature of the Christianity of the earliest days was now lost.

The Shepherd is primarily a call to repentance. The main message was that God was now granting but one repentance for post-baptismal sins committed up to that time. Hermas saw himself as commissioned to make known to the church that

> all their previous sins shall be forgiven them, and all the saints who have sinned until this day shall be forgiven, if they repent from a united heart, and put away double-mindedness from their heart. For the Master has sworn by his glory to his elect that if, after this day has been set, there still be sin, they shall not have salvation, for repentance for the righteous has an end.[8]

In another place Hermas says, "It is necessary to admit the one who sins and repents, but not many times, for to the servants of God is granted one repentance."[9] The reason why there is but one repentance is that if a person "sins and repents in an off-hand manner it is useless for such a person, for he shall hardly live."[10] Following this one repentance it is necessary that those who repent walk in the commandments, for otherwise their repentance is trivial.[11]

Although Hermas' idea that, for the baptized believer, there is only one opportunity for repentance, which must be followed by single-minded obedience, makes sense in a way, given that he believed that the final end-time tribulation was imminent,[12] it is, nevertheless, "both

---

7. McGiffert, *Creed*, 157.
8. *The Shepherd of Hermas*, Vis. 2:2;4–5; cf. Vis. 3:2;2; Mand. 4:3;4.
9. *The Shepherd of Hermas*, Mand. 4:1;8.
10. *The Shepherd of Hermas*, Mand. 4:3;6.
11. *The Shepherd of Hermas*. Sim. 6:1;3; cf. Mand. 12:3;2.
12. See Pernveden, *The Concept of the Church*, 271.

psychologically ridiculous and scripturally untenable."[13] There is truth in Thomas Torrance's comment on the theology of Hermas and his contemporaries: "salvation has become a doubtful case of enduring to the end. . . . The new life in Christ is not conceived of as a gift, but as something to be striven after."[14] That picture of a life of striving meant that God's forgiveness was rarely accessible, and the professing Christian was likely to end up tortured by despair.

Thankfully, Luther saw it differently. He was raised up by God to call the church back to the wholeness of the gospel. He recognized that "we are never without sin," but rejoiced in the truth that "there is nothing but continuous, uninterrupted forgiveness," and that it is obtained daily.[15] God "generously forgives every day every sin committed by me and every believer."[16] In Luther's threefold "every"—forgiveness for every sin for every believer every day—we hear the glory of the gospel. Day in, day out, we are confronted by a God who, in Christ, is lavishly gracious, richly merciful, staggeringly good, outlandishly kind. "Every day we ought to begin, we may begin, with the confession, 'I believe in the forgiveness of sins.'"[17]

In order fully to understand "the remission of sins," we need first to consider the nature of sin. We shall never really understand what forgiveness is until we have realized "how grievous sin is,"[18] that "sin means man's eternal lostness."[19]

The Scriptural definition of sin is found in 1 John 3:4: "sin is lawlessness." The reference here is to the law of God. Isaiah says that "the LORD is our Lawgiver" (Isa. 33:22). It is the law which he has revealed which we are obliged to obey. There is no alternative acceptable pattern for human life, because "there is one Lawgiver" (Jas. 4:12), that is to say, only one.

Sin entails breaking God's law, and since God's law is the only standard by which human behavior can be assessed, there is no fall back, we can make no excuses. Moreover, as Jim Packer points out, sin "appears in

13. Bayes, *Apostolic Fathers*, 162.
14. Torrance, *Apostolic Fathers*, 39.
15. Luther, *Larger Catechism*, 64.
16. Luther, *Enchiridion*, 80.
17. Barth, *Dogmatics*, 150.
18. Barth, *Faith*, 156.
19. Barth, *Dogmatics*, 150.

desires as well as deeds, and motives as well as actions."[20] This is because God's law prescribes appropriate inner purity as well as rightful outward holiness. Blaiklock takes the definition of "lawlessness" a step further: "the sinner acts as if no law exists to limit human conduct."[21] It is not just that we break God's law, but that we act as if God's law is non-existent, we treat it as totally irrelevant as a guide to human life.

There are those who argue that the link with the law, though etymologically implicit in the term *anomia*, has in fact dropped into the background, and that the word has come to signify "a rebellious alignment with the devil, rather than with God in Christ." On this reading the statement that "sin is lawlessness" means that sin is "not merely breaking God's law, but flagrantly opposing him."[22] This is not obviously in tune with the other uses of *anomia* in the New Testament: it often occurs in a context where God's law is involved in the discussion.[23] Furthermore, it appears to overlook the basic fact that rebellion against God is, essentially, the refusal to have him as Lawgiver.

John Stott suggests that, although 1 John 3:4 is "the clearest and most revealing" definition of sin in the New Testament, there are others. He mentions Romans 14:23, "whatever is not from faith is sin," James 4:17, "to him who knows to do good and does not do it, to him it is sin," and 1 John 5:17, "all unrighteousness is sin."[24] However, these are not so much definitions as illustrations. They are not telling us what sin is but what things are sin. If sin is, intrinsically, lawlessness, then the error in failing to live from faith is that one inevitably breaks the law. The reason why it is sin to fail to do good when one knows what is good is that it is the law which defines what is good, and therefore to fail to do the good which is known is *ipso facto* to flout the requirements of the law. The statement "unrighteousness is sin" is inevitably true, since it is the law which is the authentic outline of true righteousness.

In view of this association between sin and the breaking of God's law, Witsius calls sin "a contempt and renunciation of the dominion of God": in sinning we oppose the authority of God. Here is a recognition that to make a distinction between law-breaking and opposition to God

20. Packer, *Christian*, 68.
21. Blaiklock, *Children of Light*, 61.
22. Smalley, *1, 2, 3 John*, on 1 John 3:4; cf. Marshall, *Epistles of John*, 176–77.
23. See especially Matt. 7:23; Rom. 4:7; 6:19; Heb. 8:10; 10:17.
24. Stott, *Epistles of John*, 122.

is to create a false dichotomy. In addition Witsius notes that "sin includes a *perverseness*, a *crookedness*," which is contrary to rectitude.[25] This follows from the singularity of God's revealed law as the portrait of legitimate human life. Witsius also highlights the twofold nature of every sin, its stain and its guilt. The stain of sin arises from the "detestation and abhorrence in which God holds it" arising from his own holiness. The guilt of sin is the obligation to punishment which it involves:[26] the result of every sin is that every sinner deserves to be punished.

What the punishment for sin is the Bible makes crystal clear. The very first sanction imposed in the case of transgression was "you shall surely die" (Gen. 2:17). In Ezekiel 18:4 and 20 "a basic principle is set forth"[27] that "the soul who sins shall die." The apostle states categorically, "the wages of sin is death" (Rom. 6:23): "the ruin which follows" upon sin is its fair reward.[28]

To understand the nature of the death here in view, Calvin suggests, we should consider what is its opposite. He points out that the life from which the human race fell was one of total happiness, and one whose prospect was endless.

> Thence it follows, that under the name of "death" is comprehended all those miseries in which Adam involved himself by his defection; for as soon as he revolted from God, the fountain of life, he was cast down from his former state, in order that he might perceive the life of man without God to be wretched and lost, and therefore differing nothing from death. Hence the condition of man after sin is not improperly called both the privation of life, and death. The miseries and evils both of soul and body, with which man is beset so long as he is on earth, are a kind of entrance into death, till death itself entirely absorbs him.[29]

Haldane considers the awful nature of the eternal punishment, summed up in the single word "death," which is the proper outcome of sin:

> Its subjects will not only be bereaved of all that is good, they will also be overwhelmed with all that is terrible. As the chief good of

---

25. Witsius, *Creed*, Vol. 2, 387.
26. Witsius, *Creed*, Vol. 2, 388–90.
27. R. H. Alexander, *Ezekiel*, on Ezek. 18:1–4.
28. See C. J. Vaughan, *Romans*, 130.
29. Calvin, *Genesis*, 127.

the creature is the enjoyment of the love of God, how great must be the punishment of being deprived of the sense of his love, and oppressed with the consciousness of his hatred! The condemned will be entirely divested of every token of the protection and blessing of God, and visited with every proof of his wrath and indignation.[30]

Since "all have sinned" (Rom. 3:23), such an undying death is what we all deserve.

Calvin observes the emotional impact which consciousness of one's own sin and one's consequent liability to judicial death can have on the sinner, once the Holy Spirit's convicting work is underway: "oppressed, afflicted, and confounded by the awareness of their own sins, they are stricken by the sense of divine judgment, become displeased with themselves, and, as it were, groan and toil under a heavy burden."[31]

This convicting work is a necessary prelude to the enjoyment of forgiveness. We do, however, have to be careful to recognize that the degree of felt conviction will vary according to temperament. We must not fall into the trap of, in effect, making a particular experience or degree of conviction of sin a work which merits forgiveness.

What, then, does "remission of sins" mean? Witsius defines *forgiveness* as "the absolution of the sinner from guilt," resulting in deserved punishment being withheld.[32] This definition rightly draws attention to the two aspects involved in forgiveness. "Forgiveness implies the removal of both sins and the consequences of sin."[33]

THE REMOVAL OF GUILT

Viewed in this way forgiveness may be compared to the cancellation of a debt. God erases from his account book the record of what we owe him.[34] This is how Jesus depicts forgiveness in the parable of the forgiven, but unforgiving, servant in Matthew 18: it is like writing off a debt. Although the challenge of the parable is our duty of forgiving, it does at the same time bring out the stupendous wonder of God's forgiveness. There is no possibility that the servant can ever repay his king what he owes him.

30. Haldane, *Romans*, 265–66.
31. Calvin, *Catechism, 1538*, 20.viii, 26.
32. Witsius, *Creed*, Vol. 2, 390.
33. Van Gemeren, *Psalms*, on Ps. 85:1–2.
34. See von Balthasar, *Credo*, 89.

His debt is "astronomically high"[35] (v. 24). It would have amounted to several thousand lifetimes of earnings for the average working man.[36] We are dealing here with hyperbole to make a point: "the poor man owes the king more money than existed in circulation in the whole country at the time!"[37] However, in response to the servant's desperate plea, the master "was moved with compassion, released him, and forgave him the debt" (v. 27). Later the master reminds the servant, "I forgave you all that debt" (v. 32).

Jesus is pressing upon us the sheer magnitude of our sin: our indebtedness to God is incalculable, and nothing we could ever do, even if we were granted an infinity of eternities in which to accomplish it, could possibly settle our account with God. However, God forgives us. And this does not mean that he just waives a proportion of our debt: he forgives it all. His forgiveness is absolute, total, unrestricted, lavishly generous, colossal in its awesome completeness. Like the master in the parable, God treats us "with nearly unimaginable grace in the full dismissal of all indebtedness."[38] We are released totally from our liabilities towards God. God renounces his claim that we personally pay him everything we owe to him. And the basis of it all is his compassion.

Barth expresses this strikingly, comparing forgiveness to the deletion of a written record: "Remission and acquittal mean to cross out. God states that our sin exists. But he crosses it out."[39] Elsewhere, Barth puts it like this: "Perhaps we can best clarify the concept of forgiveness, of *remissio*, as that something has been recorded in writing, namely our life; and now a great stroke is drawn through the whole."[40]

This is similar to the picture which Paul uses in Colossians 2:13–14. He speaks of "the handwriting of requirements that was against us"; this has been "wiped out," by which is meant that God has "forgiven you all trespasses." Although Vaughan sees the handwriting as the Mosaic Law,[41] it is perhaps better to interpret it not as the Mosaic Law *tout simple*, but as the threatening sanctions of the law in case of disobedience. The law

35. Hagner, *Matthew 14–28*, on Matt. 18:24–25.
36. See Green, *Matthew*, 165; Hendriksen, *Matthew*, 705.
37. Keener, *Matthew*, 291.
38. Hagner, *Matthew 14–28*, on Matt. 18:27.
39. Barth, *Faith*, 153.
40. Barth, *Dogmatics*, 150.
41. C. Vaughan, *Colossians*, on Col. 2:13–14.

is pictured as the record of our failures.[42] This is the specific function of the law described by the apostle in Romans 3:20 and 4:15, the law as it exposes our sinfulness and highlights our vulnerability to God's wrath. However, to be forgiven is to be released from that use of the law. It is to have all the law's accusations and threats against us deleted.

The text from Colossians also emphasizes the totality of God's forgiveness: "all trespasses" without exception are forgiven. Not one sin, however serious, lies out of the reach, or wide of the scope, of God's forgiving grace. Here is a marvellous thing, a cause for exuberant joy: the record of every single sin that we have ever committed has been blotted out. This ties in with the emphasis in the explanation of the new covenant on forgiveness as God's placing of our sins forever beyond his recall by an act of his sovereign will. It is this "everlasting oblivion"[43] of sin which lies at the heart of the new covenant (Jer. 31:34; Heb. 10:17–18). Jeremiah 50:20 imagines people searching for the sins of God's people, but being unable to find them, because the LORD has forgiven them: their sins have become non-existent. This is indeed the doctrine of remission of sin "expressed in noble form": forgiveness means that sins are "completely obliterated."[44]

Perhaps the fullest Old Testament portrayals of forgiveness are found in Psalm 32:1–2 and Micah 7:18–19. The Psalm verses are quoted in Romans 4:7–8. The Romans citation stops in the middle of Psalm 32:2, recognizing that there are three parallel lines, all dealing with the theme of forgiveness. The first line alerts us to the fact that the theme is forgiveness. Each of the other two lines draws a picture, illustrating what forgiveness means.

In the first place forgiveness means that our sins are covered, hidden from God's view. When God forgives sins, he draws a veil over them, he puts a lid on them, "he buries them,"[45] so that they are no longer visible. This same picture recurs in Psalm 85:2. Secondly, forgiveness means that God stops counting our sins. He refuses to attribute them to us. He does not impute, or compute, or calculate, the quantity of our sinfulness.

---

42. See Moule, *Colossian Studies*, 156.
43. A. B. Bruce, *Hebrews*, 298.
44. Thompson, *Jeremiah*, 737–38.
45. Calvin, *Psalms*, Vol. 3, 369.

"God does not book the sin in the ledger of life against a person."[46] He tears up the record. He puts down his pen.

Plumer notes that the literal meaning of the word "forgiven" in Psalm 32:1 is "to lift up," or "to carry away." He writes: "the language must have been well understood by a pious Jew, who annually saw the service of the scapegoat solemnly performed."[47] It is true that "forgiven" translates the same Hebrew verb as that rendered "bear" in Leviticus 16:22, where the instructions regarding the scapegoat are given. Plumer is therefore right in emphasizing that the Biblical concept of forgiveness already implies the need and the provision of an atonement by a vicarious sacrifice.[48]

Micah explains forgiveness in two ways. First, it is the passing over of transgression (Mic. 7:18). Although this word was not used of the Passover as such, it is used in the story of the Passover of the Angel of death passing through the land of Egypt (Exod. 12:12, 23). Micah pictures the LORD passing through his own land, but then bypassing his people's sins, and focussing his attention on his own saving mercy. If we are right to hear an echo of Exodus 12 here, then we are again reminded of the costly nature of the forgiveness which comes freely to us. The Lamb of God, "Christ our Passover" (1 Cor. 5:7), had to die instead of us for it to be possible for our sins to be passed over.

Secondly, Micah says, God has "cast all our sins into the depths of the sea" (Mic. 7:19). They have sunk without trace. They will never be fished up. They are gone—totally and forever gone.

Viewed in this way, forgiveness is tantamount to justification, a link which is established by Acts 13:38–39. "All the righteousness of believers is contained in forgiveness of sins."[49] To be forgiven might be said to be the negative aspect of which justification is the positive aspect. "Remission does not *define* justification, though justification must embrace remission."[50] To be forgiven is to have the guilt of our sinfulness cleared; to be justified is to have our guilt replaced by the righteousness of Jesus as the reality which defines our existence before God.

---

46. Fitzmyer, *Romans*, 376.
47. Plumer, *Psalms*, 397.
48. Plumer, *Psalms*, 398, 800.
49. Calvin, *Catechism*, 1538, 20.viii, 26.
50. J. Murray, *Romans*, Vol. 1, 135.

Everett Harrison says that "forgiveness is a necessary preparation" for "the bestowal of a righteous standing before God." However, while he is right to recognize that in normal usage "forgiveness may be granted over and over, but justification is a once-for-all pronouncement on behalf of the sinner,"[51] in this context the word "forgiveness" also appears to be used in a once-for-all sense. However, Rackham errs in claiming that this forgiveness relates only to the past, while justification answers to the needs of present and future.[52] Forgiveness, considered in a once-for-all sense relates to the guilt of our entire life and existence. That is cleared decisively in the same moment that we are justified in Christ. Hallelujah!

Barth portrays the significance of forgiveness as justification in vivid terms: God "will not regard us as those who live as they live and act as they act, but says to us, 'you are justified.' For me you are no longer the sinner, but where you are there stands another. I look at this other."[53] The Heidelberg Catechism continues its definition of forgiveness by reminding me that God "graciously imparts to me the righteousness of Christ, that I may nevermore come into condemnation."[54]

THE WITHHOLDING OF PUNISHMENT

But secondly, "the remission of sins" means that the punishment which is justly merited is graciously withheld. Philip Budd, noting the root meaning of the Hebrew term for "forgive," "to lift up," concludes that the central idea is the lifting up and carrying away of sin, and particularly "the taking away of the punishment sin deserves."[55] Calvin explains forgiveness to mean "that God by his gratuitous goodness forgives and pardons the faithful their sins, so that they are not summoned to judgment nor is punishment exacted from them."[56]

There are several instances in the Old Testament where forgiveness is associated with the termination of punishment. Pharaoh begs Moses to "forgive my sin," and to "entreat the LORD your God, that he may

---

51. E. F. Harrison, *Acts*, 214.
52. Rackham, *Acts*, 217.
53. Barth, *Dogmatics*, 151.
54. *Heidelberg Catechism*, Q. 56.
55. Budd, *Numbers*, on Num. 14:18.
56. Calvin, *Catechism, 1545*, Q. 102.

take away from me this death" (Exod. 10:17). At the dedication of the temple Solomon's repeated prayer for future forgiveness is linked with the request that punishment be ended. If the punishment entails exile, then forgiveness means their restoration to their land (1 Kgs. 8:34; 2 Chr. 6:25). If the punishment is drought, then forgiveness will mean that the rains return (1 Kgs. 8:36; 2 Chr. 6:27). The LORD responds by confirming to Solomon that he will "forgive their sin and heal their land" (2 Chr. 7:14), the healing being the cessation of punishment, however greatly deserved that punishment has been.

When Joseph's brothers pretended that their father had said, "please forgive the trespass of your brothers and their sin" (Gen. 50:17), they were asking that Joseph would refrain from taking the revenge to which their guilty consciences told them that he was quite entitled. Joseph reassured them, promising provision, comfort, and kindness (Gen. 50:21). Such are the blessings which we receive from the gracious hand of our God when he forgives us. Not only does he withdraw the vengeance against sin which we deserve, but he supplies all our needs (Phil. 4:19), comforts us with love (Phil. 2:1), and lavishes kindness upon us (Titus 3:4).

Forgiveness is rendered possible by Christ. He alone, "by paying the penalty, made satisfaction,"[57] and it is "for the sake of Christ's satisfaction" that God wills not to remember our sins.[58] It was as the sinner's surety that Christ made satisfaction to God the lawgiver by taking our guilt upon himself.[59] Barth points out that "according to Calvin, sins do come under judgment to be punished, but they are not punished in our own person. There is a punishment, and a necessary punishment, but we are not those it strikes."[60]

Rather, God himself steps into our distress, makes it his own, and takes it away: "in the person of his Son, God suffers his own judgment against sin," and as a result "sin is blotted out radically, efficaciously."[61] It was "at the price of his own blood" that Jesus bought the forgiveness which to us is "freely given," and it is in his blood alone that "we ought to seek the whole cleansing of, and satisfaction for, our sins."[62] It is in this

57. Calvin, *Catechism*, 1545, Q. 103.
58. *Heidelberg Catechism*, Q. 56.
59. Witsius, *Creed*, Vol. 2, 390.
60. Barth, *Faith*, 153.
61. Barth, *Faith*, 156.
62. Calvin, *Catechism*, 1538, 20.viii, 26.

sense that remission of sins is preached in his name (Luke 24:47), and is received as his gift (Acts 5:31).

"The remission of sins" contains a challenge: it leads on to the duty of a life of obedience. To those assured of their forgiveness, Augustine says, "hold fast a good life in the commandments of God."[63] However, as Barth is at pains to insist, this is not simply to relapse into moralism, because the new life of obedience "rests on the forgiveness of sins."[64] As Calvin says, the forgiveness of sins is the foundation on which our salvation stands, from which follows the mortification of sin.[65]

How appropriately, then, does the Heidelberg Catechism entitle its third section "Of Thankfulness": having considered redemption, it then commends evangelical obedience "that with our whole life we may show ourselves thankful to God for his blessing."[66] The question by which we shall finally be judged will be, "Did you live by grace?"[67] We obey the commandments, we practise good works, not at all to increase our standing with God, but to give tangible articulation to the gratitude we feel as we contemplate the reality, I am forgiven. "As for us, no compensation from our side procures what we have from God: we receive this benefit gratuitously out of his sheer liberality."[68]

Witsius notes that to affirm the forgiveness of sins is to give glory to God, for "he can grant us the pardon of our sins in a manner that will reflect no discredit on any of his attributes, but on the contrary, afford a bright manifestation of them all."[69] It is, of course, the case, that the Biblical depictions of God often include his forgiving nature as one of his defining attributes. Readiness to forgive is one of "the basic ideas of the Hebrew Bible in its revelation of the character of God."[70]

When the Lord passed before Moses and proclaimed his name, that proclamation included the attribute, "forgiving iniquity and transgression and sin" (Exod. 34:7). It is part of the meaning of the Lord's

---

63. Augustine, *Creed*, para. 15, 700.
64. Barth, *Faith*, 158.
65. Calvin, *Catechism, 1538*, 20.viii, 26.
66. *Heidelberg Catechism*, Q. 86.
67. Barth, *Dogmatics*, 152.
68. Calvin, *Catechism, 1545*, Q. 103.
69. Witsius, *Creed*, Vol. 2, 396.
70. Allen, *Numbers*, on Num. 14:17–19.

name that he is a forgiving God.[71] Moses remembered this, and used it as an argument in pleading for Israel after their rebellion at Kadesh Barnea: "The LORD is longsuffering and abundant in mercy, forgiving iniquity and transgression" (Num. 14:18). David once addressed the LORD like this: "You, Lord, are good, and ready to forgive" (Ps. 86:5). When the Levites led the people in prayer after the rebuilding of Jerusalem, they recognized the same fact: "You are God, ready to pardon" (Neh. 9:17), "more than willing to forgive," as one commentator has suggested translating it.[72] Daniel confessed that "to the Lord our God belong mercy and forgiveness" (Dan. 9:9). So much is this ready willingness to forgive right at the heart of what it is for God to be God that it virtually becomes his name: "you were to them God-Who-Forgives" (Ps. 99:8). Forgiveness is an attribute "inseparable from his eternal essence."[73] "Thus God is the great liberal," writes Barth: "there is no other liberalism than this liberalism of God who does not want to tally up his accounts with man."[74]

Since forgiving sin is an essential feature of God as he has revealed himself in his Word, to acknowledge that he is true to his self-revelation, and therefore at one with himself as an integrated personality, in that he does forgive sins, is indeed to glorify him. It is to take him seriously as he truly is.

But all this raises a vital personal question. How may I know that my sins are forgiven? I remember, as a young boy in Sunday School, singing the chorus,

> Joy, joy, joy, with joy my heart is ringing,
> Joy, joy, joy, his love to me is known.
> My sins are all forgiven;
> I'm on my way to heaven.
> My heart is bubbling over with this joy, joy, joy.[75]

Admittedly, this is not brilliant poetry. It is little more than a ditty. And yet it profoundly captures the thrill, the breath-taking amazement that I feel in the assurance that God has forgiven—not just sins in general—but my sins, one and all, that my heavenly destiny is guaranteed, and

---

71. See Durham, *Exodus*, on Exod. 34:6–7.
72. H. G. M. Williamson, *Ezra, Nehemiah*, on Neh. 9:17.
73. Calvin, *Daniel*, 159.
74. Barth, *Faith*, 154.
75. Author unknown.

that every moment that I contemplate these sublime truths, I feel that I must burst into song, because the relieved joy of knowing that my sins are forgiven is so intense. But how may any of us have this wonderful, happy assurance?

We turn for the answer to Acts 10:43. Peter is preaching to the household of Cornelius. He urges them, "whoever believes in him will receive remission of sins." To be assured of our personal forgiveness it is sufficient and necessary to believe in Jesus, to entrust our eternal welfare to him, relying on the blood shed at Calvary as the price paid to secure forgiveness for us. Then we may rejoice with the prophet, and exclaim, "Who is a God like you, pardoning iniquity?" (Mic. 7:18).

19

The resurrection of the flesh

Although this clause of the Apostles' Creed is more familiar in the form "the resurrection of the body," the rendering given here, "the resurrection of the flesh," is the literal translation of the original Latin (*carnis resurrectionem*). Similarly, in Marcellus' Greek version, originating from fourth-century Cappadocia,[1] we read *sarkos anastasin*. The English version "the resurrection of the body" dates from 1543,[2] and has the unfortunate effect of toning down this clause, and obscuring the staggering nature of the claim that is being made. The significance of this original wording we shall consider in due course.

Although McGiffert reckons that this article is "entirely unrelated to what precedes,"[3] there is in fact a connectedness between the final three clauses of the creed. Barth sees "the forgiveness of sins, the resurrection of the flesh," and "eternal life" as representing respectively the gift of salvation under its present, future, and everlasting aspects,[4] and associates them in turn with Jesus' death, resurrection, and exaltation.[5] Pannenberg notes that since the fact of sin is demonstrated by the reality of death, "'the forgiveness of sins' means the warrant to hope beyond death for a life in communion with God."[6] This suggests that the final three clauses of the creed form a logical continuum.

The doctrine of the resurrection is proclaimed against the background of human mortality. Packer is right to insist that Scripture sees

1. Kelly, *Creeds*, 102–3.
2. McGiffert, *Creed*, 169, n. 1; Stewart, *Creeds*, 58.
3. McGiffert, *Creed*, 164.
4. Barth, *Faith*, 122.
5. Barth, *Faith*, 151.
6. Pannenberg, *Creed*, 65.

death "not as a friend but as a destroyer."[7] Death is "the last enemy" (1 Cor. 15:26). Death is the laughing, mocking certainty, the inescapable definite, that reminds us that all our achievements are ultimately nothing, and shall come to nothing. Even if our discoveries and theories and accomplishments survive us for a while, the day will come when future upheavals or the mere passage of time will leave them as archaic or as forgotten as all the great human works of past generations. In the words of the paraphrase of Psalm 90,

> Time, like an ever-rolling stream,
> Bears all its sons away;
> They fly, forgotten, as a dream
> Dies at the opening day.[8]

When I lived in Hull I used to know a man called Dennis. Whenever someone died, he had a favorite saying which would express his regret. "Life is sweet," was how the saying went. It is true for many people. To be alive in a lovely world, surrounded by the beauties of God's creation, is a sweet pleasure. To enjoy the consolations of family life, the exhilarating challenges of work and sport, the leisurely relaxation of holiday times—all these things constantly add spice to life. And yet, it is all going to come to an end. Like Job, we have to face the unpleasant, the souring, reality, "Naked I came from my mother's womb, and naked shall I return" (Job 1:21). Karl Barth expresses it starkly: "What is it, this life that ends up in the grave, the coffin? One does not like to think about it, does one, about the coffin! One would like to avoid this grave. But we will get there, and that is our life."[9]

Of course, for many people life is anything but sweet. Those who have lived and died in African famine, on the streets of Manila or Sao Paulo, in war zones, under oppressive governing regimes, with the ravages of some congenital disease—for them life itself seems to be a living death. Cranfield speaks of "all those millions of human beings who in the course of history have lived and died in hopeless wretchedness, counted as of no importance by their fellow human beings."[10] However, even where life is already an agonizing foretaste of hell, most people

---

7. Packer, *Christian*, 71.
8. From the hymn, *Our God, our help in ages past*, by Isaac Watts (1674–1748).
9. Barth, *Faith*, 170.
10. Cranfield, *Creed*, 69.

nevertheless cling in desperation to life. Life may be terrible, but death is worse. Life may be a dead end, but the fear of death haunts and tortures the living, even yet. Bereavement is no less painful in a concentration camp than in a holiday camp. Grief is just as deep in the battlefield, the minefield, the killing fields, as it is in the fields of peace and plenty.

Where do we find the answer to the problem of our human mortality? Human thinkers have come up with various different answers. Perhaps in our own culture there are three which are pertinent.

Probably the most common, and most popular, solution is the idea of the immortality of the soul. Confronted by death, even the most skeptical of people will suddenly search for comfort in the expectation that the passing of a loved one has simply transferred them to a spiritual existence in a better place. A few years ago I spent a most enjoyable day watching sheep dog trials at the Ambleside Show, held at Rydal Mount in the English Lake District. The presenter was a jovial sort of person, whose humor added some zest to the occasion. But I can still remember one remark he made. He referred to a man who had been very involved in the organization of previous trials, but who had died in the course of the previous year. Our presenter commented that this man would be enjoying today, as he looked down on us from above. That is typical of the attitude of many unbelievers.

A second way in which people try to come to terms with the sad reality of death is through the idea of reincarnation. The roots of this theory are found in animistic religion. It teaches that the soul leaves the body at death, and then seeks out another suitable body to inhabit. Hinduism took up this idea, but added an ethical dimension: the quality of life lived in the body determines the type of body to which one's soul will return for its next cycle. A good life could lead to a higher social caste, whereas a life of evil could lead to return as a mere beast.[11] This version of reincarnationism "would never be able to redeem us from entrapment in death."[12] In its modern secular form reincarnation is associated with theosophical teachers such as Rudolph Steiner. It assumes that each reincarnation represents progress towards the goal of the full perfection of the higher self.[13]

---

11. See Brow, *Religion*, 95–96.
12. Von Balthasar, *Credo*, 95.
13. See Morrison, *Serpent*, 213.

A third view, still propagated even in this age of postmodern spirituality is annihilation. Richard Dawkins quotes a passage from an essay by Bertrand Russell, which begins like this: "I believe that when I die I shall rot, and nothing of my ego will survive." Russell goes on to say that he feels no terror at the thought of annihilation.[14] Dawkins agrees: "being dead," he writes, "will be no different from being unborn," and "there is nothing to fear in that."[15] The view that death is the total end of individual existence is associated with the theory that the human being "is nothing more than a complex arrangement of molecules."[16]

The very different Christian answer to death is summed up in this clause of the creed: we believe in "the resurrection of the flesh." In the early Christian period the heresy known as gnosticism taught that the resurrection was only spiritual. For the dualistic gnostics eternal life meant escape from the realm of the flesh.[17] This error probably lies behind the words of 2 Timothy 2:18, which refers to those who "have strayed concerning the truth, saying that the resurrection is already past." "They were evidently explaining the resurrection in a spiritual sense,"[18] perhaps by allegorizing it.[19] The rejection of the doctrine of bodily resurrection was motivated by a suspicion that the flesh was intrinsically impure. Tertullian describes the gnostic "invective against the flesh" in terms such as its alleged uncleanness, worthlessness, weakness, guilt, misery, trouble, and degradation.[20]

However, the Christian hope is not a merely spiritual eternity. We do not rejoice for

> A soul out of prison released,
> And freed from its bodily chain,[21]

as one hymn rather unfortunately puts it. Biblical hope is that our physical frame will be reconstructed. In response to the gnostics Tertullian retorts that the Christian truth of the resurrection of the flesh is less

---

14. Dawkins, *Delusion*, 354.
15. Dawkins, *Delusion*, 357.
16. Brow, *Religion*, 94.
17. See McGiffert, *Creed*, 166.
18. Earle, *1 and 2 Timothy*, on 2 Tim. 2:16–18.
19. See Hendriksen, *1 and 2 Timothy and Titus*, p. 265.
20. Tertullian, *Resurrection*, 983.
21. From the hymn, *Rejoice for a brother deceased*, by Charles Wesley (1707–88).

concerned about the nature of the flesh, whether unworthy or otherwise, than about "the dignity of the Maker."[22] God made us with bodies. That is how we shall remain for all eternity.

Without the hope of resurrection, Paul tells us, Christian faith is worthless: "If in this life only we have hope in Christ, we are of all men the most miserable" (1 Cor. 15:19). The word "miserable" is derived from the root which means "mercy": unless there is bodily resurrection to look forward to, we are candidates for the sympathizing pity of our fellow human beings: "our putting up with persecutions and hardships is futile,"[23] since they are all for an illusion. Witsius comments: "This resurrection of the body is that great mystery of Christianity, without which the Gospel is vain, and our faith and hope are vain, and the consolation of those who have undergone the severest sufferings for Christ, is either small indeed, or no consolation at all."[24]

The nub of the doctrine of resurrection is that ultimately our bodies shall be "made like unto the glorious body of Christ."[25] We are destined to be "united together" with Christ "in the likeness of his resurrection" (Rom. 6:5). Every believer will be brought out of the grave, reconstituted as an individual personality, and given "active, creative and undying life, for God and with God."[26] All the pains and weaknesses of our present experience of bodily life will be forever in the past. We shall have redeemed bodies (cf. Rom. 8:23), free from deformity, illness, tiredness: "there shall be no more death, nor sorrow, nor crying, nor pain" (Rev. 21:4). The apostle Paul emphasizes this by means of a fivefold contrast between our present bodies, which are characterized by corruption, dishonor, weakness, naturalness, and mortality, and our resurrection bodies, marked by incorruption, glory, power, spirituality, and immortality (1 Cor. 15:42–44, 54). However, although there will be transformation— "we shall be changed" (1 Cor. 15:52)—there will also be "recognizable continuity with what we are now."[27]

Skeptics often ridicule the truth of the resurrection. How, they ask, can our bodies be reconstituted, given the way that the physical particles

22. Tertullian, *Resurrection*, 987.
23. Mare, *1 Corinthians*, on 1 Cor. 15:17–19.
24. Witsius, *Creed*, Vol. 2, 409.
25. *Heidelberg Catechism*, Q. 57.
26. Packer, *Christian*, 72.
27. Cranfield, *Creed*, 68.

of flesh are recycled through numerous bodies repeatedly? When I was at a rather liberal theological college, the principal once accused me of being bizarre for believing in a literal resurrection.

There is actually nothing new about such unbelief. Witsius had to face up to the same puzzle over three hundred years ago. For him the question surfaced around the issue of cannibalism. He concluded that "it is not requisite to the identity of the body, that it should consist entirely of all those parts of which it formerly consisted." Witsius was content to affirm that "the unbounded wisdom and power of God, therefore, are able so to preserve and collect those parts which are not devoured, or which, though devoured, have not passed into the substance of him who devoured them, as from them to raise the body of the dead man."[28]

Even longer ago, in the fifth century, Rufinus acknowledged the cry of the unbeliever: "How can the flesh, which has been putrefied and dissolved, or changed into dust, sometimes also swallowed up by the sea, and dispersed by the waves, be gathered up again, and again made one, and a man's body be formed anew out of it?" Rufinus responds with a counter-question, which he poses twice in different words. First, he asks: "Have you so mean an opinion of God's power that you do not believe it possible for the scattered dust of which each man's flesh was composed to be re-collected and restored to its own original fabric?" Then again, he challenges the unbeliever: "Shall divine power be thought unable to discover and distinguish the component particles belonging to each man's flesh, even though they seem to be dispersed?"[29]

Witsius and Rufinus are wise in having recourse to the power of God, and in recognizing that we exceed the bounds of legitimate enquiry when we try to penetrate into mysteries which are beyond our comprehension, and outside the scope of what God has seen fit to reveal in detail. No doubt they are taking their cue from the apostle, whose immediate response to the question, "How are the dead raised up, and with what body do they come?" is, "Foolish one," and who then asserts, "God gives it a body as he pleases" (1 Cor. 15:35–36, 38).

When will "the resurrection of the flesh" take place? Paul answers this question: it will happen "at the last trumpet" (1 Cor. 15:52), which will signal the return of the Lord (1 Thess. 4:16). Jesus too stressed that,

---

28. Witsius, *Creed*, Vol. 2, 424–5.
29. Rufinus, *Commentary*, para. 42, 1131.

in the will of his Father, he would raise up all his people "at the last day" (John 6:39–40, 44, 54).

In addition to the resurrection of those generations who have died, those alive at the time of Christ's return will be transformed: "we shall not all sleep, but we shall all be changed—in a moment, in the twinkling of an eye" (1 Cor. 15:51-52). "The dead in Christ will rise first. Then we who are alive and remain shall be caught up together with them to meet the Lord in the air. And thus we shall always be with the Lord" (1 Thess. 4:16–17). That final generation of believers will miraculously enjoy the renewing reality of resurrection without first having to undergo the experience of death. "They will then, at that very moment, receive a glorified body."[30]

This raises a further question: What happens to the person between death and the resurrection? On this point the Scriptures are quite clear. Writing to the Philippians, Paul says that "to die is gain," and that "to depart and be with Christ" is "far better" (Phil. 1:21, 23). There is an intermediate state of disembodied spiritual life in the presence of Christ, which will be an indescribably wonderful experience. In the following comment, Reymond perhaps states the obvious, but it needs to be said:

> Since it is a state "with Christ" and one "very much better" than this one, it must at least have as great an aspect of self-consciousness as we now have or the significance of our being "with Christ" and our being "very much better" would seem to have little or no significance. Cullmann's argument from the "pleasure of dreams" for a state of soul sleep as the condition of the blessed dead is not persuasive.[31]

Nevertheless, as Cranfield rightly points out, "while this state is far better than the best we experience in this present life, it is still incomplete." Cranfield notes Paul's description in 2 Corinthians 5:3 of this period of personal existence as nakedness: "it is not yet the fullness of what God has in store for us."[32] That must await the resurrection of our flesh. As Jim Packer observes, "When my body and soul separate I shall be only a shadow of what I was. My body is part of me, the apparatus of

---

30. Praamsma, *Before the Face*, 92.
31. Reymond, *New Systematic Theology*, 1017.
32. Cranfield, *Creed*, 68.

my self-expression; without it, all my power to make things, to do things and relate to my fellows is gone."[33]

Quite categorically, von Balthasar goes so far as to say, "a bodiless soul is not a human being."[34] It will only be when our bodies are resurrected that God will have completed the work of "bringing many sons to glory" (Heb. 2:10).

We must come at last to the question, Why does the creed use the word "flesh"? Christopher Stead suggests that in so doing the creed is departing from Biblical terminology, where the phrase "resurrection of the dead" is usual,[35] alongside occasional allusions to the resurrection of the body.[36] Stead even claims that the creed contradicts 1 Corinthians 15:50, "flesh and blood cannot inherit the kingdom of God."[37] However, Mare's comment on this phrase is helpful: he understands "flesh and blood" to refer in this context to our present mortal humanity: "this mortal body is perishable and cannot inherit that which is imperishable." Therefore, in order to enter God's kingdom, "the saved must have their bodies changed."[38]

Moreover, the association of resurrection with flesh is not entirely foreign to Biblical language. Job states confidently, "after my skin is destroyed, this I know, that in my flesh I shall see God" (Job 19:26). I am assuming that the traditional translation, "in my flesh," is to be preferred to the alternative, "without my flesh."[39] Despite Clines' protestations to the contrary,[40] this text seems to be affirming that "Job was convinced that even if he died, he would live again."[41]

Again, in Acts 2:31 Peter notes that the Psalmist "spoke concerning the resurrection of the Christ, that his soul was not left in Hades, nor did his flesh see corruption." Since he is "the firstfuits of those who have fallen asleep" (1 Cor. 15:20), it is not inappropriate for the creed to

---

33. Packer, *Christian*, 71.
34. Von Balthasar, *Credo*, 95.
35. Matt. 22:31; Acts 17:32; 23:6; 24:15, 21; 1 Cor. 15:12-13, 21, 42; Heb. 6:2.
36. Cf. 1 Cor. 15:44; Phil. 3:21.
37. Stead, "Apostles' Creed," 9.
38. Mare, *1 Corinthians*, on 1 Cor. 15:50.
39. So Smick, *Job*, footnote to Job 19:26; against Ellison, *Job*, 69.
40. Clines, *Job*, on Job 19:25-27; see also Peake, *Job*, 195.
41. Smick, *Job*, on Job 19:25-27; see also Still, *God—Job, and Satan*, 27.

speak of the resurrection of the flesh with reference to our eschatological hope.

But what lies behind the choice of this word? There may be truth in the suspicion that anti-gnostic or anti-Marcionite polemic is at work here.[42] However, it is more worthwhile to consider the positive implications of the term.

Cranfield exaggerates when he claims that the word "flesh" has "a bewildering variety of nuances."[43] The basic meaning of the New Testament word *sarx* and its cognates has to do with the present created order. It may refer to anything to do with the present world,[44] though more commonly it has to do with the present aspects of ordinary human existence, such as human descent,[45] the human body,[46] physical union,[47] human life and personality with all its activities and achievements,[48] or humanity as a whole.[49] The common thread is that all these things are aspects of God's creation.

However, from this basic sense a developed or extrapolated meaning arises, where "flesh" takes on negative overtones.[50] Used in this way, "flesh" becomes a way of life in which human achievements and the things of the present created order are given ultimate significance, idolised, and accorded the value of gods. It is the condition which the apostle describes in different terms in Romans 1:25, where human beings have "worshiped and served the creature rather than the Creator." "The crea-

---

42. McGiffert, *Creed*, 166–7.

43. Cranfield, *Romans*, Vol. 1, 59.

44. Rom. 15:27; 1 Cor. 9:11; 15:39; 2 Cor. 10:4; Heb. 9:10.

45. Acts 2:30; Rom. 1:3; 9:3, 5, 8; 11:14; 1 Cor. 10:18; Gal. 4:23, 29; Eph. 2:11a; Heb. 7:16.

46. Luke 24:39; John 6:51–56; Acts 2:26, 31; Rom. 2:28; 2 Cor. 7:5; Gal. 4:13–14; Eph. 2:11b,15, 29–30; Col. 2:1, 5; Heb. 2:14; 10:20; 1 Pet. 4:1; 1 John 4:2–3; 2 John 7; Rev. 17:16; 19:18, 21.

47. Matt. 19:6; Mark 10:8; 1 Cor. 6:16; Eph. 5:31.

48. Matt. 16:17; John 1:13–14; 3:6; Rom. 4:1; 1 Cor. 1:26, 29; 7:28; 2 Cor. 1:12; 3:3; 4:11; 11:18; 12:7; Gal. 1:16; 2:20; 6:12–13; Eph. 6:5, 12; Phil. 1:22, 24; 3:3–4; Col. 1:22, 24; 3:22; 1Tim. 3:16; Phlm. 1:16; Heb. 5:7; 9:13; Jas. 5:3; 1 Pet. 3:18; 4:2, 6.

49. Matt. 24:22; Mark 13:20; Luke 3:6; John 17:2: Acts 2:17; Rom. 3:20; Gal. 2:16; Heb. 12:9; 1 Pet. 1:24

50. Matt. 26:41; Mark 14:38; John 6:63; 8:15; Rom. 6:19; 7:5, 14, 18, 25; 8:1, 3–4, 6–9, 12–13; 13:14; 1 Cor. 3:1, 3–4; 5:5; 15:50; 2 Cor. 1:17; 5:16; 7:1; 10:2–3; Gal. 3:3; 5:13, 16–17, 19, 24; 6:8; Eph. 2:3; Col. 2:11, 13, 18, 23; 1 Pet. 2:11; 3:21; 2 Pet. 2:10, 18; 1 John 2:16; Jude 7–8, 23.

ture, not the Creator, is our point of orientation,"[51] or, as Thiselton puts it, "the outlook of the flesh is the outlook orientated towards the self, that which pursues its own ends in self-sufficient independence of God."[52] In Romans 8:5 the basic and extrapolated meanings come together in the words, "those who live according to the flesh set their minds on the things of the flesh." Here the first occurrence of the word "flesh" has the connotations of sin and rebellion, while in the second instance the reference is to the ordinary things of created life: to give those things quasi-divine status is to "live according to the flesh."[53]

Similarly the Old Testament term normally rendered "flesh," *bāśār*, also has these two related shades of meaning. It may refer to aspects of our humanness—the body[54] or physical union,[55] human personality,[56] relationship,[57] ability,[58] or humanity as a whole[59]—or to other created life,[60] and even to living creatures, whether human or animal, which are

---

51. Brunner, *Romans*, 69.
52. Thiselton, "Flesh," 680.
53. See Bayes, *Weakness*, 96.
54. Gen. 2:21, 23; 17:11, 13–14, 23–25; 40:19; Exod. 4:7; 28:42; 30:32; Lev. 6:10; 12:3; 13:2–4, 10–11, 13–16, 18, 24, 38–39, 43; 14:9; 15:2–3, 7, 13, 16, 19; 16:4, 24, 26, 28; 17:16; 19:28; 21:5; 22:6; Num. 8:7; 12:12; 19:7–8; Deut. 32:42; Judg. 8:7; 1 Kgs. 21:27; 2 Kgs. 5:10, 14; 6:30; Job 2:5; 4:15; 6:12; 7:5; 10:11; 13:14; 14:22; 19:20, 22; 33:21, 25; Ps. 27:2; 102:5; 109:24; Prov. 14:30; Eccl. 12:12; Isa. 9:20; 10:18; Lam. 3:4; Ezek. 11:19a; 23:20a; 36:26a; 37:6, 8; 44:7, 9; Dan. 1:15; Zech. 14:12.
55. Gen. 2:24.
56. Job 19:26; 21:6; Ps. 16:9; 63:1; 84:2; 119:120; Prov. 4:22; 5:11; Eccl. 2:3; 4:5; 5:6; 11:10; Jer. 11:15; Ezek. 11:19b; 36:26b.
57. Gen. 29:14; 37:27; Lev. 18:6; 25:49; Judg. 9:2; 2 Sam. 5:1; 19:12–13; 1 Chr. 11:1; Neh. 5:5; Isa. 58:7.
58. 2 Chr. 32:8; Job 10:4; Ps. 56:4; Isa. 17:4.
59. Gen. 6:12–13; Num. 16:22; 27:16; Deut. 5:26; Job 12:10; 34:15; Ps. 65:2; 145:21; Isa. 40:5–6; 66:16, 23–24; Jer. 12:12; 25:31; 32:27; 45:5; Ezek. 20:48; 21:4–5; Joel 2:28; Zech. 2:13.
60. Gen. 6:17, 19; 7:15–16 ,21; 8:17; 9:11, 15–17; 41:2–4, 18–19; Lev. 17:11, 14; Num. 18:15; Job 41:23; Ps. 136:25; Ezek. 10:12; 23:20b.

now dead.[61] However, "flesh" in the Old Testament may also have connotations of weakness[62] or sinfulness.[63]

When the creed speaks of "the resurrection of the flesh" it is, presumably, deliberately echoing this *double entendre* in the Biblical use of the term. The human body as part of the created order will be raised again to life with Christ, but it is the fullness of our human life and personality, our abilities and our achievements, which will be brought back from oblivion and given back to us anew on the day of resurrection.

Moreover, it is the human beings that we are who will be made new. Where "flesh" signifies "the weakness, helplessness, and transitoriness of humanity,"[64] these things will be no barrier against the resurrection power of God.

Where "flesh" speaks of our human failure, of our sinfulness and rebellion, it reminds us that the humanity which is the object of God's grace is "man such as he is and not such as he ought to have been," and that our hope is the final resurrection to glory "of the real man, miserable and sinful, and not of any ideal man."[65] The flesh which has idolized flesh will not be rejected and jettisoned by its Maker; it will be purged and purified, so that for all eternity as beings of flesh, that fleshly, idolatrous spirit will be rooted out, and our fleshly delight will rather be to worship and serve the Creator. The use of the word "flesh" emphasizes the amazing height of transformation achieved in resurrection victory. All that has gone wrong in the course of human history will be put right. "Flesh," which today is so blatantly careering towards death, will be remarkably rescued by a magnificent, dramatic and stupendously gracious intervention of God. The end of our life "is not death, but resurrection": resurrection does indeed presuppose death, "but, by mentioning only resurrection, the creed presents death as already overcome."[66]

---

61. Gen. 9:4; Exod. 12:8, 46; 16:3, 8, 12; 21:28, 31; 29:14, 31–32, 34; Lev. 4:11; 6:27; 7:15, 17–21; 8:17, 31–32; 9:11; 11:8, 11; 16:27; 26:29; Num. 11:4, 13, 18, 21, 33; 18:18; 19:5; Deut. 12:15, 20, 23, 27; 14:8; 16:4; 28:53, 55; Judg. 6:19–21; 1 Sam. 2:13, 15; 17:44; 1 Kgs. 17:6; 19:21; 2 Kgs. 4:34; 9:36; Job 31:31; Ps. 50:13; 79:2; Prov. 23:20; Isa. 22:13; 44:16, 19; 49:26; 65:4; 66:17; Jer. 7:21; 19:9; Ezek. 4:14; 11:3, 7, 11; 24:10; 32:5; 39:17–18; 40:43; Dan. 10:3; Hos. 8:13; Mic. 3:3; Hag. 2:12; Zech. 11:9, 16.

62. Ps. 78:39; Isa. 31:3; Jer. 17:5.

63. Gen. 6:3; Ps. 38:3, 7; Ezek. 16:26.

64. Cranfield, *Creed*, 67.

65. Barth, *Faith*, 162.

66. Barth, *Faith*, 162.

Rufinus evidently knew a version of the creed which read "the resurrection of this flesh." He saw this as heightening the personal nature of the confession of faith in the creed.[67] For the believer who affirms the resurrection, this is not just a theoretical expectation to do with remote times. It is not merely a vague picture of a far-off human future in general terms. It is the declaration that I know that my flesh shall be raised from the dead, that I am talking here about something intensely personal and profoundly relevant to me. And it is only as I cherish this delightful conviction that "this flesh"—this very flesh which is me—is to be raised, that I find the resources, driven by hope, to live in the present age with all its challenges, setbacks, disappointments, trials, and sufferings. In this connection Rufinus refers to Job 19:26 and 1 Corinthians 15:53–54:

> As to the addition *this* see how consonant it is with all that we have cited from the divine books. What else does Job signify in the place which we explained above, "He will raise again my skin, which is now draining in this cup of suffering," that is, which is undergoing these torments? Does he not plainly say that there will be a resurrection of this flesh, this, I mean, which is now undergoing the extremity of trials and tribulations? Moreover, when the apostle says, "this corruptible must put on incorruption, and this mortal must put on immortality," are not his words those of one who in a manner touches his body and places his finger upon it? This body, then, which is now corruptible, will by the grace of the resurrection be incorruptible, and this which is now mortal will be clothed with virtues of immortality, that, as "Christ, having been raised from the dead, dies no more: death no longer has dominion over him" (Rom. 6:9), so those who shall rise in Christ shall never again feel corruption or death, not because the nature of flesh will have been cast off, but because its condition and quality will have been changed.[68]

The doctrine of the resurrection, and the use of the word "flesh" in particular, also points beyond the final glory of the redeemed human race to the restoration of the entire creation. We have noticed that "flesh" may refer to the entire created universe, to animal life as well as human being. The renovation at the last day of that aspect of our nature which unites us to the environment in which we live, which identifies us with

---

67. Rufinus, *Commentary*, para. 43, 1132.
68. Rufinus, *Commentary*, para. 45, 1133-4.

the cosmos of which we are a part, will, in addition, be the moment when the whole of God's creation project will be restored to its pristine beauty and order, and realigned on its intended course as the vehicle of God's glory, free from corruption, decay, and the baneful outworkings of the curse of Genesis 3:17–19 (cf. Rom. 8:19–22).

Leanne Van Dyk urges us that the hope of resurrection should be a source of both relief and joy to the believer:

> The resurrection of the dead is God's resounding affirmation of the creation, a promise of final restoration for the broken creation that will heal all wounds, stitch together ripped seams, and reconcile all shattered relationships. The resurrection of the dead is God's resounding affirmation of our bodies, bodies that suffer from arthritis, diabetes, cancer, and Alzheimer's disease. These same bodies will rise to eternal life with God, restored in a way that is appropriate for eternal life with God, and also in a way appropriate for creaturely life.[69]

Because the resurrection of the flesh signals the glorious future prospect for the entire universe, the marvellous cosmic renewal which is to come, I find myself not in agreement with Calvin when he claims that this article is in the creed "to remind us that our happiness is not located on earth."[70] It may well be true that our present day happiness is not located on earth. We do "seek those things above, where Christ is, sitting at the right hand of God" (Col.3:1). However, as God's creatures, made for physical, earthly life, our goal is not disembodied existence in detachment from the earth. Our ultimate hope is that we shall live in resurrected flesh on a renewed earth, that when Christ comes from heaven, he will bring to earth with him all that makes for our everlasting happiness, and we shall find our true happiness in living in the new heavens and the new earth, "in which righteousness dwells" (2 Pet. 3:13), serving our God in new bodies, forevermore unencumbered by sin and weakness.

---

69. Van Dyk, "Conversation," 30.
70. Calvin, *Catechism, 1545*, Q. 107.

20

Eternal life

Witsius calls "eternal life" "the consequence of the resurrection,"[1] a point which is stressed by some older versions of the Apostles' Creed which read "I believe in . . . the resurrection of the flesh to eternal life." Kelly sees the addition of this final clause as a necessary assurance that the resurrection will not be a return to present mortal life, but will follow the precedent of Christ's resurrection.[2] These words form the final clause of the creed because eternal life "is in reality 'the end of our faith,' the ultimate object of our hope, the completion of our salvation, and the final issue and consummation of the whole scheme of redemption."[3]

Jim Packer refers to a skeptical comment by Bertrand Russell, who claimed to find the idea of an endless future life horrifying, on the grounds that it would be thoroughly boring. Packer suspects that this comment arises from the fact that he must have found this life boring, and could not imagine "how human existence could be made permanently interesting and worthwhile." Packer makes an insightful remark: "Here we see the blighting effects of godlessness and the black pessimism to which it leads."[4]

However, most people do not share Bertrand Russell's bleak outlook on life. Even the most ungodly of men and women cherish the hope that death will not be the end, because, as my friend Dennis used to say, "life is sweet." And for the believer, the sweetness of life is infinitely enhanced by the experience of God's grace, such that the notion that it must all come to an utter end is unthinkable. Packer expresses this admirably:

1. Witsius, *Creed*, Vol. 2, 455.
2. Kelly, *Creeds*, 387.
3. Witsius, *Creed*, Vol. 2, 455.
4. Packer, *Christian*, 75.

> This everlasting life is something to which I look forward. Why? Not because I am out of love with life here—just the reverse! My life is full of joy, from four sources—knowing God and people and the good and pleasant things that God and men under God have created and doing things which are worthwhile for God or others, or for myself as God's man. But my reach exceeds my grasp. My relationships with God and men are never as rich and full as I want them to be and I am always finding more than I thought was there in great music, great verse, great books, great lives and the great kaleidoscope of the natural order.

Packer continues by quoting a song which says, "The more I have, the more I want," and he agrees that there are countless things in life about which we feel like saying exactly that. Consequently, it is "pure delight" to anticipate the eternal continuance and increase of life's enjoyments.[5]

Witsius is no doubt right in understanding the word "eternal" as stressing the fact that the life beyond the resurrection will know no termination, because it will be a life free from sin.[6] C. H. Dodd believes that this is the significance of the phrase "eternal life" in its solitary Old Testament occurrence, in Daniel 12:2, where "the term is used for the life after death, conceived of as indefinitely, or even infinitely, prolonged."[7] Similarly, Gleason Archer notes that the Hebrew word for "eternal" here (*ôlām*) "takes on the connotation of endlessness."[8] Certainly in Genesis 3:22, where the verb "live" occurs, rather than the noun "life," the fear is that the human race might "live forever" in its sin: to prevent such a tragedy, Adam and Eve are ejected from the Garden of Eden. Jesus emphasizes the endless nature of this future life: on two occasions he too uses the verb *zaō* in distinction from the noun *zōē*, and says that anyone who feeds upon the bread of life—the Lord himself—"will live forever" (John 6:51, 58). "The words 'will live forever' clearly indicate that one cannot dissociate the quantitative idea from the concept of 'everlasting life.'"[9] Jesus also stresses the endless duration of eternal life in the words, "I give them eternal life, and they shall never perish" (John

---

5. Packer, *Christian*, 76.
6. Witsius, *Creed*, Vol. 2, 456.
7. Dodd, *Fourth Gospel*, 144.
8. Archer, *Daniel*, on Dan. 12:2.
9. Hendriksen, *John*, 241.

10:28). Morris rightly says, "It is often emphasized that the important thing about eternal life is its quality rather than its quantity. It is life of a certain kind, and not simply life that goes on for ever. While there is truth in this, yet we should not overlook the point that in fact eternal life does not end. It is this aspect that is prominent here."[10]

Nonetheless, the phrase "eternal life" taken as a whole does stand "for something more than mere continuance of life," and points to true life, the life of heaven, the life of blessing, the life of God.[11] Pannenberg puts it picturesquely when he says that "the life of the future world is not the resumption and endless prolongation of this life, along the same temporal line; it will unfold its dynamic through growth in the vertical dimension of our present life."[12] Witsius, indeed acknowledges this, but sees it as the special significance of the word "life," which he understands as "a state of the highest felicity."[13] "Eternal life" may be defined as the unending life of unending and unqualified happiness.

In John 4:14 our Lord effectively identifies eternal life with the sense of total satisfaction: "whoever drinks of the water that I shall give him will never thirst. But the water that I shall give him will become in him a fountain of water springing up into everlasting life." To thirst is to feel "the pain of an unsatisfied want."[14] Eternal life is the ultimate in happiness resulting from the God-given inner resources of the Holy Spirit, in which the believer will never thirst: he will never again know any sense of lack or frustrated longing or unfulfilled desires, but will feel completely at peace, entirely contented, and bursting with unqualified joy. Dodd aptly summarizes the Biblical concept of life in terms of "action, movement and enjoyment."[15]

Calvin equates eternal life with the kingdom of God, which, he says, will be "crammed with all brightness, joy, power, happiness."[16] Barth acknowledges that the term "eternal" speaks of something unlimited, but finds its primary meaning as belonging to the world to come, which he

---

10. Morris, *John*, 521.
11. Kelly, *Creeds*, 388.
12. Pannenberg, *Creed*, 175.
13. Witsius, *Creed*, Vol. 2, 455.
14. Westcott, *John*, 70.
15. Dodd, *Fourth Gospel*, 150.
16. Calvin, *Catechism, 1538*, 20.ix, 27.

too identifies with "the glorious kingdom of God."[17] This is in line with Jesus' promise that "there is no one who has left house or parents or brothers or wife or children, for the sake of the kingdom of God, who shall not receive many times more in this present time, and in the age to come eternal life" (Luke 18:29–30).

Packer asks how we shall spend the life of eternity in the world to come. He answers first negatively, and then positively: "Not lounge around!—but worship, work, think and communicate, enjoying activity, beauty, people and God."[18]

And it is the enjoyment of God which is the essence of eternal life. Witsius rightly insists that the full understanding of how we shall be occupied for eternity lies outside our present capacity to understand: "the nature and extent of this life can neither be conceived by the human mind in the present imperfect state, nor expressed by mortal tongues." He cites 1 John 3:2, "it has not yet been revealed what we shall be," and 1 Corinthians 2:9, "eye has not seen, nor ear heard, nor have entered into the heart of man the things which God has prepared for those who love him," a text also cited by the Heidelberg Catechism.[19] Nevertheless, Witsius goes on, God has revealed enough to give us a taste of what eternal life will involve, and the essence of it is the joy of God's immediate presence accompanied by maximum conformity to him.[20] Or, as Packer puts it, "Jesus' presence makes heaven."[21] The essence of eternal life is being with the Savior whom we love. This accurately expounds Jesus' own definition[22] of eternal life—"that they may know you, the only true God, and Jesus Christ whom you have sent" (John 17:3; cf. 1 John 5:20). To know God "transforms a man and introduces him to a different quality of living,"[23] which is indeed "eternal life." Merrill Tenney notes that here "eternal life"

> is not described in chronological terms but by a relationship. Life is active involvement with environment; death is the cessation

17. Barth, *Faith*, 172.
18. Packer, *Christian*, 76.
19. Witsius, *Creed*, Vol. 2, 457; *Heidelberg Catechism*, Q. 58; see also Calvin, *Catechism, 1538*, 20.ix, 27.
20. Witsius, *Creed*, Vol. 2, 457.
21. Packer, *Christian*, 75.
22. So Morris, *John*, 719; pace Hendriksen, *John*, 350.
23. Morris, *John*, 720.

of involvement with the environment, whether it be physical or personal. The highest kind of life is involvement with the highest kind of environment. A worm is content to live in soil; we need not only the wider environment of earth, sea, and sky but also contact with other human beings. For the complete fulfillment of our being, we must know God. This, said Jesus, constitutes eternal life. Not only is it endless, since the knowledge of God would require an eternity to develop fully, but qualitatively it must exist in an eternal dimension.[24]

However, McGrath is correct to say that "we must not think of eternal life as something that lies totally in the future. It is something we can begin to experience now."[25] He points out that "eternal life is inaugurated, but not fulfilled, in our present life as believers," and therefore the fullness of eternal life in the world to come will not be "something totally strange and unknown," but the extension and deepening of our present experience of God's love.[26] Dodd points to John 11:26, "whoever lives and believes in me shall never die," as implying that "the believer is already 'living' in a pregnant sense which excludes the possibility of ceasing to live." Hence, even before bodily death, the believer enjoys "the possession of eternal life here and now."[27] In fact, says Dodd, citing John 5:24 and 6:54, both of which texts say that the believer "has eternal life," "for John this present enjoyment of eternal life has become the controlling and all-important conception."[28]

This "eternal life," both now and forever, is obtained "in Christ Jesus our Lord" (Rom. 6:23; cf. 1 John 5:11), and is received by the inner working of the Holy Spirit: it is "of the Spirit" that we "reap everlasting life" (Gal. 6:8). Consequently, to fail to believe in the Son of God, the source of life eternal, is to be under the wrath of God (John 3:36), facing judgment and existing in the realm of death (John 5:24). Marshall notes that the statement in 1 John 5:11, "this life is in his Son," "is clearly meant to be exclusive, as verse 12 demonstrates" ("he who has the Son has life; he

---

24. Tenney, *John*, on John 17:2, 3
25. McGrath, *I Believe*, 104.
26. McGrath, *I Believe*, 105.
27. Dodd, *Fourth Gospel*, 148.
28. Dodd, *Fourth Gospel*, 149.

who does not have the Son of God does not have life"); hence it is justifiable to say that this life is found only in the Son,[29] and nowhere else.

We have noted already that eternal life consists in the knowledge of God, as Jesus indicates in John 17:3. However, we must go even further. In a rich and profound sense eternal life entails a very share in the life of God himself. Kelly refers to Aquinas who taught that "the first truth about eternal life is that a man there finds union with God, who is the reward and end of all our labors, and crowns all our desires."[30] Augustine finishes his sermon on the creed with this prayer: "God bring you safe unto himself, who is the life everlasting."[31] Calvin compares the Lord to "an inexhaustible spring," who contains in himself the fullness of eternal life.[32]

That God is the one "that lives forever" (Dan. 4:34; 12:7), or more intensively, "who lives forever and ever" (Rev. 4:9–10; 5:14; 10:6; 15:7) is a commonplace of Biblical revelation. Joyce Baldwin points out that the description of God as the one "that lives forever" "applied absolutely to God the courtly ascription to the human king."[33] On five occasions in Daniel, the polite but meaningless wish for a human king, "live for ever," is cited.[34] In Daniel 6:26, Darius recognizes that Daniel's God is "the living and eternal God." This "picks up the thought expressed in the conventional address to the human king, 'live for ever,' but asserts that there is a God of whom it is true."[35] As such this God is vastly different from, vastly superior to, the greatest of human claimants to dignity and authority. In Deuteronomy 32:40, in affirming his uniqueness as God, the LORD says, "I live for ever." This is "the one place where the LORD so speaks of himself."[36] Thus, eternal life "is the life that God himself lives as the True One; in himself, from himself, for or to himself."[37]

In the opening verses of his first epistle, the apostle John describes how, in the apostolic proclamation of the incarnation of the Word, "the

---

29. Marshall, *Epistles of John*, 241, n. 43.
30. Kelly, *Creeds*, 388.
31. Augustine, *Creed*, para. 17, 701.
32. Calvin, *Catechism, 1538*, 20.ix, 26.
33. Baldwin, *Daniel*, 115.
34. Dan. 2:4; 3:9; 5:10; 6:6, 21.
35. Baldwin, *Daniel*, 132.
36. Baldwin, *Daniel*, 208.
37. Candlish, *1 John*, Vol. 2, 324.

eternal life which was with the Father . . . was manifested to us" (1 John 1:2). However, this life in its manifestation "is not something merely theoretical, ethereal."[38] For one thing, it is revealed in the concrete human life of the person of Jesus Christ. The life which he lived in human flesh was none other than the eternal life of God. Moreover, what is in view here is a personal manifestation of eternal life to the believer, such that we enter into participation in the life which we have clearly perceived. "In Jesus Christ God's saving life has been disclosed, and made available."[39]

This availability of personal participation is signalled by the contrast between the opening and closing phrases of verse 2. The verse opens with the words, "the life was manifested." The reference is to that historical exhibition of divine life in the human life of Jesus—an objective fact, a public revelation. However, the final phrase of the verse says that this eternal life "was manifested to us." We are no longer dealing only with something public and objective, and certainly not with something detached and remote, but with something intensely personal and subjective. Our privilege is to have seen by faith the eternal life lived out by Jesus and so to have entered into fellowship with him in that eternal life. "He who is 'the eternal life which was with the Father' is 'manifested to us' as 'destroying this death.'"[40] We have become "partakers of the divine nature" (2 Pet. 1:4).

This statement of Peter's is a remarkable one. In what sense can we partake in the nature of God himself? Clearly there are ways in which this must remain forever impossible. We shall never become gods. However, we are "capable of resembling God in his immortality and incorruption,"[41] of sharing in the life which is eternal. That is our destiny, and in the present experience of eternal life we enjoy a foretaste of it.

> Blessed assurance, *Jesus* is mine:
> O what a foretaste of glory divine![42]

---

38. King, *The Fellowship*, 14.
39. Smalley, *1, 2, 3 John*, on 1 John 1:2.
40. Candlish, *1 John*, Vol. 1, 6.
41. Bauckham, *Jude, 2 Peter*, 180.
42. From the Hymn, *Blessed assurance*, by Fanny Crosby (1820–1915) [emphasis added].

2 Peter 1:4, indeed, itself defines this participation in the divine nature. The second half of the verse in its entirety reads: "that you may be partakers of the divine nature, having escaped the corruption that is in the world through lust." It is in resembling God's own incorruption, his total freedom from sinful lust, that we partake of his nature. That is the goal of our salvation. That is the essence of the life of eternity. There will be no sin in that glorious kingdom, and we shall be finally purged from sin for ever. Bengel interprets participation in the divine nature as our becoming holy.[43] The life of eternity is the life of holiness, since, in the world to come "there shall by no means enter it anything that defiles" (Rev. 21:27). Calvin sums up the sense of 2 Peter 1:4 in these words: "the image of God in holiness and righteousness is restored to us for this end, that we may at length be partakers of eternal life and glory as far as it will be necessary for our complete felicity."[44]

In this connection Karl Barth equates eternal life with glorification, and notes that "glory means the splendor of God." For us to be finally in glory means that we shall partake in God's glory; "we shall be, so to speak, draped in his light."[45] Tenney comments on Jesus' desire, articulated in his prayer in John 17:24, that "eternal life would ultimately bring his disciples to a lasting association with him in his divine glory."[46]

In a sense the creed has brought us full circle. We began by affirming our belief in the living God; we conclude by affirming our belief in the life of God, in which it is our privilege, by grace, to share. "Eternal life" is to "enjoy God forever,"[47] and that, as the Westminster Shorter Catechism reminds us, is part of "the chief end of man."[48]

The puritan, Thomas Vincent, asks, "Why ought men chiefly to desire and seek the enjoyment of God for ever?" He answers: "Because God is the chief good, and in the enjoyment of God doth consist man's chiefest happiness."[49] John Piper would add that it is by enjoying God that we glorify him, pointing out that those who first composed the Catechism spoke of man's chief end, not ends: "Glorifying God and enjoying him

---

43. Bengel, *Gnomon*, Vol. 5, 87.
44. Calvin, *Catholic Epistles*, 371.
45. Barth, *Faith*, 172.
46. Tenney, *John*, on John 17:2, 3.
47. Cranfield, *Creed*, 68.
48. *Westminster Shorter Catechism*, Q. 1, 675, 676.
49. Vincent, *Shorter Catechism Explained*, 16.

were one end in their minds, not two."[50] Piper points out that the pursuit of joy in God is mandatory for the believer.[51] "His eternal glory and our eternal pleasure unite."[52] Isaiah indicates the obligation to be happy in God when he acknowledges that God meets "him who rejoices and does righteousness" (Isa. 64:5).

In the first of this series of studies we saw how the affirmation "I believe" is a joyful, passionate commitment to the God who rewards those who seek him. In voicing this passion, we are acknowledging that the greatest reward, the only true source of our human joy, is the possession of God himself. Now, as we come to the end of our consideration of the clauses of the Apostles' Creed, we declare our belief in "eternal life": we are humbly, thankfully, gratefully, joyfully affirming that we do possess this God. He is our life; we have, by his grace alone, become sharers in his eternal life. And so as we reach the end of the creed, we find ourselves subdued by awe as we bow before the God who, in Christ, is our Redeemer. Our breath is taken away as we contemplate this stupendous mystery that our Maker has called us not just *to* himself, but *into* participation in his very nature. We have been given eternal life. And so we prostrate our hearts before the amazing magnificence of mercy.

---

50. Piper, *Desiring God*, 13–14.
51. Piper, *Desiring God*, 89.
52. Piper, *Desiring God*, 226.

21

Amen

IF WE WERE TO attend Evening Prayer in our local Parish Church, having taken part in the General Confession, heard the Old and New Testament Lessons, and praised God in the words of the Magnificat, we would then recite the Apostles' Creed. Having confessed our faith in God the Father and his works of providence and creation, in Jesus Christ his Son and his past, present and future activities for our salvation, and in the Holy Spirit and his fruits in action, culminating in "eternal life," we would then unite our voices in a resounding "Amen." In this respect the creed resembles the four gospels, each of which has "Amen" as its final word.[1]

We have completed our study of the various clauses of the Apostles' Creed. However, before we leave this tremendous document behind, we must just notice this one last thing: the creed ends with the word "Amen."

According to one Biblical Lexicon,

> the word *amen* is a most remarkable word. It was transliterated directly from the Hebrew into the Greek of the New Testament, then into Latin and into English and many other languages, so that it is practically a universal word. It has been called the best known word in human speech. The word is directly related—in fact, almost identical—to the Hebrew word for *believe* (*'āman*), or *faithful*. Thus, it came to mean "sure" or "truly," an expression of absolute trust and confidence.[2]

The universality of "Amen" is certainly true as far as European languages are concerned. We must not, however, become western chauvinists in claiming universality: the claim may need some qualification. It

---

1. In the received text of Matt. 28:20; Mark 16:20; Luke 24:53; John 21:25.
2. *Online Bible Greek Lexicon*, 281.

is beyond the scope of my knowledge to say how widespread "Amen" is in the languages of the east or the south. From my limited exposure to Asian language, I do know that the Tagalog speakers of the Philippines end their prayers with the word *siyanawa*, which accurately translates the Hebrew word "Amen," meaning "so be it." Nevertheless, the word "amen" has crept into Tagalog with a secular usage: it means "a yes man!"[3] It is also noticeable that some Tagalog Bible versions simply transliterate "Amen" in some (though not all) places where the word occurs in the Scriptures.[4]

However, the word "Amen" is not only practically universal, it is also very versatile. It serves several different functions in our religious speech, dictated by its Biblical uses. All these functions are linked with that expression of complete confidence which we have in the truth proclaimed by the Apostles' Creed, because of our absolute trust in the God to whom the creed points us. As such, "*Amen* is a consolation to our weakness."[5] We acknowledge that in us there is no truth or trustworthiness, that we are only of any import as the grace of God has laid hold of us. Our words are insignificant, unless they are informed by the word of God and empowered by the Spirit of God. By contrast, in our weakness, we look to one who is almighty power, and whose word can never fail. We say "Amen," and leave all to our God, whose strength is made perfect in weakness.

There are three main functions of the word *Amen* which I want to look at, followed by a fourth Biblical use of the term.

PRAYER

As already hinted, we are used to concluding our prayers with the word "Amen," and we add our own "Amen" when we have heard the prayers of others. "It is the expression by which a worshipper makes his own a prayer uttered by someone else."[6] There is Biblical precedent for this. When our LORD taught his disciples to pray, he finished his model prayer

---

3. Jimenez-Santiago, *Dictionary*, 21.

4. E.g. The Tagalog Popular Version, Magandang Balita Biblia (Manila: PBS, 1980), has "Amen" at Num. 5:22, but not at 1 Kgs. 1:36.

5. Barth, *Prayer and Preaching*, 113.

6. Morris, *Corinthians*, 196.

with this word (Matt. 6:13). The New Testament benedictions—prayers for the blessing of God's people—usually conclude with "Amen."[7]

The "Amen" appended to a prayer means that we are praying earnestly, that we are assured of the rightness of that for which we pray. "Prayer is not an undertaking left to chance, a voyage into the blue. It must end as it began with conviction: Yes, may it be so!"[8]

And we can and do pray with conviction because of our "certainty and assurance in the Lord to whom we pray."[9] When we say "Amen" at the end of our prayers, we are expressing this assured certainty in God. There is thus a twin significance in the use of "Amen," which is captured in Plumer's words: "it expresses a wish that what has been said may be found true, and a confidence that it shall come to pass."[10] Alan Cole puts it well: "Amen" refers "not only to the steadfast faith of the one who prays, but also to the changeless faithfulness of the one to whom the prayer is made."[11]

Not that the "Amen" has to come at the end of a prayer. When Benaiah makes his prayer-wish for Solomon as he succeeds to the throne, he puts his "Amen" at the beginning (1 Kgs. 1:36). It has been said that it is in a context like this that the word "Amen" finds its proper place, "where one person confirms the words of another, and expresses a wish for this issue of his vows or predictions."[12] John also prefaces a prayer with "Amen," as he utters his fervent wish for the coming of the Lord Jesus (Rev. 22:20).

Of the books which I have been using in my studies of the Apostles' Creed, the only one which notices the final "Amen" is the one by Alister McGrath. He suggests that the presence of the "Amen" "reminds us that the creed is as much a prayer as a statement of faith." He continues in this vein: the creed, he suggests, "is a prayer for the deepening of our faith in and commitment to the God whose greatness we have just considered.

---

7. Rom. 15:33; 16:20, 24; 2 Cor. 13:14; Gal. 6:18; Eph. 6:24; Phil. 4:23; Col. 4:18; 1 Thess. 5:28; 2 Thess. 3:18; 1 Tim. 6:21; 2 Tim. 4:22; Titus 3:15; Phlm. 25; Heb. 13:25; 1 Pet. 5:14; Rev. 22:21. All these NT prayer-wishes end with "Amen" in the received text, though in modern critical editions only Rom. 15:33.

8. Barth, *Prayer and Preaching*, 63.

9. *Theological Wordbook of the Old Testament*, 116.

10. Plumer, *Psalms*, 490.

11. Cole, *Galatians*, 37.

12. Gesenius, *Lexicon*, 36.

To say "Amen!" to the creed is to pray that the power and presence of God might touch our lives, deepen our love for him and enhance our understanding of his gospel."[13]

Peter Masters comments on the final "Amen" in the Lord's Prayer in a similar way: "it is total identification with God's kingdom purposes. It is the expression of a ransomed soul who worships, admires, accepts, and pledges himself or herself to him." It involves submission to the programme of God's kingdom as one's delight and chief interest.[14]

PRAISE

Closely related to the use of "Amen" in prayer is its place in song and praise. In Order Two for Holy Communion in *Common Worship*, the eighth element in the Service is described as praise to God for his goodness.[15] The liturgy runs as follows:

> Lift up your hearts.
> We lift them up unto the Lord.
> Let us give thanks unto our Lord God.
> It is meet and right so to do.
> It is very meet, right and our bounden duty, that we should at all times, and in all places, give thanks unto thee, O Lord, holy Father, almighty, everlasting God.
> Therefore with angels and archangels, and with all the company of heaven, we laud and magnify thy glorious name, evermore praising thee, and saying:
> Holy, holy, holy, Lord God of hosts, heaven and earth are full of thy glory. Glory be to thee, O Lord most high.

There then follows a corporate "Amen."[16] In effect the congregation is declaring, "all this is true; God really is holy and glorious; he is most worthy of praise, and we gladly unite to offer him the praise which he deserves." The apostle Paul assumes that the congregation will unite to

---

13. McGrath, *I Believe*, 105.

14. Masters, *The Lord's Pattern*, 88.

15. *Common Worship*, Holy Communion, Order Two Structure, http://www.cofe.anglican.org/worship/liturgy/commonworship/texts/hc/twostructure.html. © Archbishops' Council. Used by permission. Copyright.copyright@c-of-e.org.uk.

16. *Common Worship*, Holy Communion, Order Two, http://www.cofe.anglican.org/worship/liturgy/commonworship/texts/hc/ordertwo.html. © Archbishops' Council. Used by permission. Copyright.copyright@c-of-e.org.uk.

say "Amen," uttering "the familiar formula of assent,"[17] as they are led in the giving of thanks with understanding (1 Cor. 14:16).

On the day when the ark was brought into the tabernacle David composed a song of praise which he presented to Asaph. It is recorded in 1 Chronicles 16:8–36. It concludes with the words "Blessed be the Lord God of Israel from everlasting to everlasting." Immediately, "all the people said 'Amen!' and praised the Lord." Similarly, the words "Amen and Amen" conclude the first Book of the Psalms, following exactly the same words of praise (Ps. 41:13), and, in fact, each of the second, third and fourth Books of the Psalms ends with the double (Pss. 72:19; 89:52) or single (Ps. 106:48) "Amen" of praise. Where the "Amen" is repeated it "connotes the intensity of feeling behind the affirmation."[18] God's people responded with their "Amen" again when "Ezra blessed the Lord" (Neh. 8:6). Several times in the New Testament ascriptions of glory to God conclude with the "Amen" which confirms his praiseworthiness.[19] Indeed, "in the New Testament *amēn* is nearly always used after a doxology,"[20] where it is "a form of endorsement."[21] Gerald Hawthorne makes the following comment on this doxological "Amen": it is "that spontaneous and joyful endorsement of all that has been said. It is the 'yes' of the worshipping church to God, and acknowledgment and acceptance of the promises he has made in Jesus Christ."[22]

Perhaps this is the sense of "Amen" in Romans 1:25. Having deplored the lie which human sinfulness speaks, having lamented the world's ignominious and ridiculous substitution of created idols for the true God, Paul cannot then resist asserting God's eternal blessedness, and then appending his own "Amen" of praise to such a glorious Creator. "The "Amen" underlines Paul's commitment to this truth."[23] The function of the "Amen" in Romans 9:5 is similar.

---

17. Hodge, *Corinthians*, 291.

18. Yamauchi, *Ezra and Nehemiah*, on Neh 8:6.

19. Rom. 11:36; 16:27 (only in the received text); Gal. 1:5; Eph. 3:21; Phil. 4:20; 1 Tim. 1:17; 6:16; 2 Tim. 4:18; Heb. 13:21; 1 Pet. 4:11; 5:11; 2 Pet. 3:18 (only in the received text); Jude 25; Rev. 1:6.

20. Lincoln, *Ephesians*, on Eph. 3:20, 21.

21. Stibbs, *1 Peter*, 157.

22. Hawthorne, *Philippians*, on Phil. 4:20

23. Dunn, *Romans 1–8*, 64.

However, as in the case of prayer, so with praise, the "Amen" may come at the beginning of a doxology. Such is the case in Revelation 7:12, although here it is also repeated at the end. In Revelation 19:4, "Amen" precedes the one word ascription of praise, "Alleluia!"

J. B. Payne suggests rendering the exclamation "Amen" in a praise context as "True indeed!"[24] And that is exactly the significance of the "Amen" at end of the Apostles' Creed. Everything that the creed has said is true indeed, and therefore the Triune God in whom we have declared our faith is worthy indeed of praise. He is the sovereign Lord, the Creator of all things. He is the one who, in Jesus Christ his Son, has acted graciously and decisively at a particular historical moment for the salvation of a world which stretches across all the centuries of history. He is the God who through the years since continues to receive the intercession of his Son for that sinful but saved world, the one who, by his Holy Spirit, applies the saving work of Christ in the church and in individual experience for all eternity. Well then, "Amen!" Here is a divine story which has to evoke our profoundest praise.

ASSENT

A third way in which we use the word "Amen" is to signal our joyful assent to something which has been said, perhaps as we listen to the preaching of God's Word, or maybe, but more rarely, in ordinary conversation.

In the congregation to which I belong we used to have a dear brother called Harold. I say "used to," because, although he is still a church member, due to the frailty of old age and the incapacitating effects of illness, he has not been able to attend a service for several years now. He was always a wonderful encourager to a preacher. His own relationship with his Savior was so real and precious to him that he truly exuded joy. As the gospel was preached week by week, his "Amens" would punctuate the sermon, and the entire congregation was challenged and encouraged by his presence amongst us. Harold's "Amens" were telling us all, but more significantly, acknowledging before God, that he agreed with what was being preached, that he found the message agreeable to his spirit, that the gospel was indeed a source of comfort and joy, that the Holy Spirit had given him a lively enthusiasm for the truths of God's Word. I am in

---

24. Payne, *1 and 2 Chronicles*, on 1 Chr. 16:36.

thorough agreement with Plumer, who says that "an audible 'Amen' is no indecency in the house of God, if seasonably and reverently made."[25]

We hear this "Amen" of assent in Revelation 5:14 as a response by the four living creatures to the worship of "every creature which is in heaven and on the earth and under the earth and such as are in the sea." Jeremiah once spoke the "Amen" of assent, albeit in an ironic way,[26] to words of the false prophet, Hananiah: he wished that Hananiah's prediction could come true, but knew that it would not (Jer. 28:6). However, there is nothing ironic in John's exclamation, "Amen," as he thrills to the prospect of the Lord's return on the clouds when "every eye will see him" (Rev. 1:7): it is his "emphatic affirmation,"[27] in which he joyfully endorses the infallible truth of the second coming, and his own eager anticipation of it.

Sometimes "Amen" may be used as a signal of assent to one's own words. It then becomes a confirmation of the sincerity with which one has spoken. When Paul added his "Amen" to the words "My love be with you all in Christ Jesus" (1 Cor. 16:24), he was saying, "I really mean it, I really do love the church of God in Corinth." John's "Amen," which closes his first epistle, underscores the urgency with which he has made his final injunction, "keep yourselves from idols" (1 John 5:21).

The most notable example of someone who used "Amen" like this is our Lord himself. The familiar words from the Authorized Version, "Verily" (e.g. Matt. 5:18 and a further fifty times in the Synoptic Gospels), and, in John's gospel, "Verily, verily" (e.g. John 1:51 and a further twenty-four times), translated by the NKJV respectively as "assuredly" and "most assuredly," are actually "Amen" and "Amen, amen." Jesus is preparing his hearers for a statement of the utmost importance, and also sincerely guaranteeing his own reliability in making the statement. Hagner writes: "This prefatory usage of 'amen' is found neither in the Old Testament nor in the rabbinic literature, where the word occurs consistently as a response to a preceding statement."[28]

This is true even of Benaiah's prayer, which began with the word "Amen," and Jeremiah's opening "Amen" of assent to Hananiah: in both

25. Plumer, *Psalms*, 493.

26. R. K. Harrison, *Jeremiah and Lamentations*, 130; see also Feinberg, *Jeremiah*, on Jer. 28:5–9.

27. Aune, *Revelation 1–5*, on Rev. 1:7.

28. Hagner, *Matthew 1–13*, on Matt. 5:18.

cases they were responding to something which had been said by someone else. As the preface to a personal statement, therefore, Jesus' usage is unusual, and this singularity is surely fitting in view of the uniqueness of his person. Walter Moberley comments: "In the Old Testament *'āmēn* is always a word of response to what is said by someone else (when Jesus used it to preface his own words, his usage was entirely unprecedented and formed an important element of the unique authority with which he spoke)."[29]

Speaking from heaven in his risen glory, the ascended Christ places an "Amen" of assent to his own words in the middle of Revelation 1:18, "I am he who lives, and was dead, and behold, I am alive forevermore. Amen. And I have the keys of Hades and of Death."

When we finish our recitation of the Apostles' Creed with the word "Amen," we are giving our assent to the faith which we have confessed. "Amen" "is a good example of the nature of religious language as self-involving. To say *'āmēn* genuinely is an act of self-commitment, for it implies appropriate action on the part of the speaker."[30]

The story used to be told of a university professor who had been a professing Christian, but had become a thoroughgoing skeptic. In spite of that he still attended worship in the college chapel. Apparently, the chaplain, as he led the service would reach the point where the creed was to be recited and would pause. The reason was to allow the skeptical professor to add, in his mind, the words "It is as if" before launching into the creed, "I believe." When we say "Amen" after reciting the creed, we rule out any such mental reservation. We are saying I totally and gladly acquiesce in everything which is being proclaimed in this statement of faith. We are re-emphasizing the fact, already implied in the opening "I believe" that this is not some dry theory, some religious nicety, but the very truth to which my own heart gives personal assent, and I confess this faith with absolute sincerity.

THE GOD OF THE AMEN

The final use of "Amen" is found in Isaiah 65:16. Twice in this verse the LORD is called (in the NKJV) "the God of truth." The literal rendering would be "the God of Amen," or "the God of the Amen." Here there

---

29. Moberley, "*'mn*," 428; see also Tasker, *John*, 70.
30. Moberley, "*'mn*," 428.

is an intentional link with the verb to which "Amen" is etymologically connected, *'āman*. The connotations of this verb have to do with faithful support, assured confirmation, established trustworthiness, lasting steadfastness, but also with nurturing care, with the commitment that carries.[31] The "God of the Amen" is the God who is faithful, who is a permanent and reliable supporter of his people, whose trustworthiness is beyond question, whose word is beyond doubt, the God who cares and carries and loves with steadfast commitment, such a God "as one may safely lean upon."[32] Calvin summarizes succinctly the significance of this title: "he is faithful to his promises and steadfast to his purpose."[33] He is "the God of the Amen" in that it is always, invariably appropriate to say "Amen" to what he says: the word of the Lord cannot possibly fail.

With this text must be compared Revelation 3:14, where "the Amen" is one of the titles of Christ. Alan Johnson suggests that "Jesus is the 'Amen' in the sense that he is the perfect human, obedient response to the divine promises."[34] However, it seems more probable that David Aune is correct in seeing this title as Christologically significant "since it attributes to Christ a title associated only with God,"[35] namely the title used in Isaiah 65:16.

God is "the God of the Amen," and his personal Amen to his own purposes and promises takes embodiment in the life of Jesus Christ, "the Amen." We read in 2 Corinthians 1:20, "all the promises of God in him are Yes, and in him Amen." Alec Motyer suggests that in this text the apostle Paul is recalling and clarifying the title "the God of [the] Amen" from Isaiah 65:16: "he is the God who says 'Amen' to all his promises, affirming their reality and his trustworthiness in keeping them—the God who promised of old in Abraham that people worldwide would enter into blessing and who has kept his word."[36]

But God says "Amen," not through a long distance megaphone from heaven, but by coming to earth in person, in Jesus Christ: in his life and work, God says "Yes, Amen" to everything which his word declares.

---

31. See *Online Bible Hebrew Lexicon*, 539; *Theological Wordbook of the Old Testament*, 116.

32. Gesenius, *Lexicon*, 36.

33. Calvin, *Isaiah*, 397.

34. Johnson, *Revelation*, on Rev. 3:14.

35. Aune, *Revelation*, on Rev. 3:14.

36. Motyer, *Isaiah*, 529.

And the declarations of God's word center around the divine desire in mercy to save rebellious humanity. This desire is implicit in the Apostles' Creed.

The creed begins by defining the one in whom we believe as "God the Father almighty, Creator of heaven and earth." To make such a statement of faith is to declare that it is God who shapes our entire existence within the context of a creation over which he rules indisputably every moment.

And the great purpose in the heart of this true and living God, the ultimate shape towards which he moulds all things, is the salvation and blessing of the human family. The final part of the creed brings this out. The Father's desire is that within the communion of the church, men and women of every nation should experience the forgiveness of sins which leads to resurrection and eternal life.

And Jesus Christ, the divine Son, is God's personal "Amen," God's confirmatory assent, to his own word. He certifies God's personal desire that the world's salvation shall be fulfilled. Jesus is God's pledge of authenticity to everything he says. He is the guarantee that the promises of salvation blessing, eternal glory, resurrection joy, shall most definitely all be fulfilled in their time.

And it is in the existence of the person of Christ that the resounding "Amen" sounds out to all that God has proposed for a fallen world and a sinful human race. The key moments in his life as the incarnate Son of God, the events summarized in the middle section of the creed, together form the "Amen" to God's merciful purpose. By the Lord Jesus Christ God vocalizes his sincerity in purposing everlasting blessing for sinful humankind. Jesus' coming in the flesh, his suffering, crucifixion, death, and burial, his descent into hell, his resurrection, ascension, present heavenly ministry and future coming again are all the divine declaration that it shall be: "Amen"—humankind shall be redeemed from sin and death and hell! In the person of Jesus we are assured that "His purpose will stand. His promises are sure. His word is true."[37] Jesus is "the Amen," the final word in God's purposes of blessing for the human race. By his very existence as God incarnate, Jesus is saying, "Yes! Amen"—let it be so, it shall be so, the world must be saved for eternal joy.

Jesus Christ is the one in whom "the divine 'Yes' has come into effect as a permanent reality." All the promises of God find their fulfill-

---

37. Fortner, *Discovering Christ*, 157.

ment in him, "since he forms the climax and summation of the divine self-revelation."[38] The person of Christ is the sum total of everything that God has promised for our good. Have Jesus as your Savior, and you are guaranteed everything which God has ever promised for time and for ever. "Amen!" Cry out in genuine desire, "God, be merciful to me a sinner" (Luke 18:13), and God's reply will be "Amen"—Jesus my Son is the Savior of his people from their sins; in Christ, I give you my assent: you are accepted in my beloved. "Amen!"

I want to finish this course of studies with two quotations—a modern one, from Alister McGrath, and an ancient one, from Rufinus.

McGrath presents this challenge: "The creed will have done its job, and done it well, if it propels us out into God's world, determined to serve him with the same faithfulness and dedication as those who first used this creed all those centuries ago."[39]

Rufinus concludes his exposition of the Apostles' Creed with the prayer that, if we have followed the clauses of the Apostles' Creed with understanding,

> the Lord will grant to us, and to all who hear these words, that having kept the faith which we have received, having finished our course, we may await the crown of righteousness laid up for us, and be found among those who shall rise again to eternal life, and be delivered from confusion and eternal shame, through Christ our Lord, through whom to God the Father Almighty with the Holy Ghost is glory and dominion for ever and ever. Amen.[40]

---

38. M. J. Harris, *2 Corinthians*, on 2 Cor. 1:20.
39. McGrath, *I Believe*, 105.
40. Rufinus, *Commentary*, para. 48, 1136.

Bibliography

2 Clement. *The Second Epistle of Clement to the Corinthians.* LCL 24, 123–63.
Alexander, Joseph Addison. *A Commentary on the Acts of the Apostles.* 1857. Reprint, Edinburgh: Banner of Truth, 1963.
Alexander, Ralph H. *Ezekiel.* In *EBC.*
Allen, Ronald B. *Numbers.* In *EBC.*
Anderson, A. A. *2 Samuel.* WBC 11, 1998.
———. *The Book of Psalms: Psalms 73–150.* NCB Series. London: Oliphants, 1972.
Anselm. *Proslogion.* Translated by Sidney Norton Deane, 1903. Reprint, Chicago: Open Court, 1926. No pages. Online: http://www.Fordham.edu/halsall/basis/anselm-proslogium.html.
Archer, Gleason L. *Daniel.* In *EBC.*
Armerding, Carl E. *Obadiah, Nahum, Habakkuk.* In EBC.
Armstrong, Arthur Hilary. *An Introduction to Ancient Philosophy.* London: Methuen, 1965.
Augustine. *On the Creed.* Translated by C. L. Cornish, 1887. In *NPNF*, First Series 3, 689–730.
———. *Tractates on the Gospel According to St. John.* Translated by John Gibb and James Innes, 1888. In *NPNF*, First Series 7, 6–909.
Aune, David E. *Revelation 1–5.* WBC 52A, 1998.
Baldwin, Joyce G. *Daniel.* TOTC Series. Leicester: IVP, 1978.
Barker, Glenn W. *1, 2, 3 John.* In *EBC.*
Barker, Kenneth L. *Zechariah.* In *EBC.*
Barnes, Albert. *A Popular Family Commentary on the New Testament.* 11 vols. London: Blackie, 1868.
Barnhill, Julie Ann. *Scandalous Grace: Celebrate the Liberating and Tantalizing Realities of Divine Grace!* Carol Stream: Tyndale, 2004.
Bartels, Karl-Heinz. "*monos*." In *NIDNTT* 2, 723–5.
Barth, Karl. *Dogmatics in Outline.* 1949. Translated by G. T. Thomson. London: SCM, 1966.
———. *The Faith of the Church.* 1958. Translated by Gabriel Vahanian, 1958. Reprint, Eugene, OR: Wipf and Stock, 2006.
———. *Prayer and Preaching.* 1953, 1961. Translated by B. E. Hooke. London: SCM, 1964.
Bauckham, Richard J. *Jude, 2 Peter.* WBC 50, 1998.
Bayes, Jonathan F. *Suffering in the Theologies of the Apostolic Fathers.* Unpublished M.Phil dissertation. University of Leeds, 1988.
———. *The Weakness of the Law.* Carlisle: Paternoster, 2000.
Beasley-Murray, George R. *John.* WBC 36, 1987.
Belgic Confession of Faith. 1561. CEPC, 383–436.

Bengel, John Albert. *Gnomon of the New Testament*. 5 vols. Edinburgh: T. and T. Clark, 1858.
Berkouwer, Gerrit Cornelis. *Man: the Image of God*. Grand Rapids: Eerdmans, 1962.
Blaiklock, Edward Musgrave. *Letters to Children of Light*. Glendale: Regal, 1975.
Blum, Edwin A. *1 and 2 Peter and Jude*. In *EBC*.
Blunt, A. W. F. *The Acts of the Apostles*. The Clarendon Bible. Oxford: Clarendon, 1922.
Boer, Harry R. *An Ember Still Glowing: Humankind as the Image of God*. Grand Rapids: Eerdmans, 1990.
Boettner, Lorraine. *The Reformed Doctrine of Predestination*. Phillipsburg: Presbyterian and Reformed, 1932.
Bonhoeffer, Dietrich. *Letters and Papers from Prison*. An Abridged Edition. London: SCM, 1971.
Book of Common Prayer. 1662. No pages. Online: http://www.bcponline.
Bowen, Roger. *A Guide to Romans*. TEF Study Guide 11. London: SPCK, 1975.
Bragan, Jeris E. *Scandalous Grace*. Hagerstown: Review and Herald, 1986.
Brow, Robert. *Religion: Origins and Ideas*. London: Tyndale, 1966.
Brown, John. *Hebrews*. 1862. Reprint, Edinburgh: Banner of Truth, 1961.
———. *1 Peter*. 1848. 2 vols. Reprint, Edinburgh: Banner of Truth, 1975.
Bruce, Alexander Balmain. *The Epistle to the Hebrews*. Edinburgh: T. and T. Clark, 1908.
Bruce, Frederick Fyvie. *I and II Corinthians*. London: Marshall, Morgan and Scott, 1971.
———. *The Epistle to the Hebrews*. NICNT Series. Grand Rapids: Eerdmans, 1964.
———. "The Humanity of Jesus Christ." *JCBRF* 24 (September, 1973), 5–23.
Brunner, Emil. *The Letter to the Romans*. London: Lutterworth, 1959.
Budd, Philip J. *Numbers*. WBC 5, 1998.
Bultmann, Rudolf. *Theology of the New Testament, Vol. 1*. London: SCM, 1952.
Burrows, E. *Mark's Passion Narrative and the Epistle to the Colossians*. Baptist Union, Christian Training Programme, B4: Selected New Testament Passages. No date.
Buss, Arnold H. *Psychology—Man in Perspective*. New York: Wiley, 1973.
Calvin, John. *Catechism of the Church of Geneva*. 1545. Translated by J. K. S. Reid. The Library of Christian Classics 22: Calvin: Theological Treatises. Philadelphia: Westminster, 1954.
———. *Catechism or Institution of the Christian Religion*. 1538. Translated by F. L. Battles. Reprinted in I. J. Hesselink, *Calvin's First Catechism: A Commentary*, 1–38. Louisville: Westminster John Knox, 1997.
———. *Commentaries on the Book of the Prophet Daniel, Vol. 2*. 1561. Translated by Thomas Myers, 1852. CTS 13.
———. *Commentaries on the Catholic Epistles*. 1551. Translated by John Owen, 1855. CTS 22.
———. *Commentaries on the Epistle of Paul the Apostle to the Hebrews*. 1549. Translated by John Owen, 1853. CTS 22.
———. *Commentaries on the Epistles of Paul to the Galatians and Ephesians*. 1548. Translated by William Pringle, 1854. CTS 21.
———. *Commentaries on the First Book of Moses called Genesis, Vol. 1*. 1573. Translated by John King, 1847. CTS 1.
———. *Commentaries on the Last Four Books of Moses Arranged in the Form of a Harmony, Vol. 3*. Translated by Charles William Bingham, 1852. CTS 3.

———. *Commentaries on the Twelve Minor Prophets, Vol. 3.* Translated by John Owen, 1847. CTS 14.
———. *Commentary on the Book of the Prophet Isaiah, Vol. 4.* 1550. Translated by William Pringle, 1850. CTS 8.
———. *Commentary on the Book of Psalms, Vol. 3.* 1557. Translated by James Anderson, 1846. CTS 5.
———. *Commentary on the Book of Psalms, Vol. 4.* 1571. Translated by James Anderson, 1845. CTS 6.
———. *Commentary on the Epistles of Paul the Apostle to the Corinthians, Vol. 1.* 1546. Translated by John Pringle, 1848. CTS 20.
———. *Commentary on the Gospel According to John, Vol. 2.* 1553. Translated by William Pringle, 1847. CTS 18.
———. *Commentary on a Harmony of the Evangelists Matthew, Mark, and Luke, Vol. 1.* 1563. Translated by W. Pringle, 1845. CTS 16.
———. *Commentary upon The Acts of the Apostles, Vol. 1.* 1560. Translated by Christopher Fetherstone, 1585. Edited by Henry Berveridge. CTS 18.
———. *Institutes of the Christian Religion.* Translated by H. Beveridge, 1845. Reprint, MacDill, FL: MacDonald, no date.
Candlish, Robert S. *A Commentary on 1 John.* London: Banner of Truth, 1973.
Canons of Dort. 1619. CEPC, 550–97.
Carson, Donald A. *Matthew.* In *EBC*.
Catechism of the Catholic Church. 1997. No pages. Online: http://www.scborromeo.org/ccc.htm.
Chalke, Steve. "Cross Purposes." *Christianity Today* (September, 2004). No pages. Online: http://www.christianitymagazine.co.uk/engine.cfm?i=92&id=22&arch=1.
Chalke, Steve, and Alan Mann. *The Lost Message of Jesus.* Grand Rapids: Zondervan, 2003.
Chrysostom, John. *Homilies on the Epistles of Paul to the Corinthians.* Translated by J. Ashworth, 1889. In *NPNF*, First Series 12, 18–599.
Clement of Rome. *First Epistle to the Corinthians.* LCL 24, 1–119.
Clines, David J. A. *Job 1–20.* WBC 17, 1989.
Coad, F. Roy. *A History of the Brethren Movement.* Exeter: Paternoster, 1976.
Coenen, Lothar. "Church, Synagogue." In *NIDNTT* 1, 291–305.
Cole, R. Alan. *Exodus.* TOTC Series. Leicester: IVP, 1973.
———. *Galatians.* TNTC, First Series. Leicester: IVP, 1965.
Common Worship © The Archbishops' Council of the Church of England, 2000–2006. No pages. Online: http://www.cofe.anglican.org/worship/liturgy/commonworship/texts.
Conn, Harvie M. *Contemporary World Theology.* Phillipsburg: Presbyterian and Reformed, 1974.
Corwin, Virginia. *St. Ignatius and Christianity in Antioch.* New Haven: Yale, 1960.
Craigie, Peter C. *The Book of Deuteronomy.* NICOT Series. Grand Rapids: Eerdmans, 1976.
Cranfield, Charles E. B. *The Apostles' Creed.* London: Continuum, 2004.
———. *The Epistle to the Romans.* 2 vols. International Critical Commentary. Edinburgh: T. and T. Clark, 1975, 1979.
———. "Some Reflections on the Subject of the Virgin Birth." *SJT* 41 (1988), 177–89.

Cunningham, William. *Historical Theology, Vol. 1*. 1882. Reprint, Edmonton: Still Waters Revival Books, 1991.
Cyril of Jerusalem. *The Catechetical Lectures*. Translated by Edwin Hamilton Gifford, 1893. In *NPNF*, Second Series 7, 108–353.
Darby, John Nelson. "The Hopes of the Church of God, in Connection with the Destiny of the Jews and the Nations as Revealed in Prophecy." In JND 2: Prophetic No. 1.
———. "Lectures on the Second Coming of Christ." In JND 11: Prophetic No. 4.
Dawkins, Richard. *The God Delusion*. London: Bantam, 2006.
De Vries, John Hendrik. "Biographical Note: Abraham Kuyper, 1837–1920." In Kuyper, *Calvinism*, i–vii.
Didache. LCL 24, 303–33.
Dodd, Charles Harold. *The Interpretation of the Fourth Gospel*. Cambridge: Cambridge University Press, 1953.
Dunn, James D. G. *Romans 1–8*. WBC 38A, 1988.
———. *Romans 9–16*. WBC 38B, 1988.
Durham, John I. *Exodus*. WBC 3, 1998.
Earle, Ralph. *1 and 2 Timothy*. In *EBC*.
Ellison, H. L. *A Study of Job: From Tragedy to Triumph*. Grand Rapids: Zondervan, 1958.
Feinberg, Charles L. *Jeremiah*. In *EBC*.
Fitzmyer, Jospeh A. *Romans*. The Anchor Bible, 33. London: Doubleday, 1993.
Flew, Anthony N. *An Introduction to Western Philosophy*. London: Thames and Hudson, 1971.
Formula of Concord. 1584. CEPC, 93–180.
Fortner, Donald S. *Discovering Christ in Revelation*. Darlington: EP, 2002.
Foulkes, Francis. *Ephesians*. TNTC, First Series. London: IVP, 1963.
France, Richard T. *Matthew*. TNTC, Second Series. Leicester: IVP, 1985.
Fredericks, Daniel C. "Ecclesiastes: Theology of." In *NIDOTTE* 4, 552–5.
Fretheim, Terence E. *The Suffering of God: An Old Testament Perspective*. Philadelphia: Fortress, 1984.
———. "Yahweh." In *NIDOTTE* 4, 1295–1300.
Friedman, Richard Elliott. *The Disappearance of God*. London: TSP, 1997.
Geldenhuys, Norval. *The Gospel of Luke*. New London Commentaires. London: Marshall, Morgan and Scott, 1977.
Gesenius, William. *Hebrew and Chaldee Lexicon to the Old Testament Scriptures*. 1812. Translated by S. P. Tregelles, London: Bagster, 1868.
Gill, John. *An Exposition of the Old and New Testament*. 1763. No pages. Carluke: Online Bible on CD-Rom, Version 2.20.03, 2008.
Grant, Robert M. *The Apostolic Fathers, Vol. 4*. Camden: Nelson, 1966.
———. *Gods and the One God*. London: SPCK, 1986.
Green, H. Benedict. *The Gospel According to Matthew*. New Clarendon Bible. Oxford: Oxford University Press, 1975.
Green, Joel B., and Mark D. Baker. *Recovering the Scandal of the Cross*. Carlisle: Paternoster, 2000.
Grogan, Geoffrey W. *Isaiah*. In *EBC*.
Grosheide, Frederik Willem. *Commentary on the First Epistle to the Corinthians*. NICNT Series. Grand Rapids: Eerdmans, 1953.
Grudem, Wayne. *1 Peter*. TNTC, Second Series. Leicester: IVP, 1988.

———. *Systematic Theology*. Leicester: IVP, 1994.
Gumbel, Nicky. *Questions of Life*. Eastbourne: Kingsway, 1993.
Guthrie, Donald. *The Letter to the Hebrews*. TNTC, Second Series. Leicester: IVP, 1983.
———. *New Testament Theology*. Leicester: IVP, 1981.
———. *The Pastoral Epistles*. TNTC, First Series. Leicester: IVP, 1957.
Hagner, Donald A. *Matthew 1–13*. WBC 33A, 1993.
———. *Matthew 14–28*. WBC 33B, 1995.
Haldane, Robert. *Romans*. Reprint, Grand Rapids: MacDonald, 1958.
Hanson, R. P. C. *The Acts*. New Clarendon Bible. Oxford: Clarendon, 1967.
Harris, Murray J. *2 Corinthians*. In *EBC*.
Harris, R. Laird. *Leviticus*. In *EBC*.
Harrison, Everett F. *Acts: The Expanding Church*, Chicago: Moody, 1975.
———. *Romans*. In *EBC*.
Harrison, R. K. *Jeremiah and Lamentations*. TOTC Series. Leicester: IVP, 1973.
———. *Leviticus*. TOTC Series. Leicester: IVP, 1980.
Hawthorne, Gerald F. *Philippians*. WBC. 43, 1998.
Heidelberg Catechism. 1563. Translated by Allen O. Miller and M. Eugene Osterhaven, 1962. Reprint in *Confessions and Catechisms of the Reformation*. Edited by M. A. Noll, 133–64, Leicester: Apollos, 1991.
Hendriksen, William. *1 and 2 Timothy and Titus*. Edinburgh: Banner of Truth, 1960.
———. *Ephesians*. Edinburgh: Banner of Truth, 1972.
———. *The Gospel of John*. Edinburgh: Banner of Truth, 1954.
———. *The Gospel of Luke*. Edinburgh: Banner of Truth, 1978.
———. *The Gospel of Matthew*. Edinburgh: Banner of Truth, 1973.
———. *Romans, Vol. 2: Chapters 9–16*. Edinburgh: Banner of Truth, 1981.
Hendry, George S. "Christology." *DCT*, 51–64.
Henry, Matthew. *Commentary on the Whole Bible: Broadoak One Volume Edition*. Edited by L. F. Church. London: Marshall, Morgan and Scott, 1960.
———. *Revised Matthew Henry Commentary*. No pages. Carluke: Online Bible on CD-Rom, Version 2.20.03, 2008.
Heppe, Heinrich. *Reformed Dogmatics*, 1861. Revised by E. Bizer, 1934. Translated by G. T. Thomson. London: George Allen and Unwin, 1950.
Heron, Alasdair I. C. *A Century of Protestant Theology*. Guildford: Lutterwoth, 1980.
Hesselink, I. John. *Calvin's First Catechism: A Commentary*. Louisville: Westminster John Knox, 1997.
Hewitt, Thomas. *Hebrews*. TNTC, First Series. Leicester: IVP, 1960.
Hilary. *On the Trinity*. Translated by E. W. Watson, E. N. Bennett, and S. C. Gayford, 1898. In *NPNF*, Second Series 9, 222–597.
Hodge, Charles. *1 and 2 Corinthians*. 1857, 1859. Reprint, Edinburgh: Banner of Truth, 1974.
———. *Romans*. 1864. Reprint, Edinburgh: Banner of Truth, 1972.
———. *Systematic Theology, Vol. 1*. London: Nelson, 1880.
Hofius, Otfried. "Father." In *NIDNTT* 1, 614–21.
Hutcheson, George. *The Gospel of John*. 1657. Reprint, Edinburgh: Banner of Truth, 1972.
Ignatius of Antioch, *Epistles*. LCL 24, 165–277.
Irenaeus, *Against Heresies*. Translated by Alexander Roberts and James Donaldson, 1867. In *ANF* 1, 620–1156.

Jeremias, Joachim. *New Testament Theology*. London: SCM, 1971.
Jimenez-Santiago, Aurea. *English-Filipino, Filipino-Filipino-English Dictionary*. Manila: Merriam and Webster, 1998.
Johnson, Alan F. *Revelation*. In *EBC*.
Jones, Hywel R. "Exodus." In *NBC*, 115–39.
Jowett, John Henry. *The Epistles of St. Peter*. London: Hodder and Stoughton, 1905.
Kalland, Earl S. *Deuteronomy*. In *EBC*.
Keener, Craig S. *Matthew*. The IVP New Testament Commentary Series. Leicester: IVP, 1997.
Kelly, John Norman Davidson. *A Commentary on the Epistles of Peter and of Jude*. London: A. and C. Black, 1969.
———. *Early Christian Creeds*. Harlow: Longman, 1972.
Kendall, Robert Tillman. *Jonah*. London: Hodder and Stoughton, 1978.
Kent, Homer A. *Philippians*. In *EBC*.
Kidner, F. Derek. *Genesis*. TOTC Series. Leicester: IVP, 1967.
———. *Psalms 73–150*. TOTC Series. Leicester: IVP, 1975.
King, Guy H. *The Fellowship: an Expositional Study of 1 John*. London: Marshall, Morgan and Scott, 1954.
Kirkpatrick, Clifton. "Preface." In *CWC*, ix–xiv.
Kistemaker, Simon J. *Exposition of the Epistle to the Hebrews*. Welwyn: EP, 1984.
Klappert, Bertold. "Lord's Supper." In *NIDNTT* 2, 520–38.
Kline, Meredith G. "Genesis." In *NBC*, 79–114.
Knapp, Charles. *The Acts of the Apostles*. Murby's Larger Scripture Manuals. London: Murby, 1914.
Kuyper, Abraham. *Lectures on Calvinism*. Grand Rapids: Eerdmans, 1931.
———. *The Work of the Holy Spirit*. 1888. Translated by H. de Vries, 1900. Reprint, Grand Rapids: Eerdmans, 1979.
Ladd, George Eldon. *A Theology of the New Testament*. Guildford: Lutterworth, 1974.
Lewis, Clive Staples. *The Lion, the Witch and the Wardrobe*. Harmondsworth: Penguin, 1950.
Liddell, Henry G., and Robert Scott. *Greek-English Lexicon* (Abridged). Oxford: Clarendon, 1909.
Liefeld, Walter L. *Luke*. In *EBC*.
Lightfoot, Joseph Barber. *The Apostolic Fathers, Part 2, Vol. 2*. London: Macmillan, 1890.
Lincoln, Andrew T. *Ephesians*. WBC 42, 1990.
Lindars, Barnabas. *The Gospel of John*. NCB Series. London: Oliphants, 1972.
Lindsey, Hal. *The Late Great Planet Earth*. London: Lakeland, 1970.
Lloyd-Jones, D. Martyn. *Christian Unity: An Exposition of Ephesians 4:1–16*. Edinburgh: Banner of Truth, 1980.
———. *Romans: An Exposition of Chapter 8:17–39—The Final Perseverance of the Saints*. Edinburgh: Banner of Truth, 1975.
Longenecker, Richard N. *Acts*. In *EBC*.
Luther, Martin. *Enchiridion: The Small Catechism*. 1529. *CEPC*, 76–92.
———. *The Larger Catechism*. 1529. Translated by F. Bente and W. H. T. Dau. Albany, OR: Books for the Ages Digital Edition on CD-Rom, 1997.
Mackintosh, Charles Henry. *Notes on the Book of Exodus*. London: Pickering and Inglis, no date.

McGiffert, Arthur Cushman. *The Apostles' Creed*. 1902. Reprint, Eugene, OR: Wipf and Stock, 2001.
McGrath, Alister E. *'I Believe': Exploring the Apostles' Creed*. Downers Grove: IVP, 1997.
Mandelbaum, Jacqueline, et al. "Moment de la transplantation embryonnaire et succès de la gestation chez l'humain." *Reproduction Nutrition Development* 28, No. 6B (1988), 1763-71. Online: http://www.geocities.com/Heartland/2964/implantation2.html.
Mare, W. Harold. *1 Corinthians*. In *EBC*.
Marshall, I. Howard. *The Acts of the Apostles*. TNTC, Second Series. Leicester: IVP, 1980.
———. *The Epistles of John*. NICNT Series. Grand Rapids: Eerdmans, 1978.
Martens, Elmer A. *Plot and Purpose in the Old Testament*. Leicester: IVP, 1981.
Martin, Ralph P. *2 Corinthians*. WBC 40, 1986.
Massie, John. *Corinthians*. In *CB* 15.
Masters, Peter. *The Faith: Great Christian Truths*. London: Wakeman, 2006.
———. *The Lord's Pattern for Prayer*. London: Wakeman, 2003.
Merrill, Eugene H. "$š^e\hat{o}l$." In *NIDOTTE* 4, 6-7.
Meyer, Frederick Brotherton. *Abraham: Friend of God*. London: Lakeland, 1968.
———. *Bible Commentary*. Reprint, Wheaton: Tyndale, 1979.
———. *The Epistle to the Philippians*. London: RTS, no date.
———. *The Prophet of Hope*. London: Marshall, Morgan and Scott, 1952.
Michaels, J. Ramsey. *1 Peter*. WBC 49, 1998.
Michel, Otto. "*pistis*." In *NIDNTT* 1, 593-605.
Moberley, R. Walter L. "'*mn*," In *NIDOTTE* 1, 427-33.
Moltmann, Jürgen. *The Crucified God*. 1973. Translated by R. A. Wilson and John Bowden. London: SCM, 1974.
Morris, Leon. *The First Epistle of Paul to the Corinthians*. TNTC, First Series. Grand Rapids: Eerdmans, 1958.
———. *The Gospel According to St. Luke*. TNTC, First Series. Leicester: IVP, 1974.
———. *The Gospel According to John*. New London Commentaries. London: Marshall, Morgan and Scott, 1971.
———. *Hebrews*. In *EBC*.
Morrison, Alan. *The Serpent and the Cross*. Birmingham: K&M Books, 1994.
Motyer, J. Alec. "Messiah in the Old Testament." In *IBD* 2, 987-94.
———. *The Prophecy of Isaiah*. Leicester: IVP, 1993.
Moule, Handley C. G. *Colossian Studies*. London: Hodder and Stoughton, 1903.
———. *The High Priestly Prayer*. Grand Rapids: Baker, 1907.
———. *Philippian Studies*. London: Hodder and Stoughton, 1904.
Moulton, James Hope. *A Grammar of New Testament Greek, Vol. 1: Prolegomena*. Edinburgh: T. and T. Clark, 1908.
Muller, Richard A. *After Calvin*. Oxford: Oxford University Press, 2003.
———. *The Unaccommodated Calvin*. Oxford: Oxford University Press, 2000.
Murray, Andrew. *The Holiest of All*. London: Nisbet, 1895.
Murray, John. *The Epistle to the Romans*. 2 vols. NICNT Series. Grand Rapids: Eerdmans, 1959, 1965.
Neil, William. *The Acts of the Apostles*. NCB Series. London: Oliphants, 1973.
Nolland, John. *Luke 9:21—18:34*. WBC 35B, 1993.
———. *Luke 18:35—24:53*. WBC 35C, 1993.

Novatian. *Treatise Concerning the Trinity*. Translated by Robert Ernest Wallis. In *ANF* 5, 1227–1295.
O'Brien, Peter T. *Colossians, Philemon*. WBC 44, 1982.
Ogden, Schubert. *The Reality of God*. San Francisco: Harper and Row, 1977.
Online Bible Greek Lexicon. No pages. Carluke: Online Bible on CD-Rom, Version 2.20.03, 2008.
Online Bible Hebrew Lexicon. No pages. Carluke: Online Bible on CD-Rom, Version 2.20.03, 2008.
Oswalt, John N. "Mšh." In *NIDOTTE* 2, 1123–27.
Packer, James I. *Among God's Giants*. Eastbourne: Kingsway, 1991.
———. *I want to be a Christian*. Eastbourne: Kingsway, 1977.
———. *What did the Cross Achieve? The Logic of Penal Substitution*. Leicester: TSF, 1973.
Pannenberg, Wolfhart. *The Apostles' Creed in the Light of Today's Questions*. London: SCM, 1972.
Payne, J. Barton. *1 and 2 Chronicles*. In *EBC*.
Peake, Arthur Samuel. *Hebrews*. In *CB* 16.
———. *Job*. In *CB* 5
Pernveden, Lage. *The Concept of the Church in The Shepherd of Hermas*. Lund: Gleerup, 1966.
Pink, Arthur W. *An Exposition of Hebrews*. Grand Rapids: Baker, 1954.
Pinnock, Clark H. *Most Moved Mover*. Exeter: Paternoster, 2001.
———. "Systematic Theology." In Pinnock et al., *Openness*, 101–25.
———, et al. *The Openness of God*. Downers Grove: IVP, 1994.
Piper, John. *Desiring God*. Leicester: IVP, 1986.
Placher, William. "The Vulnerability of God." In *Toward the Future of Reformed Theology*, edited by David Willis and Michael Welker, 192–205. Grand Rapids: Eerdmans, 1999.
Plumer, William S. *Psalms*. 1867. Reprint, Edinburgh: Banner of Truth, 1975.
Polycarp. *To the Philippians*. LCL 24, 279–301.
Poole, Matthew. *Annotations upon the Holy Bible, Vol. 1*. 1683. Reprint, Edinburgh: Turnbull, 1800.
———. *A Commentary upon the Holy Bible, Vol. 3: The New Testament*. 1685. Reprint, Edinburgh: Banner of Truth, 1963.
Praamsma, Louis. *Before the Face of God*. Jordan Station: Paideia, 1987.
Pratney, William A. *The Nature and Character of God*. Minneapolis: Bethany House, 1988.
Quasten, Johannes. *Patrology*. Westminster: Christian Classics, 1984.
Rackham, Richard Belward. *The Acts of the Apostles*. Westminster Commentaries. London: Methuen, 1910.
Rengstorf, Karl Heinrich. "*Christos*." In *NIDNTT* 2, 334–43.
———. "*Iēsous*." In *NIDNTT* 2, 330–2.
Reymond, Robert L. *A New Systematic Theology of the Christian Faith*. Nashville: Nelson, 1998.
Rice, T. Richard. "Biblical Support for a New Perspective." In Pinnock, et al., *Openness*, 11–58.
Rufinus. *A Commentary on the Apostles' Creed*. Translated by W. H. Fremantle. In *NPNF*, Second Series 3, 1095–1136.

Sanday William, and Arthur C. Headlam. *The Epistle to the Romans*. International Critical Commentary. Edinburgh: T. and T. Clark, 1902.
Sanders, John E. "Summary of openness theology," *Open Theism Information Site* (2005-9). No pages. Online: http://www.opentheism.info/#foot1.
Schleiermacher, Friedrich D. E. *The Christian Faith*. 1830. Translation edited by Hugh Ross Mackintosh and James S. Stewart, Edinburgh: T. and T. Clark, 1928.
Schneider, Walter. "*krima*." In *NIDNTT* 2, 362-7.
Schoedel, William R. *Ignatius of Antioch*. Philadelphia: Fortress, 1985.
Schultz, Richard. "*špaṭ*." In *NIDOTTE* 4, 213-20.
Scottish Confession of Faith. 1560. Modern English rendering by James Bulloch, 1960. Reprinted in *Reformed Confessions of the Sixteenth Century*, edited by A. C. Cochrane, 163-84. Louisville: Westminster John Knox, 2003.
Second Helvetic Confession. 1566. No pages. Online: http://www.creeds.net/helvetic/.
Seitz, Christopher R. "Our Help is in the Name of the LORD, Maker of Heaven and Earth: Scripture and Creed in Ecumenical Trust." In *Nicene Christianity: The Future for a New Ecumenism*, edited by Christopher R. Seitz, 19-34. Grand Rapids: Brazos, 2001.
Senior, Donald. *The Passion of Jesus in the Gospel of John*. Collegeville: Michael Glazier, 1991.
———. *The Passion of Jesus in the Gospel of Luke*. Manila: St. Pauls, 1995.
———. *The Passion of Jesus in the Gospel of Mark*. Manila: St. Pauls, 1995.
———. *The Passion of Jesus in the Gospel of Matthew*. Manila: St. Pauls, 1995.
Shaw, Robert. *An Exposition of the Confession of Faith*. 1845. Reprint, Lochcarron: Christian Focus, 1980.
Shedd, William G. T. *Calvinism: Pure and Mixed*. 1893. Reprint, Edinburgh: Banner of Truth, 1986.
Shepherd of Hermas, The. LCL 25, 1-305.
Siede, Burghard. "*lambanō*." In *NIDNTT* 3, 747-51.
Sinnema, Don. *Reclaiming the Land: A Study of the Book of Joshua*. Toronto: Joy in Learning Curriculum Development and Training Centre, 1977.
Skevington Wood, Arthur. *Ephesians*. In *EBC*.
Slater, W. F. *St. Matthew*. In *CB* 12.
Smalley, Stephen S. *1, 2, 3 John*. WBC 51, 1984.
Smick, Elmer B. *Job*. In *EBC*.
Smith, David L. *A Handbook of Contemporary Theology*. Wheaton: Bridgepoint, 1992.
Smith, Sir William, and Sir John Lockwood. *Chambers Murray Latin-English Dictionary*. London: John Murray, 1976.
Spurgeon, Charles Haddon. *The Treasury of David*. 6 vols. London: Marshall, Morgan, and Scott, no date.
———. *The Treasury of the New Testament*. 4 vols. London: Marshall, Morgan and Scott, no date.
Stead, G. Christopher. "The Apostles' Creed." In *Foundation Documents of the Faith*, edited by C.S. Rodd, 1-11. Edinburgh: T. and T. Clark, 1987.
Stewart, Alexander. *Creeds and Churches: Studies in Symbolics*. London: Hodder and Stoughton, 1916.
Stibbs, Alan M. *1 Peter*. TNTC, First Series. Leicester: IVP, 1959.
Still, William. *God—Job, and Satan*. Aberdeen: Gilcomston South Church, 1978.

Stott, John R. W. *The Epistles of John*. TNTC, First Series. Grand Rapids: Eerdmans, 1964.

———. *God's New Society: The Message of Ephesians*. The Bible Speaks Today. Leicester: IVP, 1979.

Stotts, Jack L. "Introduction: Confessing After Barmen." In *Reformed Confessions: Theology from Zurich to Barmen*, by Jan Rohls. Louisville: Westminster John Knox, 1998.

Swart Ignatius, and Robin Wakely. "Ṣrr." In *NIDOTTE* 3, 853–9.

Tasker, R. V. G. *John*. TNTC, First Series. Leicester: IVP, 1960.

Tenney, Merrill C. *John*. In *EBC*.

Tertullian. *A Treatise on the Soul*. Translated by Peter Holmes. In *ANF* 3, 322–431.

———. *The Prescription Against Heretics*. Translated by Peter Holmes. In *ANF* 3, 436–84.

———. *On the Resurrection of the Flesh*. Translated by Peter Holmes. In *ANF* 3, 978–1078.

Thayer, Joseph Henry. *A Greek-English Lexicon of the New Testament*. Edinburgh: T. and T. Clark, 1901.

The Thirty-Nine Articles of Religion of the Church of England. 1562. CEPC, 486–516.

Theological Wordbook of the Old Testament. 1980. Edited by Gleason L. Archer and R. Laird Harris. I. Jurik: Theophilus Bible Software, 2003.

Thiselton, Anthony. C. "Flesh." In *NIDNTT* 1, 671–82.

Thompson, John A. *The Book of Jeremiah*. NICOT Series. Grand Rapids: Eerdmans, 1980.

Tillich, Paul. *Systematic Theology, Vol. 1*. Chicago: University of Chicago Press, 1951.

Torrance, Thomas F. *The Doctrine of Grace in the Apostolic Fathers*. Edinburgh: Oliver and Boyd, 1948.

Treasury of Scripture Knowledge. 1967. Edited by Reuben Archer Torrey. No pages. Carluke: Online Bible on CD-Rom, Version 2.20.03, 2008.

Tuente, Rudolf. "*doulos*." In *NIDNTT* 3, 592–8.

Van Dyk, Leanne. "A Conversation with the Ecumenical Creeds." *CWC*, 17–31.

Van Gemeren, Willem A. *Psalms*. In *EBC*.

Vaughan, Curtis. *Colossians*. In *EBC*.

Vaughan, Charles John. *St. Paul's Epistle to the Romans*. London: Macmillan, 1885.

Vincent, Thomas. *The Shorter Catechism Explained from Scripture*. 1674. Reprint, Edinburgh: Banner of Truth, 1980.

Von Balthasar, Hans Urs. *Credo: Meditations on the Apostles' Creed*. San Francisco: Ignatius Press, 1990.

Von Harnack, Adolf. *History of Dogma, Vol. 1*. London: Williams and Norgate, 1905.

Watts, John D. W. *Isaiah 34–66*. WBC 25, 1987.

Wenham, Gordon J. *Genesis 1–15*. WBC 1, 1987.

———. *Genesis 16–50*. WBC 2, 1994.

———. *The Book of Leviticus*. NICOT Series. Grand Rapids: Eerdmans, 1979.

Wesley, John. *Explanatory Notes upon the New Testament*. 1754. Reprint, London: Epworth, 1941.

Westcott, Brooke Foss. *The Epistle to the Hebrews*. London: Macmillam, 1889.

———. *The Gospel According to St. John*. London: Murray, 1887.

Westminster Confession of Faith and Shorter Catechism. 1646–7. CEPC, 598–673.

Westminster Larger Catechism. 1647. Reprint, *The Confession of Faith*, Glasgow: Free Presbyterian Publications, 1985.
Westminster Shorter Catechism. 1647. *CEPC*, 674–704.
Wibbing, Siegfried. "Body." In *NIDNTT* 1, 232–8.
Williams, Garry J. "Justice, Law, and Guilt." 2005. Online: http://www.eauk.org/theology/headline_issues/atonement/upload/garry_williams.pdf.
Williamson, G. I. *The Heidelberg Catechism: A Study Guide*. Phillipsburg: Presbyterian and Reformed, 1993.
———. *The Westminster Confession of Faith for Study Classes*. Philadelphia: Presbyterian and Reformed, 1964.
Williamson, Hugh Godfrey Maturin. *Ezra, Nehemiah*. *WBC* 16, 1985.
Wilson, Robert McLachlan. *Hebrews*. *NCB* Series. Grand Rapids: Eerdmans, 1987.
Witsius, Herman. *Sacred Dissertations on The Apostles' Creed*. 1681. Translated by D. Fraser, 1823. Reprint, Escondido: den Dulk, 1993.
Yamauchi, Edwin. *Ezra and Nehemiah*. In *EBC*.
Youngblood, Ronald. F. *1 and 2 Samuel*. In *EBC*.

Scripture Index

OLD TESTAMNET

Genesis

1	44	9:4	229, n. 61
1–2	42; 44	9:11	228, n. 60
1:4	44, n. 19	9:15–17	228, n. 60
1:10	44, n. 19	15:1	5
1:12	44, n. 19	17:1	34, n. 2
1:18	44, n. 19	17:1–8	38
1:21	44, n. 19	17:11	228, n. 54
1:25	44, n. 19	17:13–14	228, n. 54
1:27	24	17:23–25	228, n. 54
1:28	43	18:14	36
1:31	44	18:25	102
2:15	43	22:2–13	82
2:17	209	28:3	34, n. 2
2:21	228, n. 54	29:14	228, n. 57
2:23	228, n. 54	35:11	34, n. 2
2:24	228, n. 55	35:11–12	38
3:17–19	231	37:27	228, n. 57
3:22	233	37:35	90, n. 19
3:23–24	130	40:19	228, n. 54
4	162	41:2–4	228, n. 60
4:1	26	41:18–19	228, n. 60
6:3	229, n. 63	43:14	34, n. 2
6:6	21	48:3	34, n. 2
6:12–13	228, n. 59	50:17–21	215
6:17	228, n. 60		
6:19	228, n. 60	### Exodus	
7:15–16	228, n. 60	4:7	228, n. 54
7:21	228, n. 60	4:22	56; 189
8:17	228, n. 60	6:3	34, n. 2
8:21	192–3	10:17	215
		12:8	229, n. 61
		12:12	213
		12:13	188–9
		12:23	188; 213

Exodus-continued

12:46	229, n. 61
15:6	145
15:12	145
16:3	229, n. 61
16:8	229, n. 61
16:12	229, n. 61
20:11	46, n. 23
21:28	229, n. 61
21:31	229, n. 61
24:5-6	192
24:8	192-3
28:3	162
28:42	228, n. 54
29:14	229, n. 61
29:31-32	229, n. 61
29:34	229, n. 61
30:32	228, n. 54
31:3-5	162
31:17	46, n. 23
32	140
32:14	21
33:12-13	28
33:13	18; 30
33:14	51, n. 17
33:18	30
34:7	216
35:31-33	162
39:41	139, n. 26

Leviticus

1:9	82; 192
1:13	82; 192
1:17	192
3:5	192
3:16	192
4:5	53, n. 29
4:11	229, n. 61
4:16	53, n. 29
6:10	228, n. 54
6:22	53, n. 29
6:27	229, n. 61
7:15	229, n. 61
7:17-21	229, n. 61
7:17-18	113
8:17	229, n. 61
8:31-32	229, n. 61
9:11	229, n. 61
11:8	229, n. 61
11:11	229, n. 61
12:3	228, n. 54
13:2-4	228, n. 54
13:10-11	228, n. 54
13:13-16	228, n. 54
13:18	228, n. 54
13:24	228, n. 54
13:38-39	228, n. 54
13:43	228, n. 54
14:9	228, n. 54
15:2-3	228, n. 54
15:7	228, n. 54
15:13	228, n. 54
15:16	228, n. 54
15:19	228, n. 54
16:4	228, n. 54
16:22	213
16:24	228, n. 54
16:26	228, n. 54
16:27	229, n. 61
16:28	228, n. 54
17:11	228, n. 60
17:14	228, n. 60
17:16	228, n. 54
18:6	228, n. 57
19:6-7	113
19:28	228, n. 54
21:5	228, n. 54
21:10	139, n. 24
22:6	228, n. 54
25:49	228, n. 57
26:29	229, n. 61

Scripture Index

Numbers

5:22	242, n. 4
8:7	228, n. 54
11:4	229, n. 61
11:13	229, n. 61
11:18	229, n. 61
11:21	229, n. 61
11:33	229, n. 61
12:12	228, n. 54
14:18	217
16:22	228, n. 59
16:30–31	90, n. 20
18:15	228, n. 60
18:18	229, n. 61
19:5	229, n. 61
19:7–8	228, n. 54
23:19	20, n. 30; 21
27:16	228, n. 59
32:40	237
32:42	228, n. 54
33:1	57
33:3	197, n. 50

Deuteronomy

1:38	50
3:20	51, n. 17
5:26	228, n. 59
5:33	51
6:23	50
12:9	51, n. 17
12:10	51
12:15	229, n. 61
12:20	229, n. 61
12:23	229, n. 61
12:27	229, n. 61
14:8	229, n. 61
15:4	202
16:4	229, n. 61
21:22–23	80
25:19	51, n. 17
28:53	229, n. 61
28:55	229, n. 61
31:3	50
31:7	50
32:6	25
32:22	90, n. 20

Joshua

1:13	51, n. 17
21:44	51, n. 18
22:4	51, n. 18
23:1	51, n. 18

Judges

6:19–21	229, n. 61
8:7	228, n. 54
9:2	228, n. 57

1 Samuel

2:5	74, n. 57
2:6	90, n. 19
2:9	197, n. 50
2:10	53, n. 31
2:13	229, n. 61
2:15	229, n. 61
2:35	53, n. 31
8:9	20, n. 30
12:3	53, n. 31
12:5	53, n. 31
15:29	21
16:6	53, n. 31
17:44	229, n. 61
24:6	53, n. 31
24:10	53, n. 31
26:9	53, n. 31
26:11	53, n. 31
26:16	53, n. 31
26:23	53, n. 31

2 Samuel

1:14	53, n. 31
1:16	53, n. 31
2:5	53, n. 31
5:1	228, n. 57
7:8	34, n. 4; 39
7:14	26; 39
7:26–27	39
19:12–13	228, n. 57
19:21	53, n. 31
22:51	53, n. 31
23:1	53, n. 31

1 Kings

1:36	242, n. 4; 243
2:9	90, n. 19
8:34	215
8:36	215
17:6	229, n. 61
19:21	229, n. 61
21:27	228, n. 54

2 Kings

4:34	229, n. 61
5:10	228, n. 54
5:14	228, n. 54
6:30	228, n. 54
9:36	229, n. 61
12:10	139, n. 24
19:15	46
19:19	46
20:1–6	21
22:4	139, n. 24
22:8	139, n. 24
23:4	139, n. 24
25:18	139, n. 25

1 Chronicles

11:1	228, n. 57
11:9	34, n. 4
16:8–36	245
16:22	53, n. 30
17:13	26
22:10	26, n. 7
28:6	26, n. 7
29:10	25, n. 4

2 Chronicles

2:12	46
6:25	215
6:27	215
6:42	53, n. 31
7:14	215
22:7	53, n. 31
24:11	139, n. 24
32:8	228, n. 58
34:9	139, n. 24

Ezra

7:5	139, n. 25

Nehemiah

3:1	139, n. 24
3:20	139, n. 24
5:5	228, n. 57
5:8	26, n. 5
8:6	245
9:6	46
9:17	217
13:28	139, n. 24

Job

1:21	220
2:5	228, n. 54
4:15	228, n. 54
5:17	34, n. 3
6:12	228, n. 54
7:5	228, n. 54
8:5	34, n. 3

Scripture Index

10:4	228, n. 58	9:17	90, n. 20
10:11	228, n. 54	16:9	228, n. 56
11:7	34, n. 3	16:10	90, n. 20
11:8	90, n. 20	16:11	146
12:10	228, n. 59	17:7	146, n. 49
13:14	228, n. 54	18:5	90, n. 20
14:13	90, n. 19	18:35	145, n. 48
14:22	228, n. 54	18:50	53, n. 31
15:25	34, n. 3	20:6	53, n. 31; 145, n. 48
17:13	90, n. 19	22	107
17:16	90, n. 20	25:14	23
19:20	228, n. 54	27:2	228, n. 54
19:22	228, n. 54	28:8	53–4, n. 31
19:26	226; 228, n. 56; 230	30:3	90, n. 19
21:6	228, n. 56	31:17	90, n. 19
21:13	90, n. 19	31:23	197, n. 50
22:17	34, n. 3	32:1–2	212–3
22:25	34, n. 3	34:9	197, n. 50
23:16	34, n. 3	38:3	229, n. 63
27:2	34, n. 3	38:7	229, n. 63
27:11	34, n. 3	41:13	245
27:13	34, n. 3	43:3	5
31:31	229, n. 61	44:3	145, n. 48
32:8	34, n. 3	48:9–10	146, n. 49
33:4	34, n. 3	49:14	90, n. 19
33:21	228, n. 54	50:5	197, n. 50
33:25	228, n. 54	50:13	229, n. 61
34:10	34, n. 3	55:15	90, n. 20
34:12	34, n. 3	56:4	228, n. 58
34:15	228, n. 59	58:11	156
35:13	34, n. 3	60:5	145, n. 48
38:7	56	63:1	228, n. 56
38:36	163	63:8	145, n. 48
41:23	228, n. 60	65:2	228, n. 59
		67:4	156
Psalms		68:5	27, n. 11
		68:18	126–7; 129
2:2	53, n. 31	72:8	181
2:7	58	72:18	37
6:5	90, n. 19	72:19	245
7:8–9	156	74:11–12	145, n. 48
8:4–6	147–8	76:9	156
9:4	156	77:10	145, n. 48
		78:39	229, n. 62

Psalms-continued

78:54	145, n. 48
79:2	229, n. 61
80:15–17	146
82:8	156
84:2	228, n. 56
84:9	53, n. 31
85:2	212
86:5	217
86:13	90, n. 20
88:3–6	94
88:3	90, n. 19
88:10–12	94
89:4	26, n. 7
89:13–14	146, n. 49
89:26	26, n. 7
89:38	53, n. 31
89:51	53, n. 31
89:52	245
90	220
94:17	90, n. 18
98:1	145, n. 48
99:8	217
102:5	228, n. 54
103:13	27
105:15	53, n. 30
106:48	245
108:6	145, n. 48
109:24	228, n. 54
110:1–2	144
110:1	151
113:4–9	73–4
115:15	46
115:17	90, n. 18
116:3	90, n. 20
118:14–16	145, n. 48
119:120	228, n. 56
121:2	46
124:8	45–6
132:10	53, n. 31
132:17	53, n. 31
134:3	46
136:4	37, n. 15
136:25	228, n. 60
138:7	145, n. 48
139:2	20, n. 30
139:8	90, n. 20
139:16	20, n. 30
141:7	90, n. 19
145:21	228, n. 59
146:5–6	46
148:14	197, n. 50

Proverbs

1:12	90, n. 20
3:12	27; 31, n. 38
4:22	228, n. 56
5:11	228, n. 56
9:18	90, n. 20
14:30	228, n. 54
15:11	90, n. 20
15:24	90, n. 20
22:3	21
23:14	90, n. 20
23:20	229, n. 61
27:12	21
27:20	90, n. 20
30:16	90, n. 19

Ecclesiastes

2:3	228, n. 56
4:5	228, n. 56
5:2	123
5:6	228, n. 56
5:7	123
11:10	228, n. 56
12:1	47
12:12	228, n. 54

Isaiah

5:14	90, n. 20
7:9	11
7:11	90, n. 18

7:14	63; 66	66:16	228, n. 59
9:6	61	66:17	229, n. 61
9:20	228, n. 54	66:23–24	228, n. 59
10:18	228, n. 54		
11:2	126	**Jeremiah**	
14:9	90, n. 20		
14:15	90, n. 20	1:5	20, n. 30
17:4	228, n. 58	3:19	25, n. 4
22:13	229, n. 61	5:15–18	20
28:15	90, n. 20	7:21	229, n. 61
28:18	90, n. 20	10:12	46
28:24–29	163	11:15	228, n. 56
28:26	163	12:12	228, n. 59
31:3	229, n. 62	17:5	229, n. 62
33:22	207	19:9	229, n. 61
37:16	46	23:16	34, n. 4
37:20	46	25:15	194
38:18	90, n. 20	25:31	228, n. 59
40:5–6	228, n. 59	26:3	20
40:22–31	45	28:6	247
43:10	6	29:13	5
43:11	49	31:9	26
43:24	179	31:33	168
44:16	229, n. 61	31:34	212
44:19	229, n. 61	32:17	36; 46
44:24	46, n. 24	32:24–25	46
45:1	53, n. 31	32:27	36; 228, n. 59
45:12	46, n. 24	45:5	228, n. 59
45:18	46, n. 24	50:20	212
46:9–10	20	51:15	46
49:26	229, n. 61	52:24	139, n. 25
51:13	46, n. 24		
51:17	194	**Lamentations**	
52:10	181		
53:3	77	3:4	228, n. 54
53:12	193	4:20	53, n. 31
54:1	74, n. 57		
58:7	228, n. 57	**Ezekiel**	
63:9	70–71		
63:16	25, n. 4	4:14	229, n. 61
64:5	240	10:5	34, n. 2
64:8	25, n. 4	10:12	228, n. 60
65:4	229, n. 61	11:3	229, n. 61
65:16	248–9		

Ezekiel-continued

11:7	229, n. 61
11:11	229, n. 61
11:19	228, n. 54, n. 56
13:13	147
16:26	229, n. 63
18:4	209
18:20	209
20:48	228, n. 59
21:4–5	228, n. 59
23:20	228, n. 54, n. 60
24:10	229, n. 61
31:16–17	90, n. 20
32:5	229, n. 61
32:21	90, n. 20
32:27	90, n. 20
36:26–27	168
36:26	228, n. 54, n. 56
37:6	228, n. 54
39:17–18	229, n. 61
40:43	229, n. 61
44:7	228, n. 54
44:9	228, n. 54

Daniel

1:15	228, n. 54
2:4	237, n. 34
3:9	237, n. 34
4:34	237
5:10	237, n. 34
6:6	237, n. 34
6:21	237, n. 34
6:26	237
7:27	197, n. 50
9:9	217
9:25–26	53
9:25	53, n. 31
10:3	229, n. 61
12:2	233
12:7	237

Hosea

1:9	106
6:2	113
8:13	229, n. 61
11:1–2	106
11:8–9	106
13:14	90, n. 19

Joel

2:28	228, n. 59

Amos

4:13	54, n. 31
9:2	90, n. 20

Jonah

2:2	90, n. 20
3:10	20–21

Micah

3:3	229, n. 61
4:4	34, n. 4
5:2	37
7:18–19	212–3
7:18	218

Habakkuk

2:5	90, n. 20
3:13	54, n. 31

Haggai

1:1	139, n. 24
1:12	139, n. 24
1:14	139, n. 24
2:2	139, n. 24
2:4	139, n. 24
2:12	229, n. 61

Zechariah

2:13	228, n. 59
3:1–5	141
3:1	139, n. 24
3:8	139, n. 24
6:11	139, n. 24
9:12	116
11:9	229, n. 61
11:16	229, n. 61
14:12	228, n. 54

NEW TESTAMENT

Matthew

1:21	49
1:23	71
3:17	58
4:3	58
4:6	58
5:16	27, n. 15
5:18	247
6:8	29
6:9	27
6:13	242–3
6:14	27, n. 16
6:26	29
6:32	29
7:7–11	101
7:14	100–101
7:21	28, n. 17
7:23	208, n. 23
8:11	101
10:4	105, n. 78
10:29–31	29
11:23	90, n. 22
11:27	28
12:18	52
12:40	91
14:13–14	190
14:19	190
14:23–27	144
14:32	144
15:32–33	190
15:36	190
16:16–17	53
16:17	227, n. 48
16:18	172
16:21	112, n. 15
17:2	131
17:22	105, n. 78
17:23	112, n. 15
18:17	175
18:21–35	204; 210–11
19:6	227, n. 47
19:26	37
20:18	105, n. 78
20:19	105, n. 79; 112, n. 15
20:28	52; 101
22:14	101
22:31	226, n. 35
22:44	133; 151, n. 2
24:22	227, n. 49
26:2	105, n. 81
26:3	139, n. 23
26:15–16	105, n. 78
26:21	105, n. 78
26:23–25	105, n. 78
26:26–29	189–96
26:30	119
26:39	194
26:41	227, n. 50
26:42	194
26:45–46	105, n. 78
26:48	105, n. 78
26:54	78
26:64	133; 151
27:2	105, n. 79
27:3–4	105, n. 78
27:4	79
27:18	105, n. 79
27:19	79
27:23	79
27:24	79
27:26	105, n. 81
27:46	102

Scripture Index

Matthew-continued

27:50	81, n. 36
27:64	112, n. 15
28:17	109; 109–10, n. 7
28:18–19	149
28:20	241, n. 1

Mark

3:19	105, n. 78
6:3	59
6:34–41	190
6:46–51	144
8:2–6	190
9:3	131
9:31	105, n. 78; 112, n. 15
10:8	227, n. 47
10:23–26	100
10:24	37
10:27	37
10:33	105, n. 78, n. 79
10:34	112, n. 15
10:45	52
11:25	27, n. 16
12:36	133; 151, n. 2
13:20	227, n. 49
13:32	70
14:7	120
14:10–11	105, n. 78
!4:14	105, n. 78
14:18	105, n. 78
14:21	105, n. 78
14:22–25	189–96
14:26	119
14:36	28
14:38	227, n. 50
14:41–42	105, n. 78
14:44	105, n. 78
14:53	139, n. 23
14:62	151
15:1	105, n. 79
15:10	105, n. 79
15:14	79
15:15	105, n. 81
15:34	102
15:37	81, n. 36
15:44–45	86
16:1–3	110
16:11–14	110
16:15	184
16:19–20	149
16:19	119; 133
16:20	241, n. 1

Luke

1:28	72
1:31	49
1:37	36
1:38	73, n. 54
2:21	49
3:1–2	77
3:6	227, n. 49
3:38	56
7:12	55
8:42	55
9:22	112, n. 15
9:38	55
9:44	105, n. 78
10:15	90, n. 22
10:22	28
11:4	204
11:13	29; 101
12:32	29
13:1	78, n. 15
13:23–24	101
13:32	112, n. 15
16:22	90, n. 25
16:26	98
18:13	251
18:27	36–7; 100
18:29–30	235
18:32	105, n. 79
18:33	112, n. 15
20:20	105, n. 79
20:36	56

20:42	133	3:6	227, n. 48
22:4	105, n. 78	3:8	168
22:6	105, n. 78	3:16	55; 83
22:14	188	3:18	55
22:19–20	189–93	3:35	29, n. 32
22:21–22	105, n. 78	3:36	236
22:22	136	4:14	234
22:27	52	4:25	53
22:32	142	4:26	53
22:39	119	4:42	54
22:42	194	5:20	29, n. 32
22:48	105, n. 78	5:24	236
22:69	133	6:23	189
23:4	79	6:29	6
23:14	79	6:35	189
23:15	79	6:39–40	224–5
23:22	79	6:44	224–5
23:35	105, n. 80	6:51–56	227, n. 46
23:43	92; 94	6:51	233
23:46	92	6:54	224–5; 236
23:56	110	6:58	233
24:2–5	110	6:63	227, n. 50
24:11–12	110	6:64	105, n. 78
24:7	105, n. 79; 112, n. 15	6:71	105, n. 78
24:20	105, n. 79	7:17	6
24:21	110; 112, n. 15	7:33	120
24:27	146	7:34	123
24:37–38	110	7:39	125
24:43	111	8:15	227, n. 50
24:39	227, n. 46	8:21	120
24:46	112, n. 15	10:17	29, n. 32
24:47	215–6	10:28	233–4
24:50–51	119	11:26	236
24:51	119	12:4	105, n. 78
24:52	124–5	12:27	78
24:53	241, n. 1	12:31	156
		13:2	105, n. 78
John		13:11	105, n. 78
		13:13	61
1:13–14	227, n. 48	13:15	61
1:14	55–6	13:21	105, n. 78
1:18	29; 55	13:33	120
1:41	53	14:2	136
1:51	247	14:6	29

John-continued

14:12	120
14:16	165
14:19	116; 121
14:21	29
14:23	29
14:26	165
14:28	120; 125
14:31	29
15:5	165
15:9	29, n. 32
15:10	29
16:5	120
16:7	125
16:10	120
16:14	160–1
16:16	120
16:27	29
16:28	120
17	143
17:2	227, n. 49
17:3	235–6; 237
17:11–24	143–4
17:24	29, n. 32; 239
18:2	105, n. 78
18:5	105, n. 78
18:30	105, n. 79
18:35	105, n. 79
18:36	105, n. 80
18:38	79
19:4	79
19:6	79
19:11	105, n. 79
19:16	105, n. 81
19:30	81; 92; 105, n. 82
20:2	111
20:9	111
20:13	111
20:15	111
20:25	111; 121
20:17	29–30
20:28	62
21:20	105, n. 78
21:25	241, n. 1

Acts

1:9	119
1:10–11	122
1:11	149
1:12	119
2:2	147
2:4	129
2:17	227, n. 49
2:24	90, n. 23; 114
2:26	227, n. 46
2:27	90, n. 22
2:30	227, n. 45
2:31	90, n. 22; 226; 227, n. 46
2:33	125; 129
2:34	133
2:35	151, n. 2
2:47	172
3:13	51, n. 21; 77, n. 13
3:21	151
3:26	51
4:24	46
4:27	51, n. 21; 77, n. 13
4:29–30	46
4:30	51, n. 21
4:32	200–201
4:34–35	202
5:31	216
5:42	52, n. 22
9:22	52; 52, n. 22
10:40	112, n. 15
10:42	157
10:43	218
13:23	49, n. 7
13:33	58
13:38–39	213–4
13:38	77, n. 13
14:27	175
15:18	20, n. 30
15:22	175
17:3	52
17:28	42
17:32	111; 226, n. 35
18:5	52; 52, n. 22

18:28	52, n. 22	8:23	223
23:6	226, n. 35	8:29	180
24:15	226, n. 35	8:32	105–6
24:21	226, n. 35	8:34	135; 142
		8:35	142–3
		8:38–39	143

Romans

		9:3	227, n. 45
1:3	227, n. 45	9:5	227, n. 45; 245
1:4	58	9:8	227, n. 45
1:7	30, n. 36; 197, n. 50	10:9	60, n. 57; 112
1:24	105	10:14	99
1:25	44; 227–8; 245	11:14	227, n. 45
1:26	105	11:32	97
1:28	105	11:36	245, n. 19
2:28	227, n. 46	12:13	203
3:20	212; 227, n. 49	12:19	84
3:23	72; 210	13:14	227, n. 50
4:1	227, n. 48	14:9	158
4:7–8	212	14:23	208
4:7	208, n. 23	15:6	30, n. 37
4:15	212	15:26	202
4:24	118	15:27	227, n. 44
4:25	117	15:33	243, n. 7
5:18	97	16:1	175
6:5	223	16:20	243, n. 7
6:9	230	16:23	175
6:11	116	16:24	243, n. 7
6:19	208, n. 23; 227, n. 50	16:27	245, n. 19
6:23	209; 236		
7:5	227, n. 50		
7:14	227, n. 50	## 1 Corinthians	
7:18	227, n. 50	1:2	62; 172; 179; 197, n. 50
7:25	227, n. 50	1:3	30, n. 36
8:1	227, n. 50	1:9	186
8:3–4	227, n. 50	1:26	227, n. 48
8:5	228	1:29	227, n. 48
8:6–9	227, n. 50	2:9	235
8:9–10	125–6	3:1	227, n. 50
8:11	118	3:3–4	227, n. 50
8:12–13	227, n. 50	3:9	172
8:14	56	5:5	227, n. 50
8:15	31; 126	5:7	188; 213
8:19–22	231	6:16	227, n. 47

1 Corinthians-continued

7:28	227, n. 48
8:6	30
9:11	227, n. 44
10:16	189; 194
10:18	227, n. 45
10:32	174
11:18–22	175
11:20–34	187–97
11:22	187
12	126
12:3	60, n. 57
12:4	163
12:11	163
12:27	196–7
14:16	244–5
14:23	175
14:33	179
15:3–8	108
15:4	85; 112–3; 112, n. 15; 113–4
15:8	121
15:12–13	226, n. 35
15:14	115
15:17–19	115
15:19	223
15:20	226
15:21	226, n. 35
15:22	96
15:25	151, n. 2
15:26	220
15:35–36	224
15:38	224
15:39	227, n. 44
15:42–44	223
15:42	226, n. 35
15:44	226, n. 36
15:50	226; 227, n. 50
15:51–52	225
15:52	223–4
15:53–54	230
15:54	118; 223
16:24	247

2 Corinthians

1:2	30, n. 36
1:3	31
1:12	227, n. 48
1:17	227, n. 50
1:20	249
3:3	227, n. 48
4:11	227, n. 48
5:3	225–6
5:7	121–2
5:16	227, n. 50
5:19	54
5:20	108
6:18	34, n. 1; 39; 171
7:1	227, n. 50
7:5	227, n. 46
8:4	202
10:2–3	227, n. 50
10:4	227, n. 44
11:18	227, n. 48
11:31	30, n. 37
12:7	227, n. 48
13:14	243, n. 7

Galatians

1:3	30, n. 36
1:4	106, n. 84
1:5	245, n. 19
1:16	227, n. 48
2:16	227, n. 49
2:20	105–6; 106, n. 84; 227, n. 48
3:3	227, n. 50
3:13	80
3:16	37
3:26	56
4:4	64
4:6	31; 126
4:13–14	227, n. 46
4:23	227, n. 45
4:29	227, n. 45
5:13	227, n. 50
5:16–17	227, n. 50

5:19	227, n. 50
5:24	227, n. 50
6:8	236; 227, n. 50
6:12–13	227, n. 48
6:18	243, n. 7

Ephesians

1:2	30, n. 36
1:5	56
1:7	204
1:20–21	148
1:20	133
2:3	227, n. 50
2:11	227, n. 45, n. 46
2:14	113; 182; 193
2:15	227, n. 46
2:19	197, n. 50
2:21	172
2:29–30	227, n. 46
3:14	30, n. 37
3:16–17	130
3:21	245, n. 19
4:1–3	128
4:7–12	126–9
5:2	193
5:27	180
5:31	227, n. 47
6:5	227, n. 48
6:12	227, n. 48
6:23	30, n. 36
6:24	243, n. 7

Philippians

1:2	30, n. 36
1:19	126
1:21	225
1:22	227, n. 48
1:23	225
1:24	227, n. 48
2:1	215
2:5	59
2:10	88–91
2:11	60, n. 57
3:3–4	227, n. 48
3:10	116–7
3:20	178–9
3:21	226, n. 36
4:19	215
4:20	30, n. 36; 245, n. 19
4:23	243, n. 7

Colossians

1:2	30, n. 36; 197, n. 50
1:3	30, n. 37
1:4	180
1:14	204
1:20	113
1:22	180; 227, n. 48
1:24	227, n. 48
2:1	227, n. 46
2:5	227, n. 46
2:11	227, n. 50
2:13–14	211–2
2:13	227, n. 50
2:18	227, n. 50
2:23	227, n. 50
3:1	133; 150; 231
3:22	227, n. 48
4:16	175
4:18	243, n. 7

1 Thessalonians

1:1	30, n. 36
4:16–17	224–5
4:16	224
5:28	243, n. 7

2 Thessalonians

1:1–2	30, n. 36
1:5	156
2:16	30–31
3:18	243, n. 7

Scripture Index

1 Timothy

1:2	30, n. 36
1:17	245, n. 19
2:6	106, n. 84
3:5	175
3:15	176
3:16	227, n. 48
4:3–4	44–5; 45, n. 19
4:5	189
6:13	77, n. 13
6:16	245, n. 19
6:21	243, n. 7

2 Timothy

1:2	30, n. 36
1:5	195
1:13	184
2:18	222
4:1	157
4:18	245, n. 19
4:22	243, n. 7

Titus

1:4	30, n. 36
2:14	106, n. 84
3:4	215
3:15	243, n. 7

Philemon

3	30, n. 36
16	227, n. 48
25	243, n. 7

Hebrews

1:3	133; 134–5; 151, n. 2
1:13	133; 151, n. 2
2:5	147
2:8–9	147–8
2:8	150
2:9	121
2:10	101; 226
2:14	227, n. 46
2:17	138–41
3:1	139
4:8	51
4:13	47
4:14–15	131
4:15	61; 70; 71
5:4	139
5:7	227, n. 48
6:2	226, n. 35
6:20	136; 139
7:11	139
7:16	227, n. 45
7:25	142
7:27	142; 193
8:1	133; 136
8:10	208, n. 23
8:12	193
9:10	227, n. 44
9:12	192–3
9:13	227, n. 48
9:15	192
9:20	192
9:24–25	139
9:26	192–3
9:27	98
9:28	101; 193
10:10	193
10:12	134–5
10:13	151, n. 2
10:17–18	212
10:17	193; 208, n. 23
10:20	227, n. 46
11:1—12:3	203
11:6	4–5
11:16	51
11:39–40	94–5
11:40	51
12:1	203
12:2	134–5
12:9	31; 227, n. 49
12:22–24	198

Scripture Index 281

12:23	95
12:24	192
13:5	130
13:21	245, n. 19
13:25	243, n. 7

James

4:12	207
4:17	208
5:3	227, n. 48

1 Peter

1:2	30, n. 36
1:24	227, n. 49
2:9	172
2:11	227, n. 50
3:18–19	93
3:18	227, n. 48
3:21	227, n. 50
3:22	148–9
4:1	227, n. 46
4:2	227, n. 48
4:5	157
4:6	96; 98–9; 227, n. 48
4:11	245, n. 19
4:19	47
5:11	245, n. 19
5:14	243, n. 7

2 Peter

1:4	186; 238–9
2:4	90, n. 24
2:10	227, n. 50
2:18	227, n. 50
3:13	231
3:18	245, n. 19

1 John

1:2	237–8
1:3	31; 186
1:9	138
2:1	137–8
2:13	30
2:16	227, n. 50
3:1	31
3:2	235
3:4	207–8
4:2–3	68; 227, n. 46
4:8	14; 19
4:9	55
4:17–18	156–7
4:19	19
5:11–12	236–7
5:17	208
5:20	235
5:21	247

2 John

3	30, n. 36
7	68; 227, n. 46

Jude

1	30, n. 36
7–8	227, n. 50
23	227, n. 50
25	245, n. 19

Revelation

1:6	30, n. 36; 245, n. 19
1:7	247
1:8	34, n. 1
1:18	90, n. 22; 248
2–3	175–6
2:1	175
2:27	30, n. 37
3:5	30, n. 37
3:14	249

Revelation-continued

3:21	30, n. 37
4:8	34, n. 1
4:9–10	237
5:9	54; 182
5:14	237; 247
7:12	246
10:6	237
11:17	34, n. 1
14:12	197, n. 50
14:17	46
15:3	34, n. 1
15:7	237
16:7	34, n. 1
16:14	34, n. 1
17:16	227, n. 46
19:4	246
19:6	34, n. 1
19:15	34, n. 1
19:18	227, n. 46
19:21	227, n. 46
21:4	223
21:22	34, n. 1
21:27	239
22:20	243
22:21	243, n. 7